Getting Great Sounds: The Microphone Book

Tom Lubin

Course Technology PTR
A part of Cengage Learning

Australia • Brazil • Japan • Korea • Mexico • Singapore • Spain • United Kingdom • United States

Getting Great Sounds:
The Microphone Book
Tom Lubin

Publisher and General Manager, Course Technology PTR: Stacy L. Hiquet

Associate Director of Marketing: Sarah Panella

Manager of Editorial Services: Heather Talbot

Marketing Manager: Mark Hughes

Executive Editor: Mark Garvey

Project Editor/Copy Editor: Cathleen D. Small

Technical Reviewer: Barry Wood

Editorial Services Coordinator: Jen Blaney

Interior Layout Tech: Macmillan Publishing Solutions

Cover Designer: Luke Fletcher

Indexer: Sharon Hilgenberg

Proofreader: Brad Crawford

For product information and technology assistance, contact us at
Cengage Learning Customer & Sales Support, 1-800-354-9706

For permission to use material from this text or product, submit all requests online at **www.cengage.com/permissions**
Further permissions questions can be emailed to
permissionrequest@cengage.com

Library of Congress Control Number: 2008902404

ISBN-13: 978-1-59863-570-6

ISBN-10: 1-59863-570-0

Course Technology, a part of Cengage Learning
20 Channel Center Street
Boston, MA 02210
USA

Cengage Learning is a leading provider of customized learning solutions with office locations around the globe, including Singapore, the United Kingdom, Australia, Mexico, Brazil, and Japan. Locate your local office at:
international.cengage.com/region

Cengage Learning products are represented in Canada by Nelson Education, Ltd.

For your lifelong learning solutions, visit **courseptr.com**

Visit our corporate website at **cengage.com**

Printed in Canada
1 2 3 4 5 6 7 11 10 09

Authors dedicate books to people for lots of reasons. Sometimes it's like what The Mamas and Papas sang; it's "dedicated to the one I love"—in my case, my wife, Jenny, whose love and support is ever present. Or it's dedicated to a long-dead teacher, such as Edgar Esterwold, my high school electronics instructor, who had me build a radio and then blew it up so I could fix it. Of course, Moms and Dads get dedications. My Dad died while this book was being written, and my Mom moved into a care home. They were great parents and showed extraordinary patience during my '60s hippie/Flower Power period. I kept burning up the brakes, blowing up the engine, or rolling the car my dad gave me. Dean Thompson, then owner of Two:Dot Studios and Santa Barbara Sound, who gave me my first break as a sound engineer, and Stan Ross and Dave Gold, owners of Gold Star, who gave me my first full-time engineering job, had a lot to do with where my life went. There was Joe Saia at AAA Studios, who felt anyone had talent as long as he or she could pay for a record to be made. With Joe, I learned how to make good-sounding records for people who had little talent. Mike Gershman invited me to live in Woodstock for a year to build a studio, and then he recommended me for a job in San Fran. That was where I was hired by the two Roys—Segal and Halee, my bosses at CBS Studios. Working there was an unmatched education in sound recording. Then, as they say, there are so many people I worked with over the years at Electric Lady, Music Lab, Tewksbury, Wally Heider, and so on. I learned from everyone and was so grateful for that opportunity. This is also dedicated to Jim Riordan, a dear old friend who helped me start writing a book nearly 30 years ago, and Andy Romanoff and David LaBrun, who decided to turn that material into the Shaping Your Sound *video series. Finally, and definitely not least, Dan Alexander, my friend, once my student and then my teacher, now the expert on microphones and all things good sounding.*

Acknowledgments

I want to extend my appreciation for the assistance in creating this book to Mark Garvey, Cathleen Small, Barry Wood, and Dan Alexander for helping, guiding, and editing *Getting Great Sounds*. Also Darren Saunders and John Goldsmith at Kosmic Music (Perth) and Rob Grant at Poons Head Studios (Fremantle), who let me wander into their businesses every now and then to take pictures and have a chat. A number of people who represent manufacturers, including Ian Jones at Telefunken USA; Alan Feckanin and Anthony Zammit at Beyer Dynamic, Inc; Gregory Maxwell, Eric Bauer, Daniel O'Connell, and Ben Wagner at Griffin PR on behalf of Crown International; Andreas Sablotny at Neumann GmbH; Scott Emerton at RØDE Microphones; Mike Torlone at Harman International; Doris Germershausen at Sennheiser; Dennis Haley at Instrument Covers; Maxwell Twartz at TAG on behalf of Audio-Technica and Atlas Stands; Amalia Stephenson at Royer Labs; Dieter and Christy at K&K Sound Systems; Ewen Coldrey for Schoeps; Rip Rowan at ProRec; John Cuniberti at Reamp; Ron at Applied Microphone Technology; Bob Heil at Heil Sound; Mary Ann Giorgio at Marshall Electronics; Abigail Schommer at Latchlake Music; Sue Mulholland at Jands on behalf of Shure; and Elaine Beckett and Simon Leadley at Trackdown Scoring (Sydney). Several people contributed photos, including John Schneider, Tup Wanders, Carl Clifford, Mike Schultz, Tabitha Hawk, and Angelo Galeano. Then there are all of those I've worked with, all of those I've taught, all of those I've recorded, and all of those who have attended the hundreds of Fostex clinics and workshops I've presented. Finally, thanks to Course Technology PTR for publishing the book.

About the Author

When he was a kid, all **Tom Lubin** was interested in was sound and then recording. His uncle got him a wire recorder (before tape) when he was 11 and a simple record cutter when he was 14. He got a kit amp mail order from Kansas City to drive the cutter head. All this meant that he was pretty technical for a kid. He could make cables and connectors and wire things up. So when Tom started hanging out in studios, they knew he could fix headphones and mic leads, and they let him come back. And he kept coming back.

There were only a few places on the planet where there were sound studios. Tom was fortunate to grow up in one of them—Hollywood. When he was 15, he called RCA Studios and asked whether he could watch a session. The studio manager invited him down and bought him lunch. A kid being interested in recording was novel. Tom visited lots of studios and started hanging out at those that would let him. There were no schools teaching recording and very few books. He learned by watching and standing behind people with great ears. And every now and then, Tom got to play with the gear. When he was 17, Wally Heider hired Tom to drive his truck from Hollywood to Tahoe to record Bill Cosby. That weekend ended badly. Tom crashed the roof of the truck into a sign, Wally caught him playing the master tapes to girls in the chorus line, and on the way home, Tom blew up the truck's engine by going too fast. Tom learned a lot that weekend and managed to do better in his next job.

Tom engineered in great studios for years; taught sound; edited a sound production magazine; had a rock-and-roll hotel; toured the U.S. for years for Fostex, talking about home studios; and made some instructional videos on recording—all the while still making records. In 1987, Tom moved to Australia and was involved increasingly in film, TV, games, animation, puppetry, digital media, and training for these industries. A couple of years ago, he took a year off to take stock of where he had been and what he might do with the time he had left. Deep inside, he remained just a rock-and-roller who still liked to record and turn the speakers up. It was time to finish the book he had started 30 years ago. This is that book. Turning it down is never an option.

Contents

Chapter 3
Understanding Sound and Hearing 43

Chapter 4
Polarity, Phase Cancellation, and Reverb 65

Chapter 5
Impedance and Balance 83

Chapter 6 Hum 101, DIs, and Related Transducers 91

Chapter 7 Accessories and Necessary Hardware 107

Chapter 8 Stereo Microphone Techniques 123

Chapter 9 The Recording Session 139

Chapter 13
Miking Solo Acoustic Instruments and Vocals 217

Chapter 14
Miking Classical Acoustic Sections 241

Appendix A
Compressors and Limiters: A Brief Overview 265

Appendix B
An EQ Primer 273

Index. 283

Introduction

Virtually everything in the universe has a cyclical vibration. The essence of all things great and small is conveyed by their emerging vibrations. The excursion from positive to negative (up and down, back and forth) could be no more than the thickness of a molecular fraction or a distance measured in light years. The time it takes to complete one cycle may be the shortest instant or an eternity—or any moment in between.

Have you heard someone say that something (or someone) has "vibed them out?" Some vibrations (or auras), such as fear, may be very subtle and not easily sensed by man, though animals can pick them up. Other vibrations are very tangible, as vibes go, such as light and sound. Our bodies reflect light vibrations that our eyes can see; our vocal chords generate sound vibrations. Our lips and fingers can control vibrating bodies that make up the universe of musical instruments. Our ears sense these vibrations in the atmosphere and transduce this energy into electrical pulses that our brain understands to be sound.

Microphones are the first link in the amplification and processing of acoustic sound. Microphones capture the ever-changing instant of atmospheric pressure that passes by them. They are the windows through which we observe what someone has heard, what someone has played, what someone has said, and what someone has sung.

Microphones are transducers. They change acoustic sound vibration into an oscillating electrical signal. They also uniquely transduce meaning. The most elusive vibrations—and the ones most sought after—are those that emerge from and are touched by the human soul. Central to capturing this elusive soul, this hidden spirit, are microphones. Somewhere within the sound they capture is the soul that differentiates a recording that moves the listener from one that does not. What makes it happen in one case but not in another?

When someone uses a microphone, he attempts to enhance each sound's essence by selecting the microphone that brings out the desired "best" view of the sound, much as a painter might use different brushes and paints, pencils, or chalks to create textures. For example, the mic that is above the cymbals or on the hi-hat may not be the best choice for the toms, kick, or snare of a drum set. The best microphone for a given sound is the one that picks up the vibrations of an instrument as the player always imagined his performance should sound.

The path to the perfect sound is a journey that includes the technology that follows the microphone's signal path and the acoustic environment that surrounds the sound source and precedes the microphone.

A great vocal microphone captures an elusive quality that lets a singer hear himself the way he has always imagined he could sound. When he sings into *that* mic, he feels like he's on a cloud, surrounded by an aura, like he's wearing golden slippers. The microphone's view of the sound becomes part of the artist's trademark. What are the golden slippers for any given person? For some, they're a rare condenser/tube microphone. For others, the magic may be captured with one of the latest models. Every singer's golden slippers will vary depending on how the artist hears himself and what will unlock and capture that magic. The answer is simple and complex—a matter of palpable hardware and magic.

I hope you will find this book helpful as you endeavor to capture that elusive soul in all that you record.

1 The Development of the Microphone

I like learning about where and how things began. In this chapter, you'll look at the beginnings of the microphone, who invented it, and what they were trying to do with it. You'll explore some landmark developments in the history of the microphone, be introduced to a bit of the technical details, and hear a few interesting stories about the early history of the microphone. It all starts with one of the most important inventions of the 20th century.

Bell and the Telephone

In the early 1860s, a Frenchman named Leon Scott, working at the Massachusetts Institute of Technology (in Cambridge, Massachusetts), came up with a device called a *phonautograph* for tracing vocal patterns. A thin hog's-bristle quill was attached to the center of a flexible diaphragm at the back of a tapered horn that concentrated the sound. The other end of the quill was a sharp, fine stylus. A piece of smoked glass would travel past the stylus as the sound entering the horn scratched a wavy line into the soot. An impression of the sound had been captured. A later version of the device positioned the stylus against a cylinder of heavy paper coated with soot. The cylinder was rotated by hand, as the sound to be captured entered the horn, and an image of the vibrations was recorded. Leon Scott's device was not a marketable product, aside from its scientific applications, but it did point the way toward later inventions—the microphone and the phonograph, or gramophone.

Alexander Graham Bell (1847–1922), a Scottish-born scientist and inventor, had been working in Boston (in the early 1870s) with deaf-mute people and was looking for some means of capturing and portraying speech (see Figure 1.1). He was attracted to the research that was going on at MIT and to Scott's work from the previous decade. On seeing Scott's sound vibration drawings, Bell concluded that such a device would be perfect to show those who couldn't hear what their speech looked like. At MIT, Bell was able to review its library of the work done over the previous hundred years by Helmholtz, Oerstead, Sturgeon, Faraday, Volta, and others. Bell was able to use a century of observations and isolated electroacoustic phenomena to then make a cornerstone invention.

In about 1875, Bell took two metal bars and wrapped wire around each of them. He set them out of magnetic reach of one another and then connected them in series with a battery. Attached to the front of each of the windings was a thin metal diaphragm with the freedom to vibrate

Figure 1.1 Alexander Graham Bell demonstrating his telephone microphone.

close to the coil of wire. Bell attached a sound-gathering horn to the front of one of the diaphragms and a sound-projecting horn to the surface of the other. When he spoke into the sound-gathering horn, the metal diaphragm vibrated and altered the magnetic field of the nearby electromagnet. This caused the current flowing through the wire to fluctuate in sympathy with the slight changes in the magnetic path. The undulating current traveled to the second winding and created a corresponding fluctuation in its magnetic field, causing the diaphragm near the second winding to vibrate sympathetically and reproduce the sound that had been gathered at the other end. Bell had invented the microphone and speaker. The telephone and electronic sound transmission had become a reality.

On January 14, 1876, Alexander Graham Bell filed his patent for the telephone and became a giant in the field of communication and a legendary figure in history. It was an invention whose time had come (see Figure 1.2). Amazingly, later that same day, a man named Elisha Gray, a co-founder of Western Electric, also filed a patent for essentially the same invention, which he had independently developed. It would take 10 years before Bell was awarded free title to the telephone patent. In that time, the Bell Telephone Company (then called American Bell) would acquire controlling interest in Western Electric.

Microphones Grow Up

For the first time, microphones (and speakers) made electroacoustic communication between two points possible. However, the points still had to be reasonably close to one another because prior to the invention of electronic amplification, the signal the microphone generated dissipated quickly.

The Quest for Better Sound

Starting at the end of the 19th century and throughout the early 20th century, there was a continuous flow of new inventions and refinements in all forms of electromechanical technology,

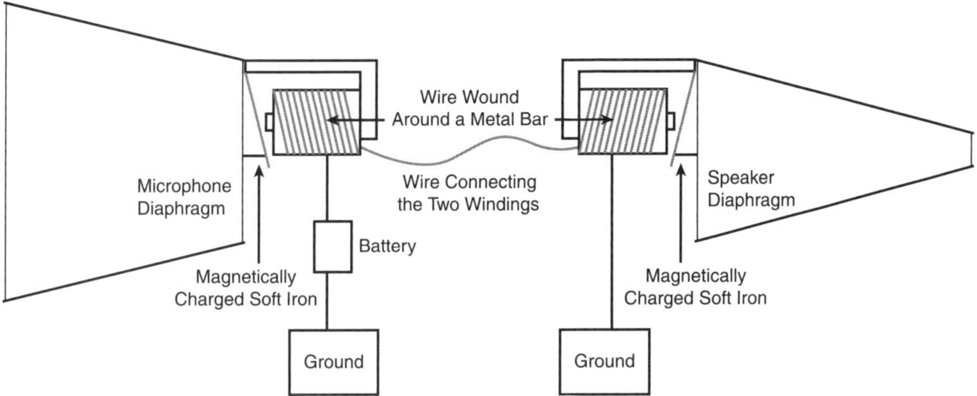

Figure 1.2 Bell's original patent drawing for the telephone. As the microphone diaphragm vibrated, it moved a hinged magnetic bar at one end of a coil that was connected to a battery. The mic coil was connected in series with another coil whose field sympathetically changed with changes in the first coil. This caused a bar connected to the speaker diaphragm to vibrate and make sound. And so Bell told his assistant, "Mr. Watson, come here—I want to see you."

including microphones. The ongoing quest in microphone design was to increase the output of the microphone so the signal would travel farther, and, if possible, extend the frequency response to higher frequencies. But, for the purposes of the telephone, the microphone response didn't actually have to be that good. Musical instruments generate sound from very low frequencies to beyond 20,000 Hz, and of course the ear can hear frequencies nearly that high, but most speech sounds are between 1,000 Hz and 4,000 Hz. (For a brief explanation of frequencies, see the sidebar in this chapter titled "Bandwidth and Frequency.")

The challenge was this: For a microphone to reproduce higher frequencies, it needs to be highly flexible or compliant in order to respond to the more rapid vibrations of higher frequencies. The conundrum in the days before amplification was that when the metal was made thinner to be more flexible, the microphone would generate a lower output, because in Bell's design the output was directly related to the thickness and size of the diaphragm. (More on this when we get to how ribbon microphones work in Chapter 2, "Microphone Types, Patterns, and Uses.") Higher frequency response *and* higher output was impossible to achieve until there was some way of amplifying the small signals that early microphones were capable of generating.

Edison and the Vacuum Tube Amplifier

The beginning of the vacuum tube amplifier had its origins in the lab of another great inventor, Thomas Edison. While perfecting the electric light, Edison discovered a phenomenon that pointed the way toward the amplifier tube. In 1883, four years after he created the light bulb, Edison was disturbed by how the glass housing of the bulb became clouded as particles of the copper filament seemed to boil off and attach to the inside surface of the bulb. He decided to put an additional metal plate into the lamp, hoping that the particles would be attracted to the metal instead of the glass surface. In the course of his experiments, he discovered that when the bulb was on, electric current would flow between the positive side of the filament and the collecting plate. He didn't know why this was happening, but he noted it in his workbook as the "Edison effect." In 1904, seven years after J. J. Thompson discovered the existence of the electron, another English scientist, J. Ambrose Fleming, came up with the correct explanation for the Edison effect. In the vacuum of the glass casing, the heated filament does not burn up (because of a lack of combustible oxygen), but electrons leap from the heated wire and are then attracted to the plate. The electrically heated filament was named the *emitter* (of the electrons), and the positively charged plate was named the *collector*. Fleming called the assembly a *diode* (because it had two electrodes—an emitter and a collector) and patented it in 1904 (see Figure 1.3). This discovery had little immediate impact, but in 1906, an American scientist, Lee de Forest, perfected a method for controlling a high electron flow with a weak positive voltage. He placed a fine metal screen between the emitter and the collector, and by connecting the screen to a weak positive voltage, he could control the much greater electron flow. This caused the electron beam to accelerate sympathetically with voltage changes applied to the screen. The screen itself was physically so light that very few of the electrons were actually attracted to it. Nearly all of the electrons flowed through to the collector.

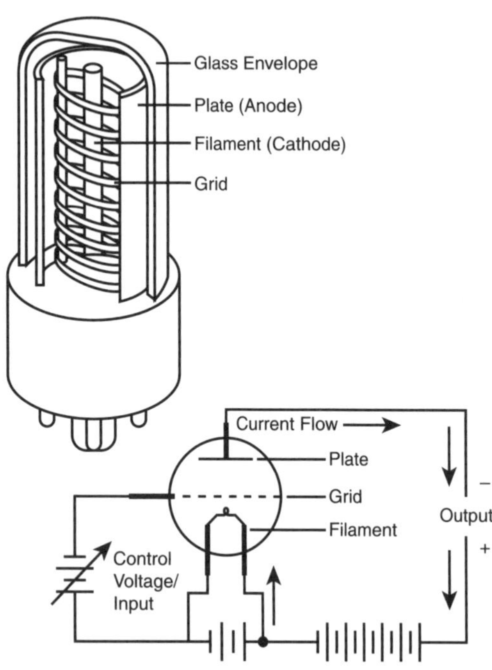

Figure 1.3 A vacuum tube and its schematic. High current traveling between the anode and the cathode can be controlled by very low current applied to the screen, thus amplification occurs.

Of greatest importance was the fact that the high current beam of electrons between the emitter and the collector could be modulated or controlled by a much lower alternating signal (in this case, low-level audio) connected to the screen that separated them. In other words, a very weak signal voltage to the screen would cause an identical modulation of a significantly greater current flow from the emitter to the collector. The electron amplifier tube was a reality. De Forest patented his triode (it had three electrodes—emitter, collector, screen) tube in 1906 and called it an *Audion* (see Figure 1.4). In much of the world, this device was called an *electron valve*. In the U.K., Fleming successfully challenged de Forest's patent, but it was reversed 40 years later. In the U.S. there was no such challenge.

Photo courtesy of Mike Schultz.

Figure 1.4 Lee de Forest's triode tube (Audion) from 1906.

In 1913, Western Electric obtained exclusive rights to de Forest's Audion tube design. Over the next several years, it made many improvements to the amplifier. By the early '20s, Western Electric's design teams had connected the microphone to a de Forest amplifier and used the output to drive an electric record-cutting system. They also made sound mixers that allowed the signal from several microphones to be mixed together. The microphone's low output could be amplified, and it was now being used to pick up the wide frequency range of instruments and singing.

Twentieth-Century Developments

The pioneers of sound technology understood that microphones had to be perfected in order to achieve high-quality transmission. In the early days, the principal microphone manufacturers were large communication labs, such as Telefunken, Western Electric, the BBC, Bell Labs, CBS, and RCA. Significant performance improvements were being made by the late 1920s, when the Western Electric 630 "Eightball" (see Figure 1.5) was the first microphone capable of picking up 10,000 cycles. At the time, this was considered an excellent high-frequency response. This microphone resembled a black eight ball, with a two-inch chrome ring surrounding a black grill covering the opening on one side.

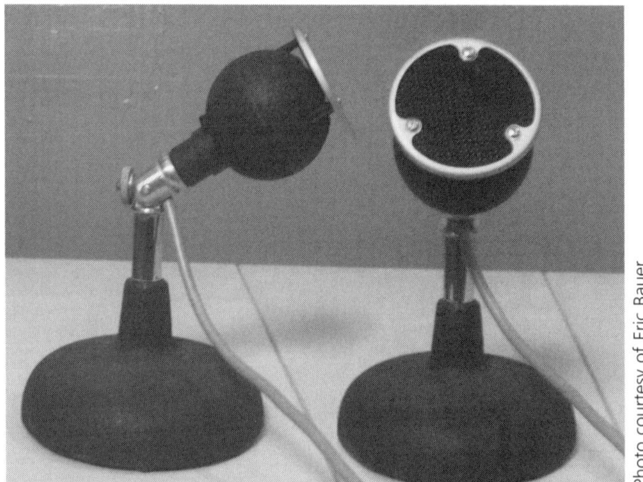

Photo courtesy of Eric Bauer.

Figure 1.5 Western Electric 630 moving-coil microphone—the "Eightball."

Bandwidth and Frequency Sound travels in waves or cycles of sound pressure. These pressure waves push and pull our eardrums. *Frequency* is the measure of how many oscillations or cyclical pressure changes occur in a second (see Figure 1.6). *Bandwidth* is the range of frequencies that the ear, a microphone, or a piece of electronic equipment can hear, pick up, or amplify (see Figure 1.7). For instance, the ear can hear a bandwidth from 30 cycles or Hertz (Hz) to 18,000 Hz. On the other hand, a subwoofer speaker has a limited bandwidth of 30 Hz to 200 Hz. There's much more on bandwidth, frequency, and how our ears work in Chapter 3, "Understanding Sound and Hearing."

Today's oldest technologies were new in the early 20th century. The carbon compression used in the Western Electric 600A and other mics of the mid-'20s (see Figure 1.8) was leading-edge innovation at the time. The diaphragm's movement put pressure on a large quantity of pinhead-sized spheres of conductive carbon, through which a voltage would be passed. The continually varying pressure on the carbon would change its resistance, thus modulating the current passing through it in response to the sound. Carbon mics remained common in telephones into the '60s, but for high-quality applications, carbon mics were soon replaced by better designs such as the Eightball.

The early 20th century was a time when it seemed every day would bring new materials and manufacturing techniques. Synthetic magnets that could be molded into shapes and were more

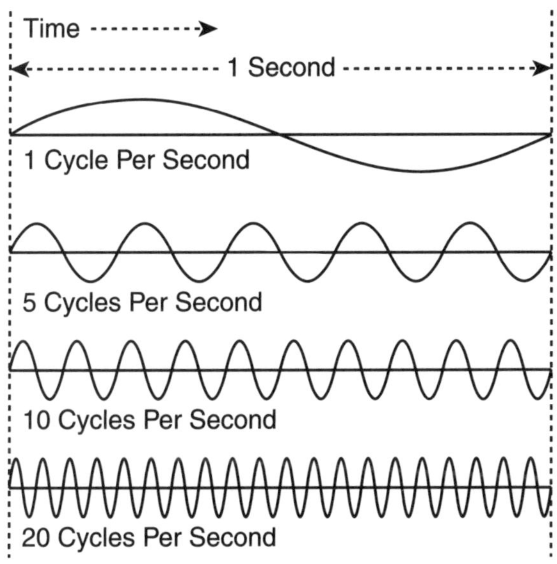

Figure 1.6 Frequency = cycles per second, or Hertz. As the frequency goes up, so does the pitch, and the wavelength is shorter.

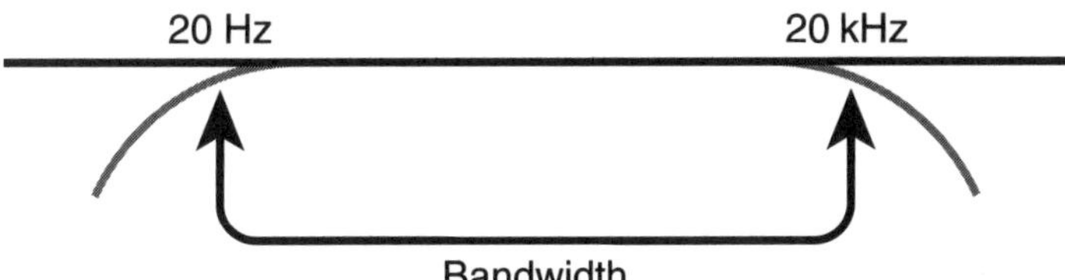

Figure 1.7 Bandwidth from 20 Hz to 20 kHz. Outside the bandwidth, the response rolls off.

powerful meant that the diaphragm could be smaller and still generate the same amount of output. Diaphragm material no longer needed to be metal when a way to make a very small coil and attach it to the rear of the diaphragm was perfected. A means of spraying a metal surface one molecule thick onto a thin synthetic membrane was a critical step in the development of highly responsive condenser microphones. And what metal was best? Silver, nickel, gold, alloys of various types—all were tried. A great deal of research also went into optimizing the diameter of the diaphragm—should it be big or small? (More on that in the next chapter.) What was the best way to create a housing for the diaphragm so that it picked up the sound all around the mic—or conversely, from just in front of it? The need for a microphone to pick up a single sound at some distance was pursued by many, because it was critical in a range of uses, including film, radio, and the military.

In the '30s, RCA was the first broadcast company to bring out microphones that were widely used in the developing radio, record, and film industries (RCA 44 and 77 ribbon microphones—see Figure 1.9). Their use was a key factor in the rapid improvements in sound quality in these three industries. The RCA mics were used widely for many years. By the '40s, RCA ribbon mics

Collection and photos courtesy of John Schneider.

Figure 1.8 A collection of microphones from the '20s to the '70s.

1: The RCA 77DX is the "classic" 1950s studio microphone. Its origin was the 77-A designed by Dr. Harry F. Olson sometime during the late 1920s or early 1930s; 2: Shown are three carbon microphones from the early 1930s, made by Universal, Shure, and Turner (L to R). Turner was a major microphone manufacturer from the late '20s to the late '70s. These would have been used for public address or communications purposes, rather than for broadcasting; 3: This professional carbon microphone was widely used in early radio broadcasting. The microphone is housed in a Western Electric 1B desktop housing and has reasonable fidelity; 4: The Shure 55S is the "junior" version of the 55 dynamic microphone. It is still sold by Shure Brothers today (55SH Series II), with an improved mic element; 5: The Electro-Voice 630 (bottom) was a popular omnidirectional dynamic PA mic. The 664 (center) was a directional mic popular for use in PA systems in the 1960s. The microphone at the top is the 666, a professional low-impedance version of the 664, designed for studio use. The 666 was exceptionally durable. Salespeople would use it to hammer nails into pine timber, then plug it in and demonstrate that it hadn't been hurt; 6: This classic RCA 44BX microphone was the second of a series of ribbon "velocity" mics made by RCA; 7: Many microphone manufacturers in the '40s and '50s styled their microphones in art deco designs. From left to right: Turner models 22D, 33D, BX , 25X, and 211; 8. The Western Electric 639 "Bird Cage" has both dynamic and ribbon elements. The user could select either element or a combination of both. It was commonly used as a radio studio mic in the '40s and '50s; 9: The DR330 ribbon microphone made in the '50s by the American Microphone Company. It's shown here with matching desk stand. It had a switchable pattern select; 10: The Shure 55 Unidyne was the classic 1950s rock-and-roll microphone, used by Elvis Presley and most of the other big stars. It was introduced in 1939. The external design was based in part on the front grille of a 1937 Cadillac; 11: The Western Electric 633A was a popular dynamic studio microphone, commonly referred to as the "Salt Shaker." It was omnidirectional unless equipped with an optional baffle that fit over the front of the microphone; 12: On the left is one of the first Shure microphones (early '30s). On the right is the 520DX "Green Bullet," favored even today by harmonica artists; 13: This Tannoy omnidirectional dynamic microphone was used in the British Parliament starting in the early '40s; 14: Electro-Voice V1 and V2 velocity (ribbon) microphones were EV's answer to RCA's 44B ribbon microphone. The V2 appeared in the early '40s and had a directional or nondirectional pattern select; 15: The Turner 101A was a broadcast-quality ribbon/dynamic microphone made by Turner. The two elements were combined to create a cardioid pattern; 16: The RCA 4-A-1 condenser microphone, showing on the right side of the box the gas-filled condenser element. The interior of the mic box contained a three-tube mic preamplifier. This condenser mic was used in the 1930s; 17: The Western Electric 618A dynamic microphone was known as the "Fireside Chat" mic because it was the model that FDR used in his Depression-era radio broadcasts. This mic was made in 1934; 18: The RCA BK-1A "Ice Cream Cone" dynamic studio microphone was introduced around 1950. It was a high-fidelity, semidirectional dynamic microphone that was considered suitable for reproducing music or speech. It was nondirectional when in the vertical position and became semidirectional when used horizontally; 19: Electro-Voice microphones from the '60s; 20: RCA 88A dynamic mic and stand. This mic came to market in 1938 and was a common radio broadcast mic; 21: A Western Electric 600A double-button carbon broadcast mic circa 1925; 22: The Turner 34X crystal mic has a classic "Buck Rogers" art deco styling. The exterior of this mic has been re-created in the Heil Sound Fin. The Fin is designed for all recording applications. It's a large-diameter dynamic microphone. There are four blue LED lamps mounted inside, causing the microphone to glow through the windscreen, just to be cool; 23: The Astatic D104 was the classic mic used by ham radio operators because of its crisp sound. It appeared in 1933. The companion desk stand has a push-to-talk handle grip; 24: Shure SM33 and 300 ribbon mics. The SM33 has a super-cardioid response. Introduced in 1965, it was widely used in broadcast and most notably became famous as the mic used by Johnny Carson from the late '60s throughout the '70s. Shure had inscribed it with "Johnny's mic. . . Not Ed's. . . Not Fred's" (referring to Ed McMahon, the announcer, and Fred De Cordova, the producer). The 300 was introduced in the late '70s and is fixed bidirectional; 25: Turner models 87 ribbon mic and 999 dynamic mic; 26: The Western Electric 630 "Eightball" omnidirectional dynamic studio mic. The element pickup faced upward when mounted, as shown; 27: RCA 40. This mic was the beginning of the RCA ribbon "velocity" mics manufactured by RCA in the early 1930s. It was succeeded by the improved models 44BX and 77DX.

Figure 1.9 L to R: Contemporary ribbon microphone AEA R84 in the tradition of the classic RCA 77 (mid '30s) and RCA 44 (early '30s). The 77 went through seven different models and was made up until 1973.

were capable of a 16-kHz bandwidth. These mics were the standard of the industry for many years. Advanced versions of these models are still made.

Because microphones could be made in small factories, in the early '30s, despite the Depression, many small companies successfully manufactured "sound" equipment. Quite a few made mics, but only a few rose above the rest—these included Electro-Voice, Shure Brothers, Astatic, Turner, American, Beyer, and Neumann. By the early '40s, these specialty companies as well as a few national broadcasters had designed and manufactured very good microphones. Larger companies also began to market microphones designed for them by these smaller manufacturers.

Feeling the Pressure The capsule or diaphragm of a microphone is in fact a sophisticated and sensitive barometer that responds to very slight atmospheric pressure changes against its surface. By comparison, a weatherman's barometer, which slowly changes with the prevailing atmospheric pressure, is very crude in its ability to pick up slight or rapid atmospheric changes. Obviously, a microphone and the human ear are significantly more sensitive. Some mics are nearly as sensitive as the human ear, which is also a barometric pressure sensor (of sorts). When a microphone is within an environment, a pressure wave that is vibrating at an audible frequency will push the diaphragm when the wave of compressed air molecules passes the diaphragm. This is followed by a rarefaction of air molecules that creates a vacuum that pulls the diaphragm (see Figure 1.10). How frequently the pressure changes determines the frequency or pitch of the sound, and the intensity of the pressure determines its loudness. Microphones sense these slight pressure changes in the environment, which is why they will also respond if wind blows across them. (More on how we hear in Chapter 3.)

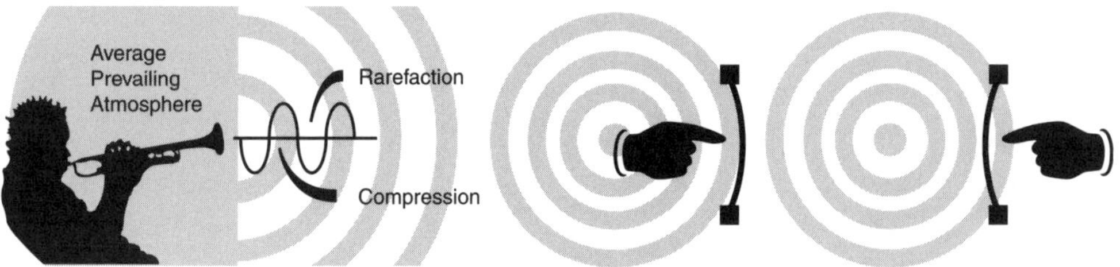

Figure 1.10 Sound waves radiate from the source of the sound as a series of compressed and rarefied air molecules. A diaphragm or the ear responds to these passing changes in atmospheric pressure.

Microphones Today

Over the years, manufacturers have changed designs, improved performance, updated old versions, and brought out a continuous flow of new models. The old models were not always changed for reasons of quality, but for marketing purposes. When the prevailing market for a particular microphone reached a saturation point, or the older manufacturing techniques or hand-built components became too expensive, the manufacturer would introduce a new and improved model. In some cases the change was inconsequential; in other cases, major overhauls occurred.

Although microphones in general have been continually improving, one cannot assume that each new model by a particular manufacturer is an improvement over the previous model. In many cases it is not a matter of improvement—both may be very good, but each sounds different, and either may be the microphone of choice for a given situation and the likes and dislikes of those using them. Put another way, for a given situation, one microphone or the other will be the best choice for the desired sound. Today, there are hundreds of models made by dozens of manufacturers. Some modern mics are excellent (see Figure 1.11), and some are less so, but the majority fail to match the standards set by the classic benchmarks of broadcast technology.

A substantial number of classic tube microphones developed between 1946 and 1962 are exceptional. Consequently, certain vintage microphones continue to be the first choice of many audio engineers. So popular are some of these old mics that in recent years several manufacturers have released microphones designed to emulate or reproduce the characteristics of popular models from earlier eras. A particularly good example is the Telefunken Ela M 251, as well as some of the other mics that have been re-created in the past couple of years by Telefunken USA (see Figure 1.12). (More on them in Chapter 2, "Microphones, Types, Patterns, and Uses.")

Photo courtesy of Audio-Technica.

Figure 1.11 Audio-Technica 4047. An excellent large-diaphragm cardioid condenser that is widely used in commercial studios.

Photo courtesy of Telefunken USA.

Figure 1.12 Telefunken U 47M. This is a meticulous re-creation of the classic tube microphone first developed in 1946. This microphone has selectable omni and cardioid patterns.

There are three common design approaches used by almost all modern microphone manufacturers. Later in this book, I'll cover these microphones types in great detail, but it will be helpful to get these terms straight from the start:

- A *moving-coil* or *dynamic* microphone has a diaphragm with a coil of wire attached to it. The coil of wire is in a magnetic field, and a signal is generated as the diaphragm vibrates.

It is durable and most commonly used in PA (live) applications and certain recording applications. High-frequency response is not the forte of the dynamic mic.

- A *ribbon* microphone has a thin metal diaphragm that is in a magnetic field to create an output as the "ribbon" vibrates. Ribbon mics are more likely to be found in studio applications, but a few designs are robust enough for live applications. They have a unique sound for instruments such as horns.
- A *condenser* microphone does not use magnets, but an electronically charged diaphragm. As the diaphragm vibrates, the charge changes, and this is amplified for an output. Condenser mics have internal amplifiers and are used widely in studios because they have a wide frequency response. This design is also used in most built-in microphones found in all forms of electronic devices. They require a power source, and although some of the studio condenser mics are fragile to varying degrees (older models in particular), many new models are sufficiently robust for the road.

Accepting that microphones are an important part of getting a great sound, it must be stressed that if the quality of the sound entering the mic isn't good to start with, the choice of microphone or the use of EQ or other signal processing won't make it wonderful. No amount of microphone fiddling or knob twiddling will make a bad sound great.

Microphones are the first link in the sound chain. Sound is most pure at the point of conversion, where it is changed from airborne atmospheric vibration to electron oscillation. Advances in microphone design in the first part of the 20th century meant that by the late '40s, some microphones were so good that they continue to be used today. But critical to their development were advances in materials and manufacturing processes—and, of course, the invention and development of the vacuum tube. In the next chapter, we'll look at how a microphone works, as well as a variety of parameters that affect how each one sounds and operates.

2 Microphone Types, Patterns, and Uses

The world of microphones is a jargon-filled one. In this chapter, you'll sort through some of the special language used to talk about mics, and you'll learn more about what microphones are, how the different types work, and some of their special characteristics. Along the way, I will begin to describe ways of using microphones to help you capture the sound you can hear in your head.

Microphones have a number of common features. Figure 2.1, of a RØDE NT2-A microphone, points to common features found on most microphones and some that are only found on condenser microphones. This chapter will explain universal characteristics and the differences between microphone types.

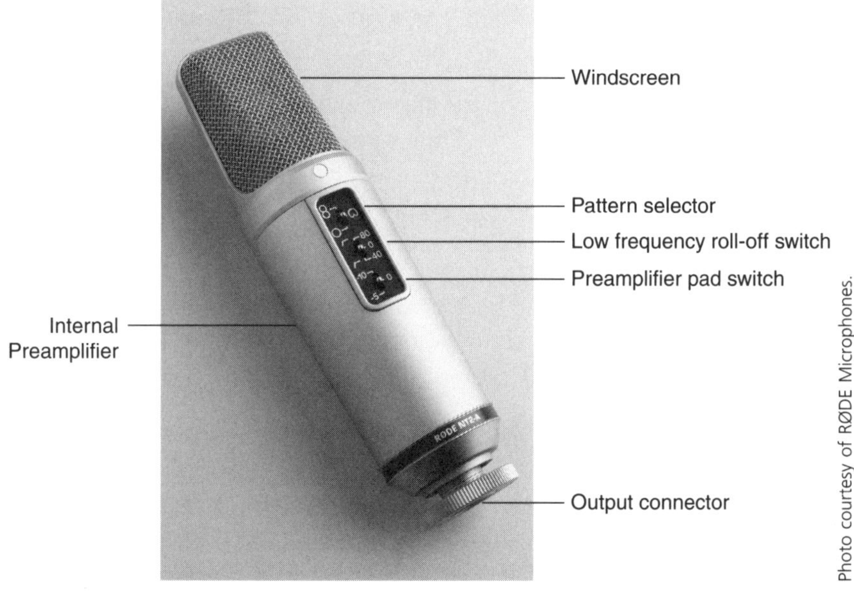

Figure 2.1 Common features of a microphone.

Three Types of Transducers

Microphones are *transducers*—that is, they change one form of energy into another. Microphones convert the energy of acoustic sound vibration into oscillating electrical energy, which can then be picked up and amplified in various ways. As mentioned previously, one of the earliest methods of converting sound into electrical energy was by varying the pressure on carbon particles. Modern microphones use three common methods of transduction: moving-coil, ribbon, and condenser. The first two methods use electromagnetic principles and are passive devices with no internal amplification. The sound causes fluctuations in a magnetic field that generates an alternating audio signal. Condensers use *capacitive* principles, where sound varies the number of electrons that are held in an electronic storage circuit. That variation is internally amplified as an audio signal. Although all three designs are used for all types of applications, moving-coil microphones are the most common type found in PA (live) applications, and condensers are the most widely used type for recording in the studio because of their low noise and high output across the entire audio spectrum.

Many microphones look the same physically but sound quite dissimilar because of differences in enclosure design (the housing), transducer type, and the design and construction of the capsule (the transducer or capsule and its surrounding housing). In the case of condenser microphones, differences in the design of the internal amplifier are also a factor in the sound. The output transformer inside the microphone (if there is one) also has an influence on the sound. (More on transformers in Chapter 5, "Impedance and Balance.")

Moving-Coil or Dynamic Microphones

This group is more accurately called *pressure-gradient* microphones. They are similar in design to a speaker (see Figure 2.2). A moving-coil microphone has a spooled coil of very fine wire connected to its diaphragm (usually at the back). The diaphragm is positioned over a magnet that has a circular channel molded into it. The coil at the rear of the diaphragm sits inside that channel. As the diaphragm moves, the coil breaks magnetic lines of force spanning the gap of the

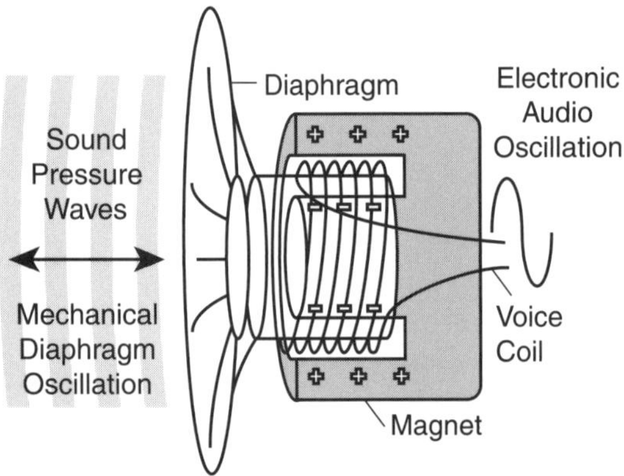

Figure 2.2 Components of a moving-coil microphone.

channel in the magnet, and an electron flow is generated in the windings of the coil. When the diaphragm changes direction, the magnetic lines of force are broken in the opposite direction, and the flow of the electrons through the coil reverses direction. This oscillating electron flow shadows the acoustic sound waves. How often the diaphragm changes direction reflects the frequency or pitch, and how far it travels in a given instant determines how great the output signal will be during that instant.

Generally, as a group, moving-coil diaphragms have the greatest amount of mass, although every model has a different compliance (the diaphragm's ability to respond to rapid changes in frequency or loudness—more on this when we talk about transient response later in this chapter and in Chapter 3, "Understanding Sound and Hearing." Variable factors include the diaphragm material, its thickness, how it is hinged (so that it can move), the size and weight of the coil, and so on. Moving-coil mics are also commonly called *dynamic* microphones because the conductor moves with the sound waves. Two of the most popular dynamic microphones ever made are the Shure SM57 and SM58 (see Figure 2.3). The SM57 and SM58 are identical except that the 58 has a built-in substantial windscreen and is preferred for vocalists, while the 57 does not and is preferred for instruments.

Figure 2.3 Shure SM57 and SM58 moving-coil or dynamic microphones.

Ribbon Microphones

A ribbon mic also uses magnetic principles, but in this case, the diaphragm is also the electrical conductor that breaks the lines of force in the magnetic field. The ribbon, a thin corrugated length of metal, is held at its ends and positioned between two magnetic fields of opposing polarity (see Figure 2.4). As it vibrates back and forth in the magnetic field, an alternating electrical current is generated in the ribbon diaphragm. The classic RCA 44 and 77 are ribbon mics. In order for the ribbon to have enough compliance, it must be thin and highly flexible. At the same time, it must be long enough so that as it vibrates, sufficient numbers of magnetic flux lines are broken to generate a high enough output signal. The conflicting factor of compliance while achieving sufficient output has meant that ribbon microphones have a reputation for low average output.

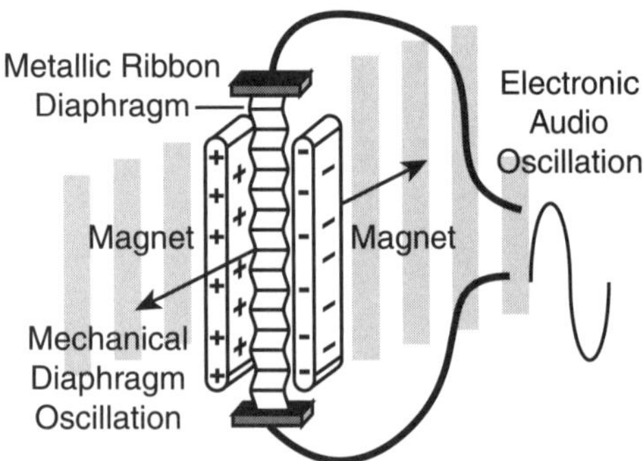

Figure 2.4 Illustration of the components of a ribbon microphone.

Ribbon microphones have traditionally been more fragile than moving-coil types. Because the ribbon was so long and thin, if it was hit with a high-velocity sound pressure wave, it could stretch, break, or snap. (Old RCA 44s and 77s are not good choices for kick drum miking—though the 77DX was a popular kick drum mic at the legendary Gold Star Studios; they loved the sound and would constantly replace the ribbon.) However, in recent years, some manufacturers have developed ribbon technology to the point that modern ribbon mics are reasonably durable and can be used on drums and as PA vocal mics.

To achieve both durability and higher output, modern ribbons are shorter and are suspended in an extremely intense magnetic field. Ribbon microphones such as the classic Beyer M160, M260, M130, and M500 all have good output in durable and compact handheld designs.

The Achilles' heel of ribbon microphones has always been output level, but in recent years a new group of ribbon microphones that have internal preamplifiers has appeared. These include the Golden Age R1, the AEA A440, the Groove Tubes VELO 8T, and several models from Royer (see Figure 2.5).

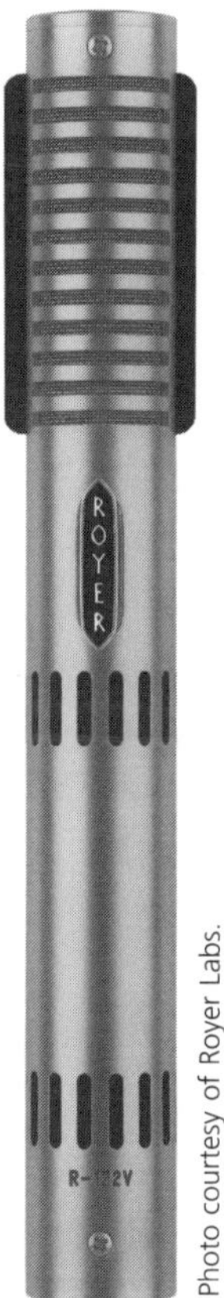

Photo courtesy of Royer Labs.

Figure 2.5 Royer R-122V. Ribbon bidirectional diaphragm with an internal tube preamp.

A ribbon mic is much more compliant, has much less mass, and generally has better transient response than a moving-coil design. Noting a relationship between the length of the ribbon and the degree of wavelength cancellation as earlier described, the longer the ribbon, the better the low-frequency response; conversely, the shorter the ribbon, the better the high-frequency response.

What Is Frequency Response? *Frequency response* refers to the range of frequencies (or bandwidth) that a microphone (or other electronic device) can accurately transduce or reproduce.

Condenser Microphones

The term *condenser* goes back to the beginning of the electronic revolution (in the early 1900s). The word itself is seldom used in modern electronics, but the device is a key component of all electronic designs. Condensers are now more commonly called *capacitors*, which is, in fact, more descriptive due to their ability to hold an electron charge. Without power applied to them, they do eventually lose their charge, but some types of capacitors can hold a charge for a long while. In a power supply, capacitors act as an electron reservoir so that as the AC power oscillates from positive to negative and back to positive, the capacitors continually store and then release electrons to smooth out the electrical valleys between the mountains to convert alternating current into what is used inside electronic devices—direct current (DC). A capacitor consists of two or more conductive (some form of metal) plates that are parallel to each other and separated by an insulator, such as air in the case of old radio tuners and microphones. The amount of electron capacitance that can be stored varies with the size and material of the plates, the insulating material (called a *dielectric*), and the distance between the conductive plates.

The diaphragm of the condenser microphone consists of a fixed rear plate and a movable front plate (the diaphragm), with the result that as the diaphragm vibrates, the electron charge, or electron capacity, is constantly changing (see Figure 2.6). The movable "plate" is usually a 3- to 10-micron thin piece of Mylar that has been spattered with an incredibly fine spray of silver, gold, or nickel alloy to make it conductive. (For reference, a human hair is about 40 microns thick.)

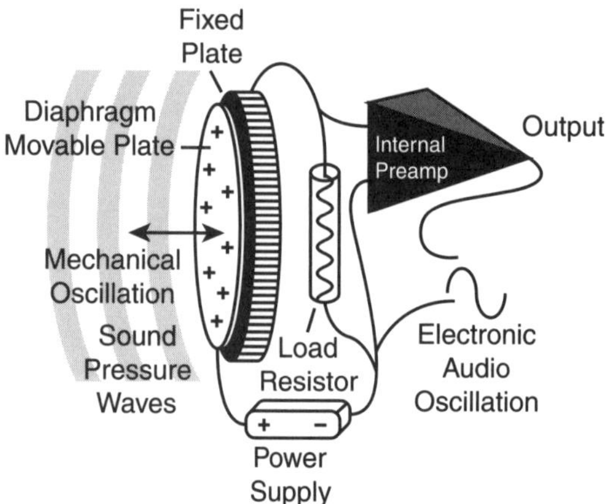

Figure 2.6 Illustration of the components of a condenser microphone.

All condenser microphones require an amplifier within a few centimeters of the capsule, so inside all of them you'll find a high-gain preamplifier that raises the constantly changing output of the condenser to a "standard mic" level balanced output. (Some microphones will have a transformer output; others will use a balanced IC output.) Without this amplifier, the signal would be so low that it would dissipate before reaching the mixing desk (see Figure 2.7). The condenser capsule is connected in series with a resistor and a DC power source. Sound vibrates the movable plate, causing the distance between the back plate and the diaphragm to constantly

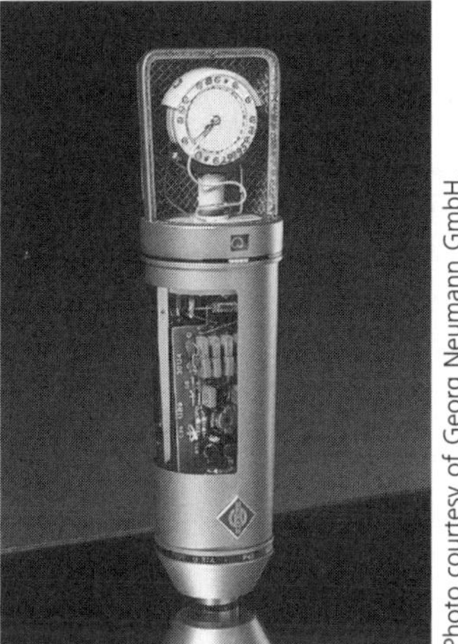
Photo courtesy of Georg Neumann GmbH.

Figure 2.7 The capsule and internal preamp in a U 87.

change, which causes the electron charge between the two plates to also change. Since the power-supply voltage remains constant, the total voltage across the condenser in series with the resistor also stays the same. When the electron capacitance of the condenser changes, the electrons flow into or out of it. The relationship of the voltage drop across the resistor compared to the capsule is also ever changing. The condenser microphone's internal preamp amplifies the constantly changing voltage fluctuation across the resistor.

Some condenser microphones have electret capsules that have a permanently charged diaphragm. However, with time, the cheaper versions of this type of condenser capsule can lose their charge and sensitivity. An electret mic will still need an internal microphone preamplifier and either an internal battery or an external power supply to provide power.

The design of the internal preamplifier also plays a part in the sound. For instance, the same handmade capsule is used in the original Telefunken Ela M 251, AKG C 12, C 12 A, C 24, 412, 414 E, and early 414 EBs. In the midst of the 414 EB product run, AKG started using a machine to make these capsules, which sound different again compared to the handmade capsules. Over the years, this same capsule has been used by AKG in many of their large-diaphragm condenser microphones. However, a dramatic difference can be heard between the 414, which has an internal amplifier of a transistor design, and "the Tube" (C 12 VR), which is amplified by a contemporary nine-pin miniature vacuum tube. Both of these sound quite different compared to the mics that came before them in part due to difference in amplifier design and the change in capsule manufacturing—the 412 (early transistorized), the C 12 A ("nuvistor"—a type of sub-miniature, peanut-sized vacuum tube), and the first large-diaphragm mics made by AKG, the C 12 and C 24 and the legendary Telefunken Ela M 251 and 252 (nine-pin miniature vacuum tube).

The New Telefunken Fewer than 1,600 Tele 251/250 microphones were made (circa 1960). The 251/250 was designed by AKG for Telefunken, who, at the time, were more or less the RCA or Westinghouse of Europe. In 1960, a new 251 would have cost about $250. That was a lot of money at the time, but today, if you can find someone willing to part with one, you might be looking at a price tag approaching $20,000 for an original model in top condition. A few years ago the Telefunken name was reborn in the U.S., as was the Ela M model designation. According to Telefunken USA, the company's research and development team spent more than a year "reverse engineering [the mic], networking with the people who use them and the people who repair them, and meticulously documenting every part down to the last screw.... Every measurement remains metric, and each part meets the original German spec." Although old Ela M 251s vary greatly in sonic quality, engineers have embraced the reissue as comparable to the best original (see Figure 2.8).

Photo courtesy of Telefunken USA.

Figure 2.8 A modern Ela M 251. What was old is new again.

Needless to say, a condenser microphone requires a power source for its internal preamplifier. Most transistorized condenser microphones use something called *phantom power*, which is provided through the microphone lead. (Chapter 5, "Impedance and Balance," explains how phantom power works.) Tube microphones like the Ela M 251 use external supplies to provide the high voltages to the tube. Condensers that are commonly used for field work or wireless application have provision for internal batteries. Battery supplies are easy to deal with for live performance and/or recording, but an external supply usually results in better specs because the external supply has a much greater voltage potential and is more consistent than a battery.

Photo courtesy of Dan Alexander.

Figure 2.9 An array of Neumann tube microphones.

Tube Condensers

When transistors first appeared in condenser microphones, manufacturers claimed that solid-state components would eventually replace the tubes found in earlier designs. Tube microphones have never become obsolete with the best engineers—those who knew good sound when they heard it. In recent years, the tube sound has become widely popular again, and there are an increasing number of new models on the market. As with all equipment, read what others have to say about them and trust your ears when trying them out.

Specs and Musicality: Why Tubes Sound Better In the early 1970s, Russell Hamm wrote a paper that seemed to answer why tube mics just seemed to sound better than other types. He measured the quality of the harmonic distortion and found that tubes created primarily even-order harmonic distortion (such as 2nd, 4th, and so on), while transistors were mostly odd-order harmonics (3rd, 5th, and, to a lesser degree, 7th order). He suggested the reason that tubes sounded better, even though their measured distortion was usually higher compared to transistors, was that tube distortion closely paralleled musical intervals. Tubes also have a different way of handling overload conditions. As an input signal pushes a tube toward its maximum output, the distortion tends to have a smoother transition compared to transistors. Third, as the tube amplifier reaches its maximum output, the signal tends to compress the peaks more smoothly compared to transistors. Tubes also use such high voltages that quick transients and peaks are more easily accommodated.

Then there are days when I choose to believe that musical soul can more easily dwell in the space inside a vacuum tube than in the solid interior of a transistor.

Some of the best-known tube mics are (or were) made by Neumann (see Figure 2.9), AKG, Calrec, Telefunken (made by Neumann, AKG, and Schoeps), Sony, Schoeps, and Sennheiser.

In the '70s and '80s, a next generation of tube mic makers appeared with Groove Tubes, RØDE, PML, Manley Labs, Pearl, Oktava, and a few others. In the mid '90s another wave appeared, including ADK, Alesis, Audio-Technica, Blue, Brauner, CAD/CTI Audio, Carvin, Curtis Technology, DPA Microphones, Lawson, Marshall Electronic, AEA, Royer, Microtech Gefell, RTT, Soundelux, Studio Projects, and Yorkville.

Pickup Patterns

Every microphone will pick up sounds coming from some directions better than those coming from other directions. This intentional directional characteristic of the microphone, referred to as its *pickup pattern*, is primarily determined by the design of the housing around the capsule. A few early microphones provided different patterns or directionality by physically attaching rings and other implements around the microphone's opening. Today, most manufacturers use the same capsule mounted in different housings to create a line of mics (or interchangeable capsules), each with a different directional pattern. Pattern selection is one of the tools the engineer uses to creatively control which sounds will be picked up and which sounds will be rejected by the microphone.

The term *polar pattern* is used to describe a microphone's directional characteristics. Most often this is illustrated as a flat drawing, with the microphone's capsule at the center of the illustration. In fact, the microphone pattern is spherical in nature, and its characteristics act on sound coming from all around. Directional patterns are most sensitive to sound that is directly in front of the microphone. To be exactly in front of a cardioid microphone (at right angles to the capsule) is to be *on axis*, and moving away from this point is described as being *off axis*. On or off axis provides context for the description of a microphone's ability to pick up sound—for instance, the on-axis response as opposed to the off-axis response.

There are basically three patterns: omni, figure eight, and cardioid, with four variations on the cardioid pattern (cardioid, supercardioid, hypercardioid, and shotgun). Any of the capsule types can be made to have any of these specific directional characteristics. Most mics have only one pattern, but many are variable. Usually the selection is made electronically, but sometimes it is made by a mechanical adjustment.

Omni or Non-Directional

If the microphone housing is enclosed so the back of the diaphragm is not exposed to the air, then the front of the microphone will respond equally to sound pressure waves regardless of the direction of their origin. A microphone with this housing design will have an omni pattern. It will pick up sound from any direction, and its pattern can be represented by a sphere with the mic in the center. There may be a slight high-frequency dip in the response for sound coming from directly behind the mic because the microphone's body partially blocks the very short, high-frequency wavelength, but by and large an omni or non-directional mic has a spherical pickup pattern (see Figure 2.10).

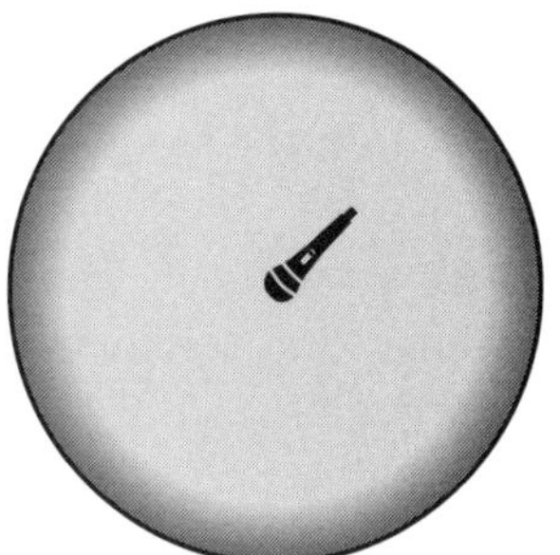

Figure 2.10 Omnidirectional pickup pattern.

Omni mics are commonly used when one or two mics are needed to pick up everything that's generating sound in a room—for instance, if you want to capture not only the sound coming from an organ, but also the reverberations of the organ's sound in the space. In such cases, a couple of omni mics might be used for stereo. Omni mics are also used when you want a room mic to pick up what everyone is saying in a room, or to capture the natural reverb or ambience of the space (which may be blended back into the final mix for added "liveness"). A pair of omnis (or more for surround) might be used outdoors for recording sound effects and atmospheres for film and TV production.

Omni mics tend to be used sparingly in recording, because the common practice of multiple-mic placement is best handled when the mics are directional. My preference for an omni mic for location work is a small-diaphragm condenser AKG 451 with an omni capsule. In the studio I would use one of a variety of large-diaphragm condensers, such as a U 87, AKG 414, or similar (see Figure 2.11).

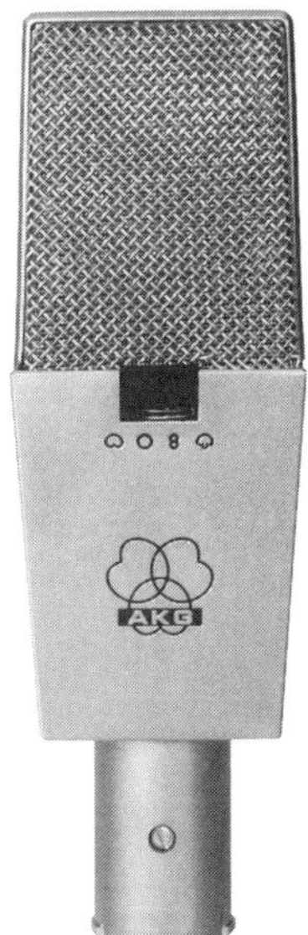

Figure 2.11 AKG 414 condenser. One of the most universally used high-end studio microphones. It can accommodate all patterns by a selector switch. It is transistor amplified and can be used on almost anything, including vocals.

Figure Eight or Bidirectional

When both sides of the diaphragm are exposed, sound that arrives on axis from the front and back will be picked up, but sound arriving from the sides (or at right angles to the diaphragm) will create equal but opposite pressure on the diaphragm and result in no net movement. Thus, sound from the side will not generate an output (see Figure 2.12). This arrangement results in a bidirectional or figure eight pickup pattern. Ribbon microphones are particularly suited for bidirectional operation, while moving-coil mics have seldom been so. Selectable pattern condenser mics often have a bidirectional selection.

Figure 2.12 Bidirectional pickup pattern.

Bidirectional microphones are my favorite when I have two of anything doing the same part—two horns, two background singers, and so on. The musicians stand facing one another with the microphone between them. I like to use a large-diaphragm condenser selected to bidirectional, or for horns possibly an RCA 44 or one of the modern ribbons. Instead of using two microphones, I also like a single bidirectional between a pair of similar drums, such as a couple of congas, bongos, or tom toms (see Figure 2.13). It picks up both drums, and at the same time has a high degree of rejection of all the other percussion sounds that are usually going on in the vicinity of the pair of drums.

Figure 2.13 Neumann U 87 in bidirectional mode between a pair of rack toms.

Selectable Patterns Most condenser mics with selectable patterns have two capsules back to back. In some designs the dual diaphragms are attached to opposite sides of a single backplate. The backplate(s) are perforated to provide a "porting." In other designs there is a separate backplate for each of the two diaphragms. The two capsules are wired out of phase with one another for bidirectional operation and in phase for omni. One of the two capsules is disconnected to provide a broad cardioid pattern (see Figure 2.14). A number of selectable pattern condensers replace the selector switch with a continuously variable control.

Condenser microphones that are designed as cardioid usually have a porting similar to other mics. In a few cases, such as the Sony C-37A and the Groove Tubes M3A, the pattern (directional and omni) can be changed by the mechanical opening and closing of the port.

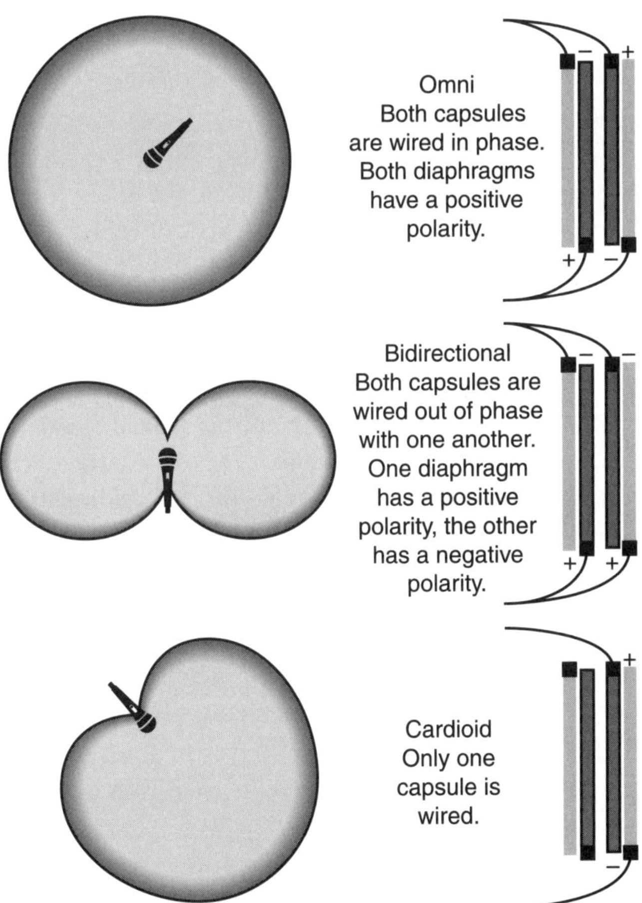

Figure 2.14 How condenser microphones have selectable patterns.

Cardioid or Unidirectional Microphones

A cardioid pattern will (to varying degrees) pick up sound in front of the diaphragm while rejecting sound coming from behind it. Cardioid means *heart-shaped*, which is how the pattern got its name (see Figure 2.15).

Figure 2.15 Basic cardioid pattern.

A cardioid pattern is created by the use of *ports*, which are openings behind the capsule that, on some models, extend all along the body of the mic. All cardioid microphones have some type of port design. Ports are openings to internal acoustic labyrinths or paths that lead to the back of the capsule's diaphragm. The length of the port determines the frequencies that are most effectively rejected. The greatest off-axis rejection occurs at frequencies that have a half wavelength equal to the length of the port path. The ports allow sound coming from behind the mic to arrive at the back of the diaphragm at the same time that it arrives at the front. This causes the sound coming from the rear to exert equal but opposite pressure on the capsule, so no output is generated (see the top of Figure 2.16).

Sound coming from in front of the mic will first strike the capsule and then enter the ports. This sound will eventually arrive at the back of the capsule, but because it has traveled twice the distance, the phase shift will be doubled. This will cause the sound from the front to be reinforced by the porting and labyrinth. In other words, if the port distance creates 180 degrees of phase-shift delay for sound originating from the rear, sound coming from the front will experience 360 degrees of phase-shift delay and will arrive at the back of the diaphragm with the same relative phase compared to sound originating in front of the mic. (See the bottom of Figure 2.16.) Since wavelength will get longer as the frequency goes down, the acoustical phase shift provided by the ports will become less and less effective with lower frequencies. For this reason, a highly directional shotgun microphone will have extremely long porting of two to three feet. The longer the port's path, the better the low-frequency directionality of the microphone.

Phase The *phase relationship* between two signals refers to the physical position of the peaks and valleys of the two waveforms in relation to each other at any given moment. If two identical waves start and end their cycles at the same time, the signals are said to be *in phase*. Phase is measured in degrees, and a cycle can be divided into 360°. See Figure 2.17.

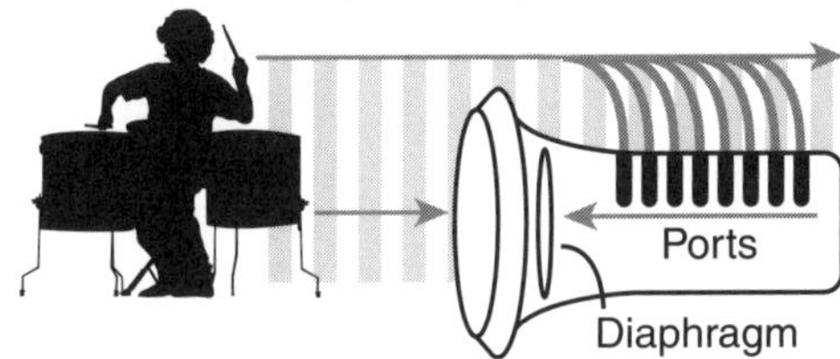

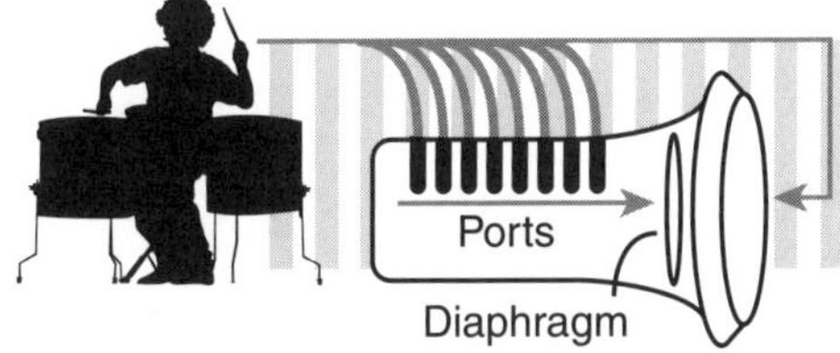

Figure 2.16 How ports work to create a cardioid pattern.

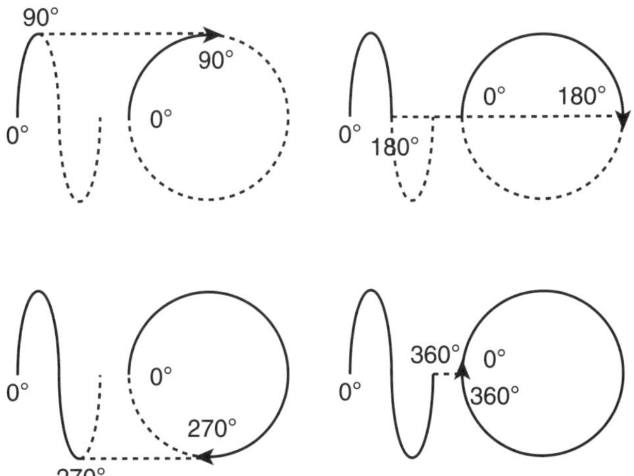

Figure 2.17 Relative phase of a wave.

Two signals with 180° phase difference are said to be *out of phase*. That is, when one signal is at a compression peak, the other is at a trough peak. If two signals are of the same frequency and amplitude but are 180 degrees out of phase, and they are combined, they'll cancel each other out. If a signal is 360° later in time, it can be said to be back in relative phase, but 360° out of real phase.

If our two in-phase signals are of the same frequency and equal in amplitude, then their addition will result in a signal of the same frequency that is 6 dB greater in amplitude. (More on dB in Chapter 3, "Understanding Sound and Hearing.") However, each wave is generated one after another, so time becomes a variable. In other words, each wave, though identical to the other in shape, loudness, and frequency, will be different in time. Two waves may be identical to one another in terms of relative phase, but different by thousands of degrees in what is called *real phase*. Partial cancellation of a signal is quite common with signals of different phase, frequency, or amplitude. This partial cancellation or addition can occur acoustically (waves in air) or electronically (currents in electronic circuits). See Figure 2.18.

Phase cancellation becomes a very big deal when two or more microphones are placed on the same instrument—for instance, a stereo pair on a piano or guitar, or the many microphones that are on a set of drums. It is also a significant problem if microphones are wired out of phase. This subject will be fully explored in Chapter 4, "Polarity, Phase Cancellation, and Reverb," under the heading "Polarity."

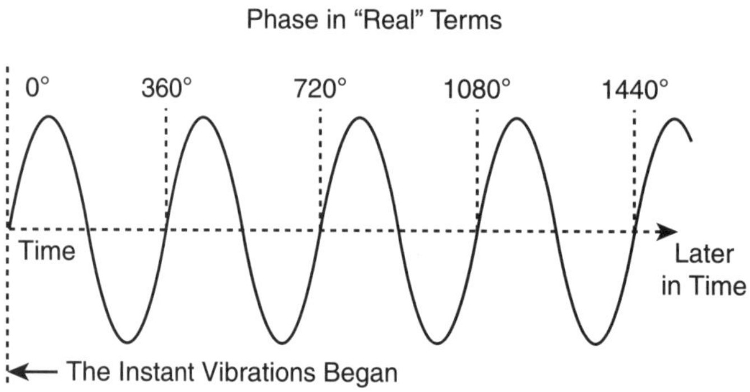

Figure 2.18 Real phase of a sound wave.

While there is a wide variety of cardioid patterns, there are three descriptive variations for cardioid: supercardioid (see Figure 2.19), hypercardioid (see Figure 2.20), and shotgun (see Figure 2.21). As you move from the first to the last, the pickup patterns become increasingly narrower in their on-axis directional characteristic. Note that a narrower cardioid shape on-axis to the microphone typically creates a longer tail in the pickup pattern toward the rear of the pattern.

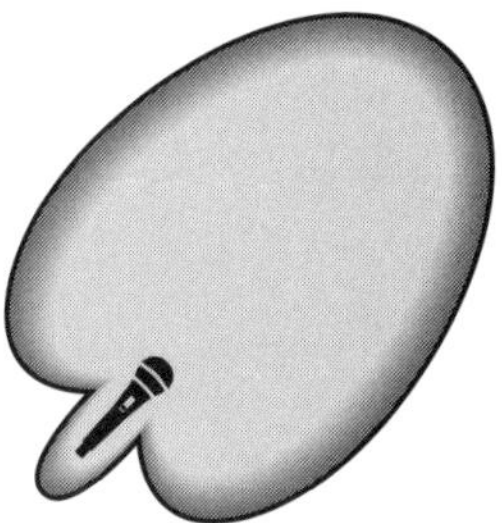

Figure 2.19 Supercardioid pattern.

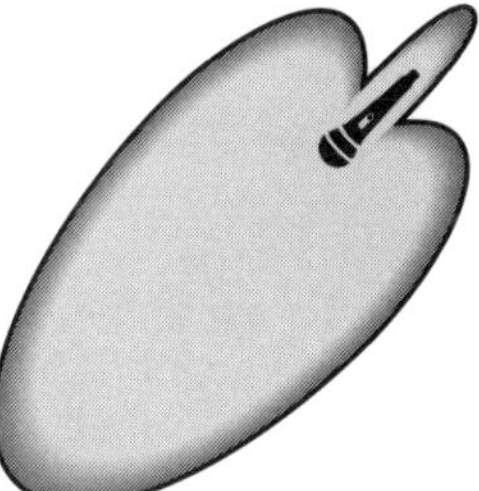

Figure 2.20 Hypercardioid pattern.

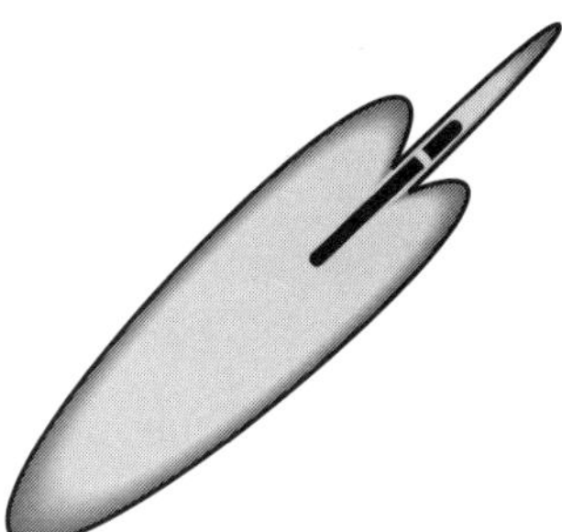

Figure 2.21 Shotgun pattern.

Watch the Ports Many directional microphones have elongated ports along their housings (see Figure 2.22). If that style of microphone is not put into its holder correctly, the clip can block the ports and cause the mic to lose pattern performance. This design is not very suitable for handheld applications because the hand blocks the ports and changes the directional characteristic of the microphone. In a live performance, this turns a directional mic into a non-directional one that is more prone to go into wild feedback. It will also sound pretty bad. Singers who try to stop feedback by covering the front of the mic cause the feedback to increase because all the sound now enters the microphone through the ports without the sound-cancelling properties of a cardioid.

Photo courtesy of RØDE Microphones.

Figure 2.22 RØDE NTG-3 shotgun. Note the long row of ports that create the highly directional pattern.

The Right Microphone for Every Job

Different microphones are used for different purposes. The choice of which mic to use depends on many factors. A partial list of these considerations includes:

- Frequency range of the sound source (type of instrument, a voice, sound effects)
- The nature of the sound (a percussive sound; a large, vibrating single source, such as a piano; a quiet temple bell; a screamin' guitar; a string section)
- The level of background noises in the recording area (passing buses, air conditioning, wind, rain on a tin roof)
- The acoustics (good acoustics that are a part of the recording of an orchestra, bad acoustics of a jazz club)
- The approach to the recording (multi-mic, simple stereo, news gathering in which the sound is on the move and intelligibility is key, a lecture that includes questions from the audience)
- Purpose of the recording (spoken word, film atmospheres, music recording, podcasts)
- Planned output (mono, stereo, 5.1)
- The style of the recording (for instance, if you want a drum sound like that of Buddy Rich in the '50s or a '60s Motown rhythm-section sound)
- Size of the sound source (one guitar player, a band in live concert, symphony, musical play)
- Location of recording (fixed, outdoors, on location in a jungle, swamp, boat, ocean, desert)
- Durability, reliability, available power (on location in an isolated area, for instance, or high humidity)
- And, of course, the pragmatic consideration of what microphones happen to be available and your budget

A given microphone may be the preferred choice for a particular sound but not necessarily the best choice in every situation. However, a microphone that is generally accepted as suitable for vocals will probably be good for most acoustic work (piano, guitar, violin, and so on). All of the microphone manufacturers mentioned earlier make microphones suitable for vocal recordings. As for me, I could seldom pass up the sound of an Ela M 251 for vocals. That being said, at other times I have used the Neumann U 87, U 67, U 47, and KM 56; the AKG C 12 A and 414; and a couple of the RØDE mics, to name a few. And then there have been the rare times when what should have been an unsuitable mic happens to be the sound everyone is looking for. For sounds where a less-dominant bottom (or bass) is required, I prefer an AKG 451, one of the Neumann KM series, or a small-capsule AT condenser.

There are also a great many microphones that are not good choices for recording vocals but that work well for recording drums or guitar. For example, the Shure SM58 and 57 don't have particularly good high-frequency or transient response, but these "weaknesses" may make them ideal on drums and electric guitar amps, though not suitable for cymbals. On the other hand, they are a staple of live performance because they can be held right against the lips, and they seldom pop or go into feedback (when the sound coming from the speakers is uncontrollably re-amplified through the mic, creating an ear-splitting howling noise). They are also very nearly indestructible.

Many microphones can be used for both performing and recording, but recording microphones are generally brighter, broader in frequency response, and more sensitive, and hence prone to feedback, or they can be too sensitive for close-range vocals and prone to popping and crackling on sounds of S's, T's, and P's. The criteria for a P.A. microphone—a mic used for live performance—include not only how it sounds but also its ability to reject feedback. Good-quality P.A. mics can be used for many recording applications, but if you're serious about recording, you should think about acquiring at least two or three good recording microphones—in particular, a good vocal mic or two that can also be used on higher frequency or percussive instruments, such as cymbals or acoustic guitar. If you're not recording live drums, you'll probably never use more than two or three mics for most sessions. But if you are emotionally attached to acoustic drums and you want to mic them as most studio engineers would, you'll need at least a matched pair of bright microphones for cymbal overheads and another bright mic for the hi-hat. Those mics that are widely used for live work will often be suitable on the toms, snare, and kick. The drum overhead mics can also serve well on acoustic guitar, piano, or mixed percussion.

The best way to choose a recording microphone is in a studio environment where a recording can be made and the playback can be evaluated. It may take a few attempts with the same mic to get a feel for how it will perform on a given sound source. In the case of vocals, different microphone techniques should be tried, and for instruments, different placements.

What you hear in a microphone is quite subjective. Some of it is a bit like describing the color of a blue sky, but here goes. I'll try to suggest the sorts of things I listen for when trying out an unknown mic.

- How does the pickup pattern measure up? If omni, does the mic seem to pick up full-bandwidth sound from all around the mic? If cardioid, how well does it pick up sound on and slightly off axis compared to sound that's coming from behind the mic?
- How much low-frequency rumble does the mic pick up from any direction (coming from the acoustics, building rumble, band next door, and so on)?
- Compared to the level of the sound coming from the microphone, how much electronic noise seems to be generated by the mic? This is also described as *signal to noise*, and it's a problem if you are recording a quiet instrument and you need to turn up the mic preamp a lot.
- How well does the mic handle very loud sounds (such as a kick drum or amplified guitar)?
- How well does the mic pick up sound that is some distance away, or, conversely, close to the mic?
- For PA, how prone is the mic to go into feedback when it's near the speakers? How prone is it to pop when the mic is close to the mouth?
- How much mechanical noise or floor vibration is picked up through the mic stand, or in the case of handheld mics, how much noise is created from hand-holding?
- How open is the sound? For instance, when an acoustic guitar is strummed, is the sound expansive and does the sustain seem to linger and extend into the decay of the surrounding reverb?
- How well does the mic reproduce the attack of percussion sounds (triangles, drum, cymbals, and so on)?

But how do you get your hands on mics to try them out? The most pragmatic and common way comes down to building a relationship with the place where you buy your gear. I understand getting the best price on anything is imperative when you don't have much money, but if that's your only consideration, you may find little interest from a local store that would otherwise be willing to help if you're a good customer. Having spent years working with music stores and recording-supply retailers, I have found that try-before-you-buy is a common policy extended to serious regular customers. Even if they don't have it in stock, they can often ask the manufacturer's rep for a demo model to try out for a day or so. Depending on the mic, renting them for a short term is also possible.

Another way to learn about mics, though one step removed, is through videos such as *Shaping Your Sound with Microphones, Mixers, and Multitrack Recording* (Hal Leonard, 2002) by yours truly. There are also many A/V demos online from YouTube and on the websites of many mic manufacturers.

In the later chapters, when we're talking about specific microphone applications, I will be making some specific mic suggestions (as well as sharing those of some of my engineering buddies).

Physical Law #1: The Smaller, the Brighter

Because a microphone responds to net atmospheric pressure change on its surface, if the diaphragm diameter is not sufficiently small, high-frequency sound waves with very short wavelengths will create offsetting pressures on the surface of the diaphragm (see Figure 2.23). In theory the summing of the positive and negative movement totals no net movement, and consequently, no output will be generated, i.e., acoustic phase cancellation. In reality, the cancellation is more erratic due to differences in every wave, but it will create a rigidness and lack of smoothness in the sound.

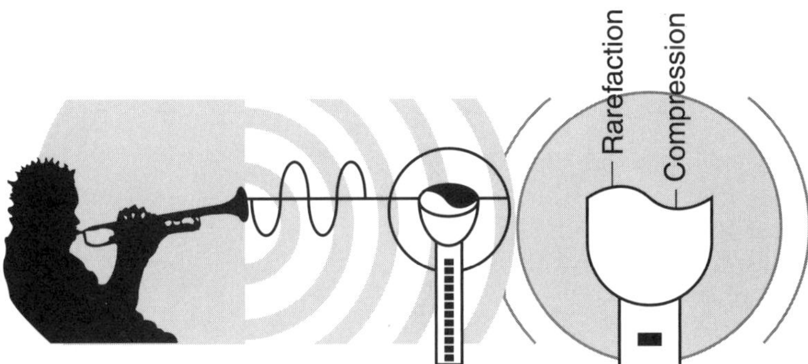

Figure 2.23 High-frequency sound waves generate equal but opposite pressures on the surface of a larger diaphragm, causing some cancellation and a reduction of those frequencies.

For example, frequencies above 10 kHz have wavelengths that are sufficiently short to generate opposing pressures on the surface of most diaphragms. The larger the capsule, the lower the frequency at which this cancellation is a factor, and many microphone capsules are large enough to be affected. This can cause them to have an uneven high-frequency response beginning at approximately the frequency that has a half wavelength equal to the diameter of the microphone's diaphragm. From that frequency upward, the diaphragm will experience an ever-increasing amount of opposing pressure. When the diaphragm diameter equals one wavelength, the counterpressure will be nearly equal.

In reality, no sound wave is perfectly symmetrical, nor is a diaphragm so compliant that it perfectly mirrors the precise pressure differences (or gradient) across its surface, so cancellation is never complete or total. However, a general principle of microphone design is that the smaller the diameter of the diaphragm, the better the high-frequency response and the higher the frequency at which the microphone begins to experience some degree of phase cancellation. It is for this reason that PZM mics (pressure-zone microphones are described in Chapter 4) and sound level meters use an extremely small-diameter capsule. Conversely, in general, a large diaphragm will give a more solid low-frequency response compared to a small diaphragm (see Figure 2.24). Recall that a diaphragm responds to net atmospheric change at any given instant. As a low-frequency pressure wave passes the capsule, a small diaphragm will experience very little physical movement from one moment to the next. On the other hand, a large diaphragm "sees" a greater "sample" at any given instant, so to speak. Consequently, a small diaphragm is generally brighter and more brilliant for recording upper-register sounds, and a larger diaphragm is richer for recording low-register sounds.

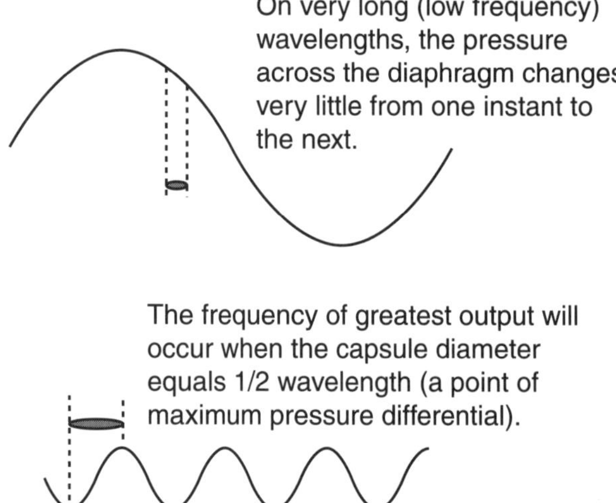

Figure 2.24 In general, large diaphragm diameter equals better low-frequency response, while smaller diaphragm diameter equals better high-frequency response.

It may be hard to choose the best size diaphragm for a given situation. Obviously, every mic has other factors that influence its sound, but as a rule, small-capsule mics will usually sound brighter while larger capsule mics tend to have more body. A female vocalist with a high voice might need a larger diaphragm to bring out the low range of her voice and reduce any unwanted harshness, for example.

Physical Law #2: The Bigger, the Slower

Large or heavy diaphragms or those that are less compliant are less able to instantly respond to very quick transients or high frequencies. The physical laws of mass in motion state that a large mass requires more time to get going, and then inertia comes into play, making it harder to slow down and change direction. The "compliance" of the flexible hinges that hold the diaphragm will also affect the transient response. A microphone with relatively large mass will not pick up high frequencies as well, and percussive transients will be slowed down. This might not be bad if, for instance, a little bit of electromechanical compression is desired on drums. In other words, a Shure 58 or 57 or AKG D 112 on the tom-toms or kick will not respond to the rapid attack of the stick or beater, thus compressing the transient and bringing out the drum's sustain and fatness.

On the other hand, a lighter and more compliant capsule (such as a small-capsule condenser) will have a better transient response. Condenser microphones are the most compliant design because their mass is so small. Ribbons microphones are nearly as compliant. In general, a moving-coil dynamic microphone is the least compliant, though there are several dynamics that are fairly bright with reasonably good transient response.

Microphones and Transient Response

A transient is the leading edge and initial attack of a sound's envelope (see Figure 2.25). (An envelope is a graph of time versus loudness; more on this in Chapter 3.) The beginning of a sound event is usually a transient—for instance, the crack of the snare. A moment before the drum is struck, there aren't any vibrations, and then, when the stick hits the head, the sound is as loud as it will ever be. If a microphone by its deficiencies of design cannot respond to this sudden change in pressure, it will not have a good transient response, and the signal it generates will have less attack and percussiveness. Mics with a bad transient response may lack clarity no matter how much the treble (high-frequency) control in the mixing desk is boosted.

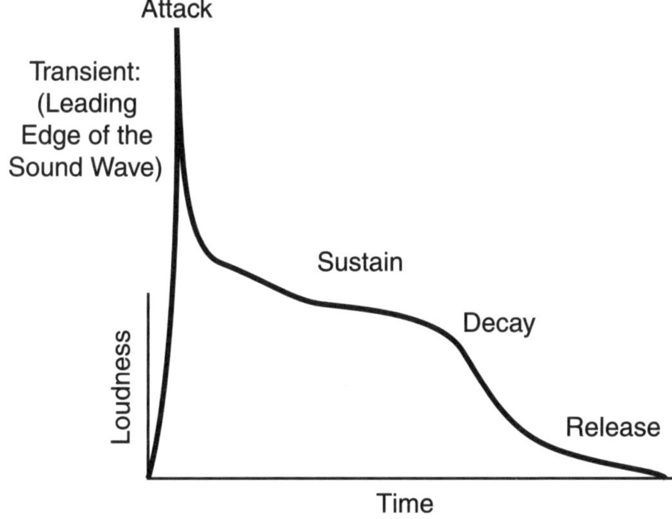

Figure 2.25 An illustration of a sound envelope.

Often, transient response is adversely affected by a thick windscreen, as commonly found on many microphones designed for PA vocal applications, where it is expected that the singer will have his or her lips right against the microphone. When choosing a microphone intended to be used for both P.A. and recording, select one that has a removable windscreen. (You can simply unscrew many of them.) Take it off for recording and leave it on when it is used for P.A. When recording vocals, a more transparent form of windscreen is preferable; it is described in Chapter 7, "Accessories and Necessary Hardware."

Off-Axis Coloration

When evaluating the polar pattern of any microphone, and in particular a cardioid mic, the off-axis response is a significant factor in its sound and suitability for various applications. Off-axis coloration describes how the polar pattern of the microphone changes depending on the frequency being picked up (see Figure 2.26). In other words, what frequencies does the microphone pick up in its off-axis area? Many cardioid mics are quite directional at high frequency but relatively non-directional at low frequency, causing them to pick up significant amounts of low-frequency rumble from any direction. For this reason, a bidirectional or omnidirectional mic may be a better choice for recording vocals because these patterns have a minimum of off-axis coloration. Although there will be more leakage (room sounds), it is full range and not predominantly low-frequency rumble. Obviously, you would only do this if the singer were the only thing being recorded at the time.

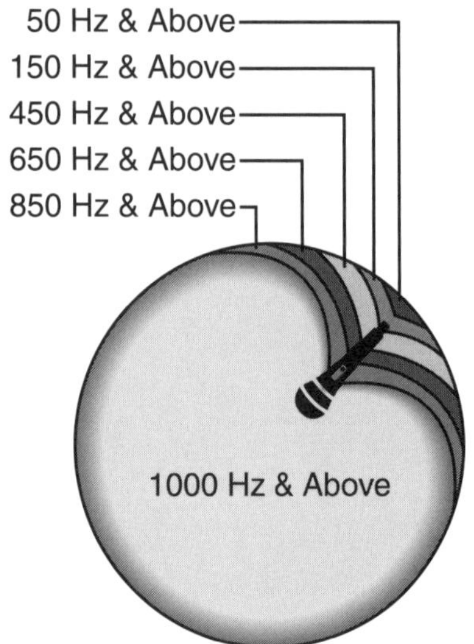

Figure 2.26 Illustration of a cardioid pattern with off-axis coloration.

Sensitivity and the Proximity Effect

A microphone's *sensitivity* refers to how well it picks up sound at a distance and to how high a sound-pressure level the microphone can take before it distorts. The character and quality of the mic's sound will also vary depending on the sound's distance from the mic. Most microphones sound dramatically different when they are close to the sound source from how they sound at a distance from the source. This is called the *proximity effect*, and it is caused by the ports reinforcing the low-frequency waves. On many microphones there is a low-frequency roll-off switch to compensate for the proximity boost caused by close miking or by the singer holding the mic right up against his mouth. Proximity can be useful for many miking effects. A mic with a fair amount of proximity, positioned right near the drums, can enhance the depth of the sound. Sticking a mic right up against a guitar amp speaker cone will generate similar results. Proximity effect is used for FM DJ-type vocals, and a great many popular music songs have been recorded with the vocalist close to the microphone to take advantage of the natural boost in low frequencies.

Spec Sheets

Specification sheets are data prepared by the manufacturer that quantify the microphone's physical dimensions, technical details, and performance. Figure 2.27 shows an example of a good microphone spec sheet. Some microphones will also come with a frequency response curve for that microphone. Manufacturer spec sheets are a decent indicator of how a mic may sound; however, when reading a spec sheet, you need to keep in mind that there are many different ways of interpreting or presenting the same information. It's not that the specifications are different from the product's reality or that a manufacturer is lying (at least we would hope not), but it is a matter of how the information is presented. For example, are the specs typical or best case? One manufacturer's best-case specs might look a lot better than another that guarantees the specs are typical minimums. In reality, when a direct comparison is made between the two straight out of the box, there may or may not be little difference.

Distortion, noise, and sensitivity figures will also differ, depending on reference levels and the type of signals used for the measurements. Frequency-response measurements are generally made with a sine wave as the source, but in reality, musical sound more closely resembles a square wave (see Figure 2.28). Regardless of the frequency of the sound, the quick attack of a note (or event) requires that the mic respond immediately to the transient. A microphone might more easily follow the curve of a high-frequency sine wave but round off the edges of a square wave regardless of its frequency (see Figure 2.29). The manufacturer may (or may not) include qualifying information in the fine print of the specs.

Often, a reality of manufacturing is that the initial performance specifications are measured on an engineering prototype so the spec sheets can be printed while the mic is being mass-produced. Sometimes a spec sheet will say "preliminary specifications," and sometimes it won't. In fairness, products may in fact perform better than specified, since the real product is often an improvement over the prototype that was tested for the spec.

Equally useful, most manufacturers also have a microphone guide that suggests which of their mics to use on specific instruments, voices, or sounds, and some provide such guidance in sound and video examples on their websites.

The point is, published specifications can only provide an *indication* of performance. The acid test is to plug in the microphone and determine how it sounds to you. There are many times when the deficiencies of a mic might actually enhance the desired quality of a given sound.

Features

- Live condenser vocal microphone
- Feedback rejecting super-cardioid pick up pattern
- Locking on/off switch
- Heavy duty metal body
- High level of RF rejection
- Low handling noise
- Designed and manufactured in Australia
- Full 10 year warranty*

Specifications

Acoustic Principle	Pressure gradient	Directional Pattern	Super-Cardioid
Frequency Range	35Hz ~ 20,000Hz	Sensitivity	-44dB ±2dB re 1V/Pa (6.3mV @ 94 dB SPL) @ 1kHz
Nominal Impedence	50Ω	Equivalent Noise	23dBA SPL (A - weighted per IEC651)
Maximum Output	+5.2dBu (@ 1% THD into 1kΩ)	Dynamic Range	118dB (per IEC651)
Maximum SPL	141dB (@ 1kHz, 1% THD into 1kΩ load)	Signal/Noise	71dB SPL (A - weighted per IEC651)
Power Req.	24/48V Phantom Power	Dimensions	Length - 187mm Diameter - 47mm
Output Connection	3 pin XLR, balanced output between Pin 2 (+), Pin 3 (-) and Pin 1 (ground)	Shipping Weight	545g
Net Weight	308g		

Frequency Response

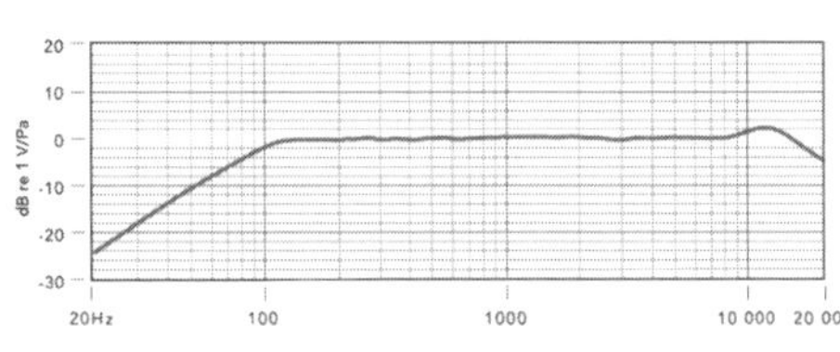

Polar Pattern

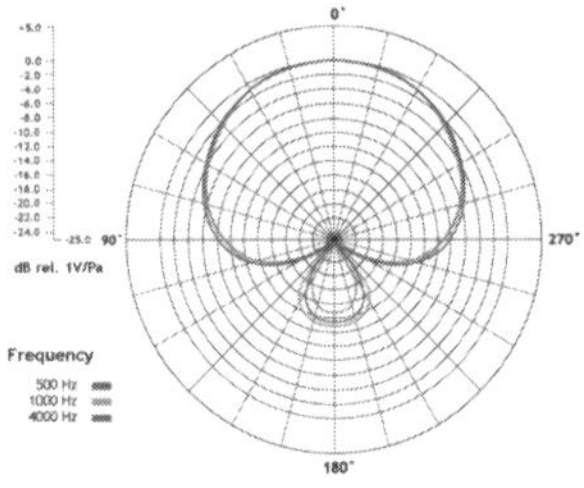

M2 Live Condenser Microphone www.rodemic.com RØDE MICROPHONES

Courtesy of RØDE Microphones.

Figure 2.27 Typical specification sheet.

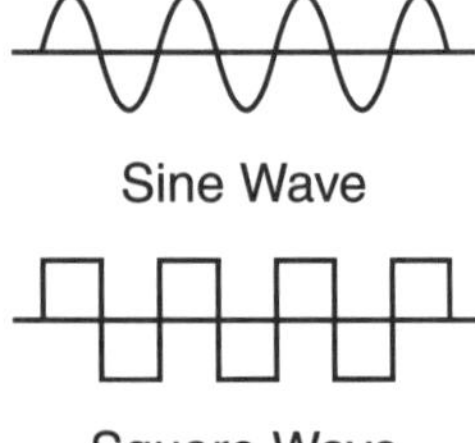

Figure 2.28 Sound is more like a square wave.

Figure 2.29 A poor mic or amp will round off the corners of a square wave and the attack of a sound transient.

The legendary U 47 is a unique case in point. Though its frequency response is far from flat, and it has some intrinsic distortion, countless singers have embraced its sound while recording innumerable hit records.

Storing Microphones

Microphones need to be stored when they're not in use. When they are left standing in the studio, they tend to attract cigarette smoke and extremely fine dust and become coated with a film that builds up the diaphragm's mass, lowers its compliance, and causes a general loss of response. The attraction is either electrostatic or magnetic, depending on the type of transducer. The problem is made worse if the mic's internal dust/wind screen has any slight tear. I prefer to keep all the mics in the manufacturer's boxes, stored in a pigeonholed cabinet. Jewelry or cigar boxes can be found at flea markets for mics that don't have boxes. I've often seen foam rubber cut out to cradle mics, but it tends to deteriorate and generate dust. Line the boxes with a cushion of cloth. If the microphone came with a cloth bag, use it. Keep any special connectors or the microphone's holder with the mic. It's alarming how many times a holder that is unique to the mic gets lost. Never leave batteries in a mic if it's not going to be used for a while.

If there is a bit of humidity where you are, keep electronic moisture absorber pillows (the little things that come with new electronics) in each box. Get a couple of hand-carry shopping baskets to ensure that a number of microphones can be safely carried from the cabinet to the studio.

Now that we've looked at how microphones work, in the next chapter we'll consider the other side of the equation—how sound works and how we hear.

3 Understanding Sound and Hearing

Using microphones to get great sound requires more than simply knowing their specs or knowing where to place them in relation to a particular instrument, sound, and vocalists. Getting great sounds begins with understanding how sound itself works. It also helps to know as much as you can about how your ears work. This chapter looks at sound and how humans hear.

How Sound Works

The word *sound* is used to describe the brain's interpretation of stimuli arriving at the ear in the form of air pressure variations. In fact, any physical disturbance, alteration, or pulsation of pressure capable of being detected by the ear is sound. In general, such a disturbance reaches the ears by traveling through air. Sound waves do not travel through a vacuum. In order to transmit sound, a medium possessing matter (such as air molecules) and elasticity is required.

Sound Waves

Sound is created by atmospheric pressure variation caused by the vibrations of objects such as strings, drum heads, reeds, or vocal chords. When an object is tooted, whistled, plunked, or boomed out of its stationary state, there arises an internal elastic restoring force of stiffness. It is the action of this force, combined with the inertia of the system, that enables an object to vibrate back and forth across its at-rest position until all the energy that initially set up the vibration has dissipated.

These vibrations push, then pull, air molecules that are initially at rest against the now-vibrating body. The vibrating waves of air move outward from the object, like ripples from a rock thrown into a pond, and if the excursions (back and forth movements) of the vibrating object are great enough and at a frequency that's within the range of human hearing, the vibrations in the air will reach our eardrums and be interpreted as sound. The individual vibrating particles of air that transmit a sound wave do not change their average positions. The sound is transmitted by many individual molecules bouncing in waves off their neighbors, and then back toward their position of rest, and the cycle repeats until the vibrating body stops moving (see Figure 3.1). The average maximum distance the individual particles move from their rest or equilibrium position is called the *displacement amplitude*. For most sound waves, the displacements are quite small. For example, the air particles one meter from a vibrating dinner gong may undergo a maximum displacement of a fraction of a millimeter.

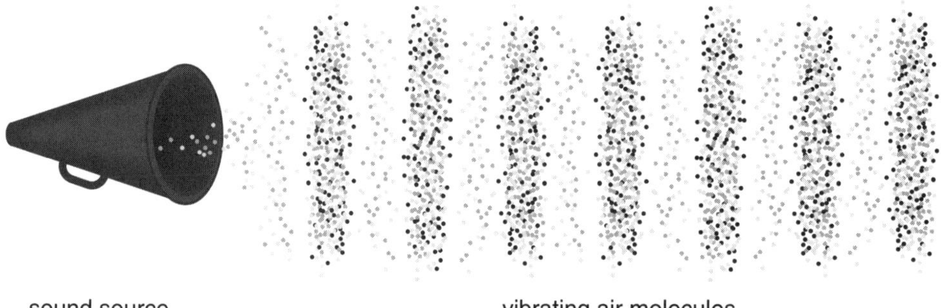

Figure 3.1 Sound is a generated by small alternating changes in atmospheric pressure.

The greater the movement of a vibrating body (in other words, the sound source) the greater the displacement of the air particles from the resting or equilibrium position and the louder the resulting sound. Because it is in motion, this energy is called *kinetic energy*, and small amounts of it dissipate with each bounce, hence the sound decreases in loudness the farther it is from the source. Compared to the average prevailing air pressure, as the sound travels away from the sound source, the pressure waves are made up of recurring concentrations of air molecules called *compressions*, followed by areas of relatively thinly grouped molecules called *rarefactions*. The greater the periodic air pressure wave, the louder the sound. *Amplitude* is the term used for loudness and is the measure from the maximum of compression pressure to the maximum of rarefaction pressure of the wave (known as *peak-to-peak amplitude*). See Figure 3.2. A graph of one complete cycle of a wave is called a *waveform*.

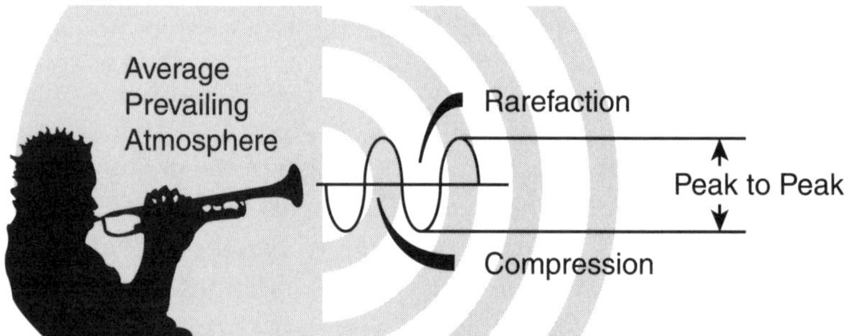

Figure 3.2 Sound waves are regularly recurring fluctuations in atmospheric pressure above and below an average prevailing pressure. From the maximum high pressure to the minimum of pressure is called peak to peak on a graphical representation of the sound wave.

One complete variation of compression through to rarefaction and back to normal air pressure again is called a *cycle*. How many times a second the vibrating body changes direction determines the sound wave's frequency and is heard as a note's primary pitch. *Frequency* can be defined as the rate of recurrence of a vibration (or the compressions and rarefaction of air) measured in cycles per second. The way of measuring cycles of sound waves was discovered by a scientist named Heinrich Hertz, and thus cycles per second are known as *Hertz* (*Hz*).

Speed of Sound and Wavelength

How fast do these waves of energy travel? Not very fast, actually. In fact, because sound travels so slowly, delay, echo, and reverberation occur, all of which are important elements of the experience of sound. If sound traveled faster, its reflections would return so quickly as to be indistinguishable from the originating, or direct, sound.

Sound travels only about 344 meters per second, or 1,126 feet per second (768 miles per hour) in air at room temperature (20°C or 68°F). See Figure 3.3. In warmer air, sound travels slightly faster. In cooler air, it slows down a bit. The speed also changes ever so slightly with variations

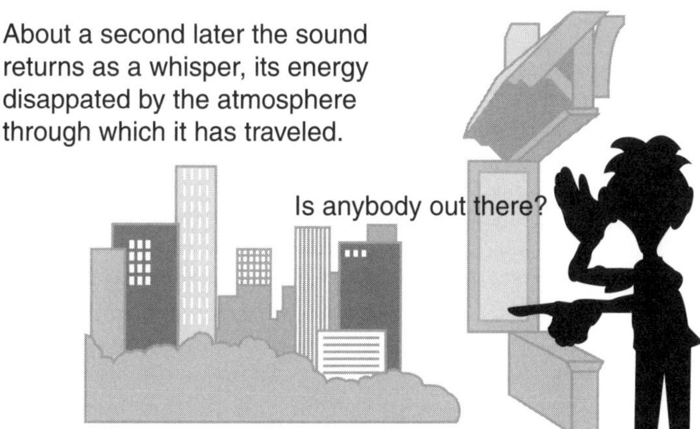

Figure 3.3 Sound travels in dry air (68°F) at 768 mph, or 1,126 ft/s.

in relative humidity. Sound travels much faster in liquids and solids than it does in air. But as the density of these materials increases, the distance that the sound will travel is reduced. In other words, sound travels quickly through steel, but it doesn't travel very far due to the density of the steel. Understanding how quickly sound travels from one place to another will be a surprisingly useful bit of knowledge when it comes to mic placement, because the distance between mics and their relationship to a sound source affects how the various sounds entering the microphones will combine in a mix.

The wavelength of a wave is the physical distance between the beginning and the end of a cycle, or between corresponding points on adjacent cycles. The formula for figuring wavelength looks like this:

Wavelength = Speed of sound / Frequency

Therefore, the distance between two compressions of sequential cycles is equal to the wavelength, and the distance from positive peak to negative peak of one cycle is equal to half the wavelength. Wavelength has important implications with regard to how sound behaves under certain architectural conditions, such as when reflecting off walls and corners and propagating through doorways. Wavelength is also of great concern in the conversion of energy by transducers, such as microphones and speakers. Low frequencies have long wavelengths, while high frequencies have short wavelengths. As described in Chapter 2, the size of the diameter of the microphone capsule is a factor in how well that microphone will respond to various frequencies. Figure 3.4 gives a few examples of frequency versus wavelength (at 68°F).

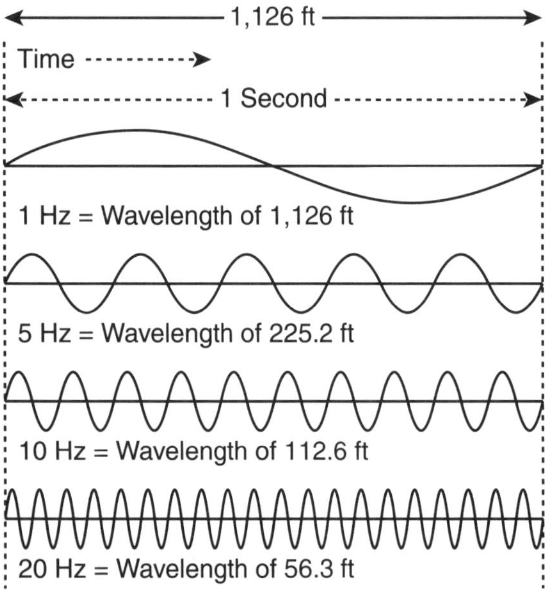

Figure 3.4 As the frequency goes up, so does the pitch, and the shorter the wavelength is in real space. (In dry air, 68°F.)

The real and relative phases of a sound wave were explained in Chapter 2, and it might be useful to have another look at that explanation. In Chapter 4, "Polarity, Phase Cancellation, and Reverb," there is also much more information on phase.

The Doppler Effect: A Leslie Speaker If a sound source is moving toward or away from you, the wave it creates is shortened as it's coming toward you and is stretched when it moves away. If you're standing near a railway line, and a train happens to blow its horn as it passes, the train's horn goes up in pitch as it comes toward you, then goes down as it moves away. Perhaps the best example is the classic Leslie speaker cabinet (see Figure 3.5) that most rock and jazz organ players (The Doors, Jimmy Smith, Booker T and the MGs) used through the '60s and '70s. The speaker itself is also a popular sound for guitarists such as Joe Walsh and Santana. It has two speakers. The treble speaker faces up, and the bass speaker faces down. Rotating horns positioned over the speakers focus the sound and cause it to come toward the listener and then go away as the horn rotates.

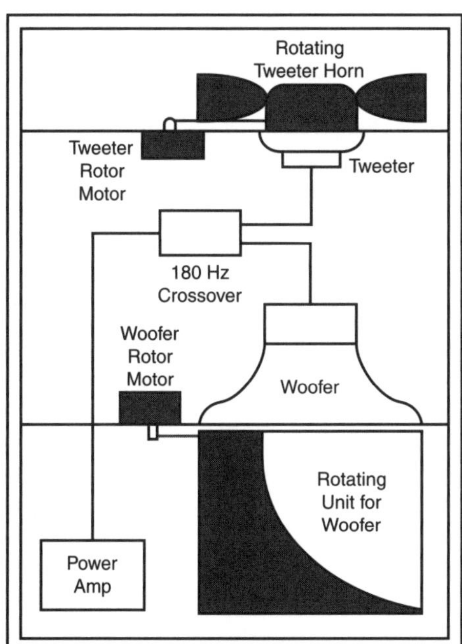

Figure 3.5 A Leslie cabinet has two rotating horns (high and low) so the sound from the two speakers is going away, then moving toward the listener (or the microphone). The speed of the rotor motors and the horns' rotation can be varied by the player.

Harmonics and Overtones

Consider a mass attached to a string so that the weight is constrained to move back and forth in only one plane. If the mass is displaced from its rest or equilibrium position and then released, it will go into motion—think of a pendulum. The frequency of the pendulum's movement, or vibration, is constant, and the displacement of the mass from its rest position is a sinusoidal function of time. A sinusoidal or sine wave is a smoothly curved wave that represents but a single frequency throughout its cycle (see Figure 3.6).

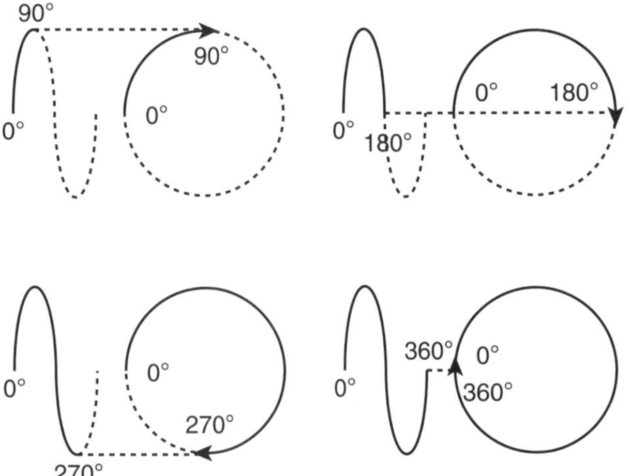

Figure 3.6 Sine wave degrees compared to the degrees of a circle.

If we graph this displacement from its rest position over time, as with a mounted tuning fork, we produce our familiar sine wave, the simplest type of wave. Such a wave, if produced at an audible frequency, produces a pure tone of a certain pitch.

But musical instruments rarely produce pure, single sine waves. For instance, the complex pattern of vibrations generated by a bowed violin string or a voice is not one simple tone, but rather a complex collection of frequencies that can be dissected into an equivalent composite pattern of simple harmonic vibrations. Harmonics are a series of tones that are integral multiples of the primary or fundamental frequency that corresponds to the pitch of a note (see Figure 3.7). The fundamental frequency is known as the *first harmonic*; an overtone of twice this frequency is the *second harmonic*; and so on. For example, a first harmonic of 200 Hz has a second harmonic of 400 Hz and a third harmonic of 600 Hz, and so on (see Figure 3.8).

The harmonics of a note, plus any other vibrations created in the generation of a fundamental note, are called *overtones*. The overtones common to any given instrument are the unique result of the materials, geometry, and construction of that particular instrument, as well as the way in which it is played and the acoustics of the space in which it is played. That's why a D note played on a piano sounds different than a D note played on a flute—the instrument's complex overtones

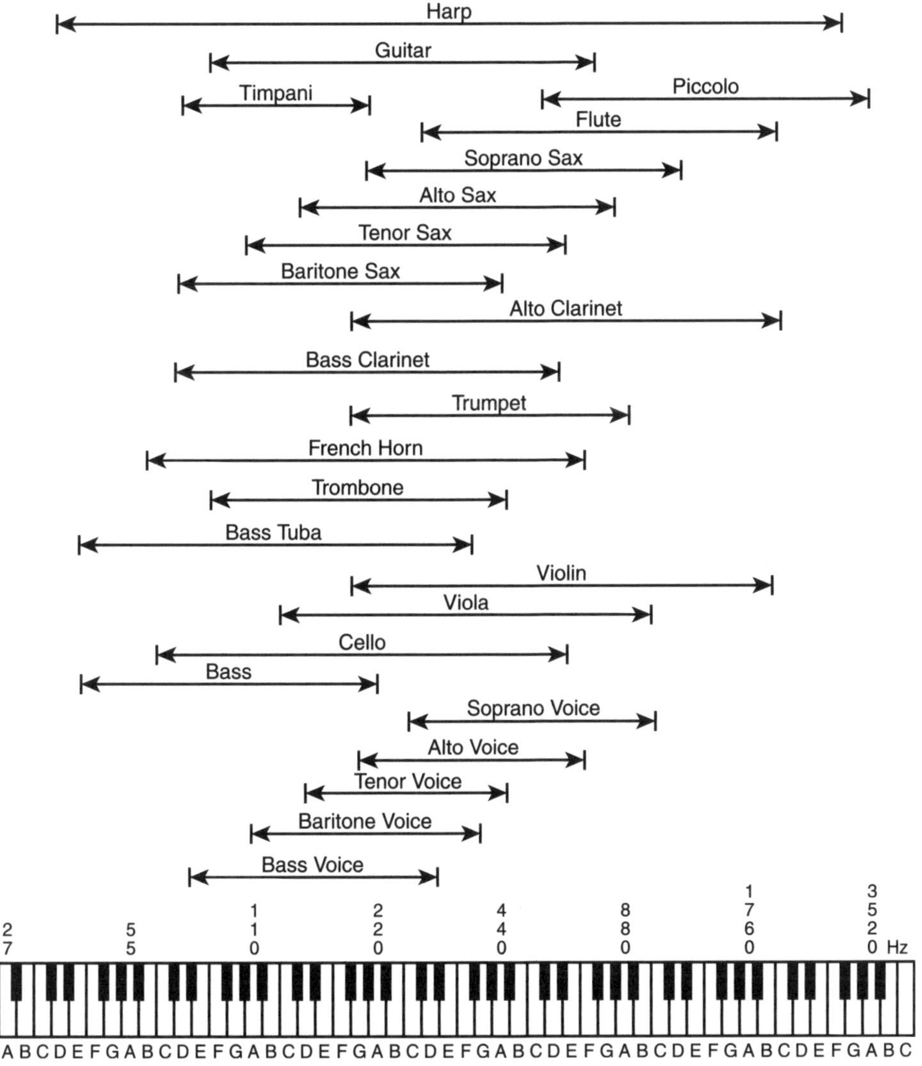

Figure 3.7 Fundamental frequency range of instruments.

shape the sound. This difference is known as an instrument's *timbre* and allows us to differentiate between two tones of equal intensity levels and fundamental frequencies on different instruments. Timbre, like pitch, is a complex characteristic, although it is primarily determined by the waveform of the tone being sounded, its frequency, and intensity. Timbre has been described in many ways, including mellow, brassy, muddy, and sharp, but it is difficult to formulate a definitive set of units to describe timbre. Nor will two seemingly identical instruments create an

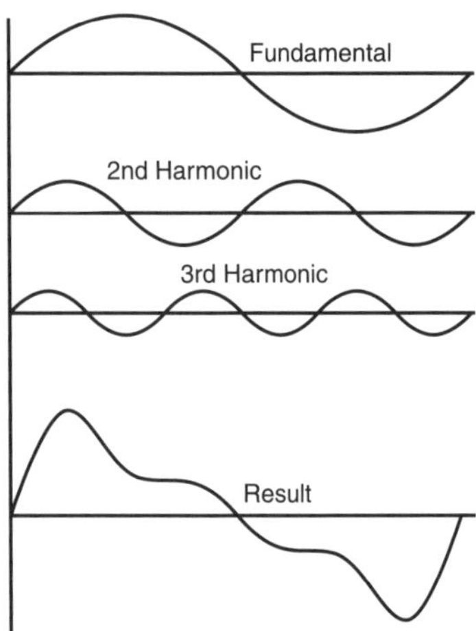

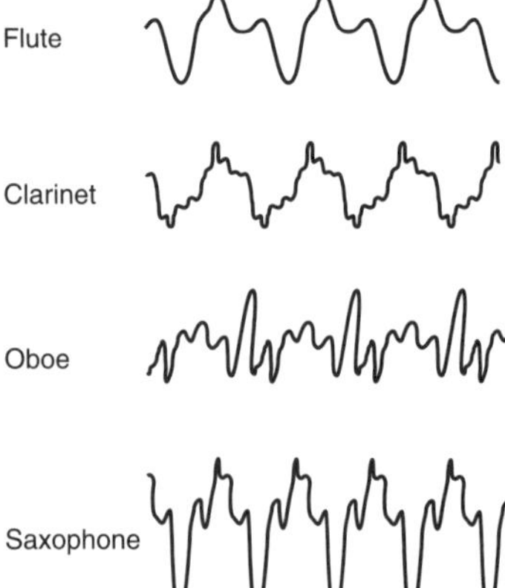

Figure 3.8 Fundamental plus harmonics to create the wave shape of different instruments for the same note (flute, clarinet, oboe, saxophone).

identical sound. It is for this reason that, for example, the best sampler technology used to reproduce a violin section will not sound like a real violin section with its multitude of instrument and performance variables.

Some instruments, however, such as bells, xylophones, drums, and other percussion instruments, have overtones that are not harmonically related to the fundamental frequency. However, these overtones and their relative amplitudes create the fullness of the sound and help determine its characteristics. The harmonics present in a sound and the relative amplitudes of these harmonics can be shown graphically by what is known as a *harmonic spectrum*.

Formants The harmonics that are generated when a fundamental note is played are seldom evenly spaced, nor do they decrease in loudness at regular, identical intervals as they rise in frequency. In other words, the second harmonic is not necessarily louder than the third, nor is the fourth necessarily softer then the third. In fact, some harmonics may be missing entirely. Nearly all musical instruments have small clusters of harmonics interspersed with areas where there are few or no harmonics. These clusters of harmonics are called *formants* (see Figure 3.9). For example, a formant might encompass a range from the 2nd to the 7th harmonic. Then the harmonic content might be very weak until the 11th harmonic, where another formant begins and extends to the 13th, and so on. Formants exist because the vibrating member (that is, the string, reed, diaphragm, vocal cords, and so on) of the musical instrument interacts with the physical structure of the instrument, the player's technique, and the resistance of the atmosphere (which could be the outside environment or that which is inside the instrument). For the same reason, the loudness of each unique harmonic, in relation to the fundamental, will vary with the note and the instrument. Formant clusters will also vary with the unique construction of that particular instrument and the note(s) played (see Figure 3.10). Formants are a key element of any musical sound and an important part of what the microphone must capture in order for the instrument's sound to seem complete.

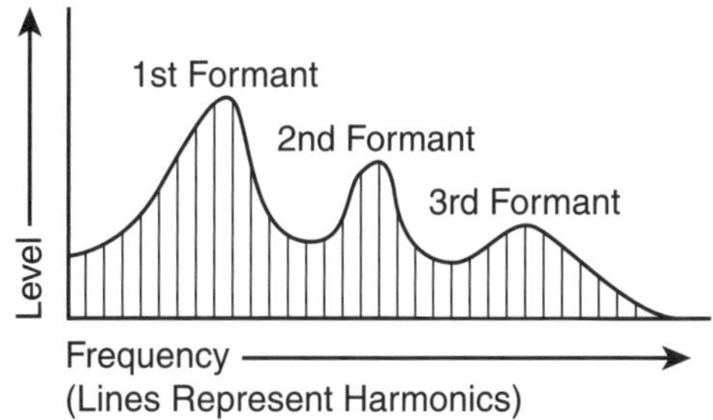

Figure 3.9 Formants are clusters of harmonics.

The loss in level of the overtones and harmonics (formants) of a sound accounts for the dullness of an old guitar string or the deadness of an old drum head. Also, both the content of the harmonics and the overtones experience change through the course of the note's duration.

As noted earlier, overtones have a lot to do with establishing the unique sounds of particular instruments. How these overtones cluster, how loud they are in relation to one another, and how the dominant overtone frequencies change over time all contribute to determining an instrument's timbre or characteristic sound.

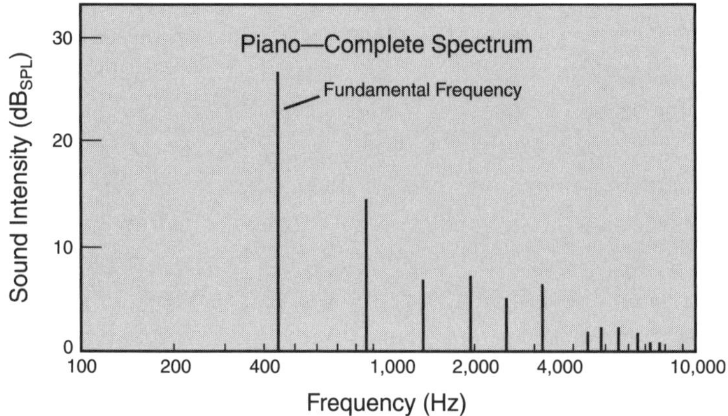

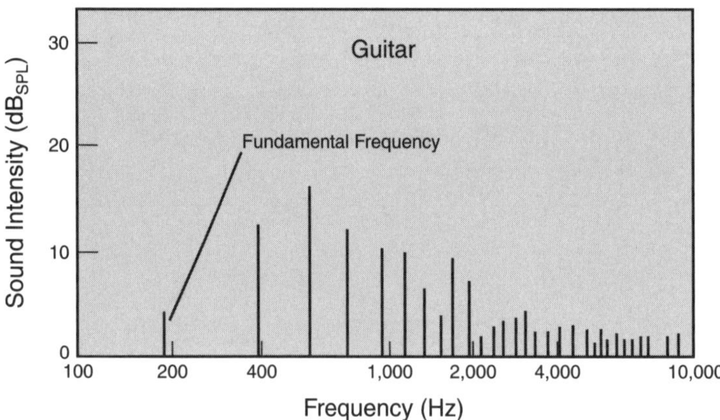

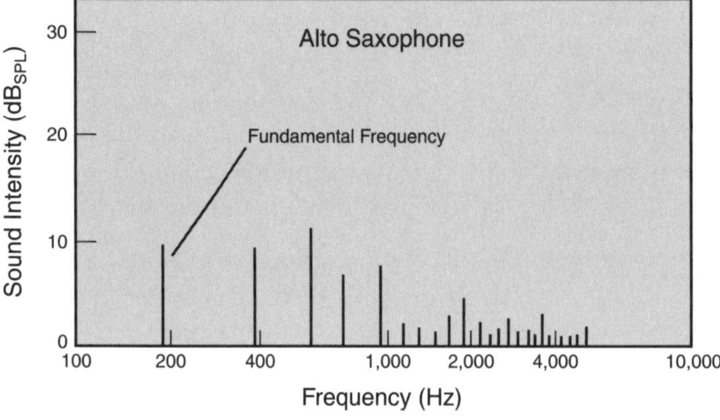

Figure 3.10 The relative loudness of harmonics for different instruments (piano, guitar, alto sax).

Measuring Amplitude: The Decibel

To be able to measure any aspect of audio, a unit of measurement of sound had to be developed. The dB unit came into existence in the late 19th century through more of Alexander Graham Bell's research into human hearing. By then it had become possible to measure the slight variations in atmospheric pressure that transmit sound through the air. A significant challenge was relating this measurement to what the average person could hear.

To determine the threshold of hearing, a large sample of people was asked to subjectively judge what they could and could not hear. At the same time the sound pressure was measured. The generated sound was lowered by small increments until most of those tested could not hear it. From this point, the sound was slowly increased to determine the quietest sound that most of those tested could hear. All of the sample data was averaged and became the threshold of hearing. This does not suggest that there are no sound vibrations occurring below this point, but that the level is too small to be heard by the average person. Which is also to say that some people have more sensitive hearing than others.

The researchers also wanted to come up with some idea of human hearing's ability to distinguish loudness relationships. They asked those tested to tell when it seemed as though one sound was twice as loud as another similar sound. For the average person, they found that the sound pressure level had to be increased by 10 times to be perceived as twice as loud. With each doubling of the perceived loudness, the sound pressure level went up another 10 times. In other words, compared to the sound pressure level starting point, the first doubling of perceived loudness required 10 times the original barometric pressure level, the next doubling was 100 times the original, the third doubling was 1,000 times greater, the fourth was 10,000 times the original, and so on.

The ear had no trouble coping with loud sounds that were 100 billion times the sound pressure level of the quietest sound that could be heard. But to try to directly relate human hearing to barometric sound pressure meant using measurements in the millions and billions of units. Another outcome of the research that was not wasted on Bell was the fact that perceived hearing was not linear, but logarithmic. From this observation, it was concluded that humans hear loudness variations logarithmically, and a measuring system could be based on the well-established logarithm 10 to the power of 2. This new sound unit was named after Alexander Graham Bell—the decibel ("deci" being the Greek word for 10).

When something is made twice as loud, the sound pressure will have increased by 10 dB. When the loudness is doubled again, the sound pressure is increased by another 10 dB for a total of 20 dB louder than the original loudness. Moving up from 0 dB SPL, which is the threshold of hearing (for the average person—at least in Bell's day), rustling leaves are about 20 dB SPL, a quiet studio is 30 to 40 dB SPL, conversational speech is about 60 dB SPL, and your garden-variety rock band somewhere between 100 and 110 dB SPL. See Figure 3.11.

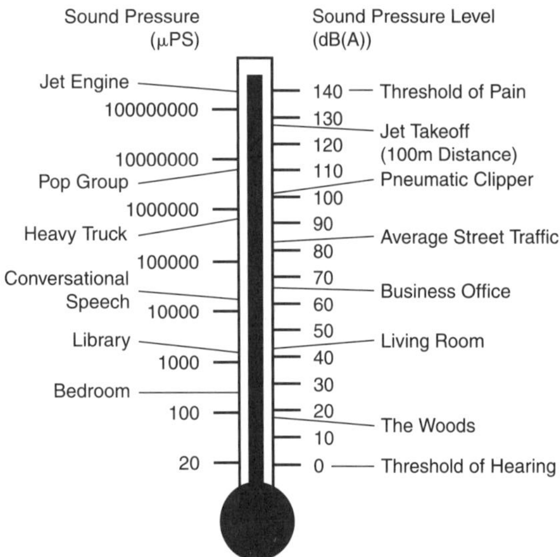

Figure 3.11 Sound pressure levels and hearing.

Once the dB unit was defined in relationship to the threshold of hearing, a variety of other dB scales were developed for other purposes. In each of these cases, the scale was redefined to a specific reference or point of comparison. Without this reference the dB scale is meaningless. The original dB scale was referenced to SPL (*sound pressure level*). Another example, the dBm, establishes a 0-dB reference point as one milliwatt of electrical power dissipated into a 600-ohm resistive load. There's also dBV which references 0 dB to 1 volt. Both of these are commonly used in electronic specifications. A bit of useful information is that if you double an electrical signal, it will show a 6-dB increase on a sound meter. When you're mixing and you pan a signal, such as the vocal or bass, to the center of a stereo mix, what you're doing is sending an equal amount of vocal or bass to both the left and right channels. When the stereo mix is combined into a mono mix (such as when it goes out to a poolside PA or to much of AM radio), the vocals and bass will be 6-dB louder than those sounds that are only in the left or right channel. Even though everything in stereo or 5.1 is a common mixing mode, it is still a good idea to see how the stereo mix sounds in mono.

Variation in loudness is also measured in dB, and if measured over time, it is referred to as *dynamics*. The range of amplitude, or loudness, an instrument or device can produce, from its quietest to its loudest, is known as its *dynamic range*. By drawing a chart of a sound's loudness over the passage of time, you create an illustration of a sound envelope.

Envelopes

Sound envelopes were briefly explained in Chapter 2. The envelope, the representation of a sound's amplitude over time, is usually broken down into four regions of activity. These four regions are known as ADSR, for attack, decay, sustain, and release (see Figure 3.12).

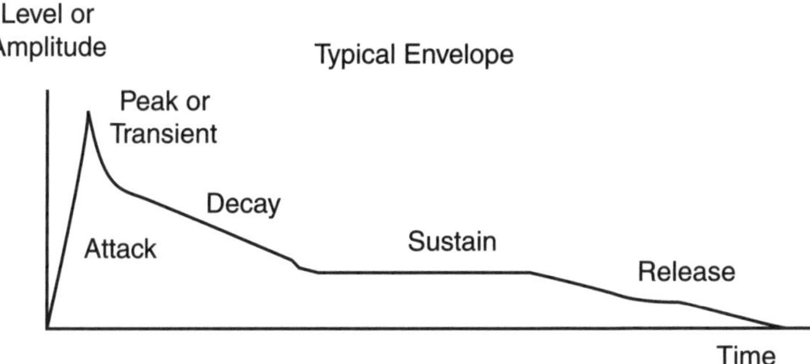

Figure 3.12 A typical envelope.

- **Attack.** This is the time it takes for the beginning of the sound to reach its peak. For many instruments it is nearly instantaneous. This element of the sound is often referred to as the *transient*.
- **Decay.** This is the time it takes for the sound to drop from the peak of the attack to the sustain level.
- **Sustain.** This is the region of the envelope that shows the constant loudness from the decay, to the end of the sound when it releases.
- **Release.** This is the time it takes for the sound to fade away after a sustain comes to an end.

A sound with a short attack time and a fast initial decay is characterized as being percussive, while a slower attack and gradual decay produce a smoother, gentler sound. Figure 3.12 illustrates the elements of an envelope, but not all sound envelopes would have all ADSR aspects, or one or more may have little prominence. Figure 3.13 shows four examples of different envelopes. As mentioned a moment ago, the leading edge of the attack is also described as the *transient*. For most sounds, the attack or leading edge of the sound is actually an amalgam of all

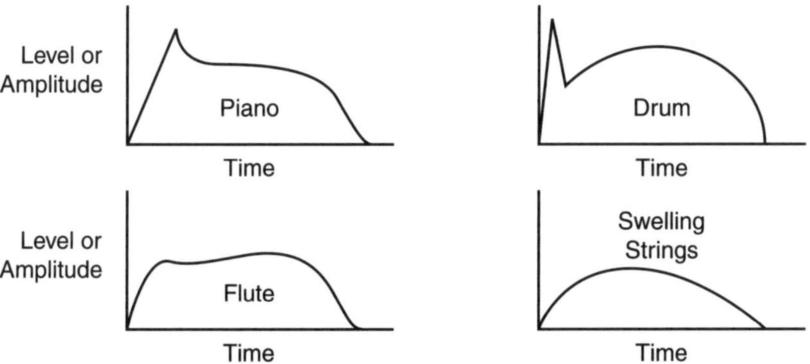

Figure 3.13 A comparison of typical envelopes of four common instruments.

frequencies and is noise. To explain, a bow going across a string is initially a noise until the string begins to vibrate at a frequency. It is this noise that gives the attack of the note. This short transient contributes to the character of the sound more than the loudness. The transient provides much of the brightness and clarity of a sound.

Having Great Ears

When it comes down to it, great engineers make decisions based on their personal experience of hearing. So if we spend time on how microphones work and how to use them, it's probably worth spending some time on how the ear works and how we experience hearing. Great engineers and producers are often described as having great ears. In fact, George Martin, legendary producer for The Beatles (and so much more), wrote a biography called *All You Need Is Ears.*

Anatomy of the Ear

The ear consists of three separate sections: the outer, the middle, and the inner ear (see Figure 3.14).

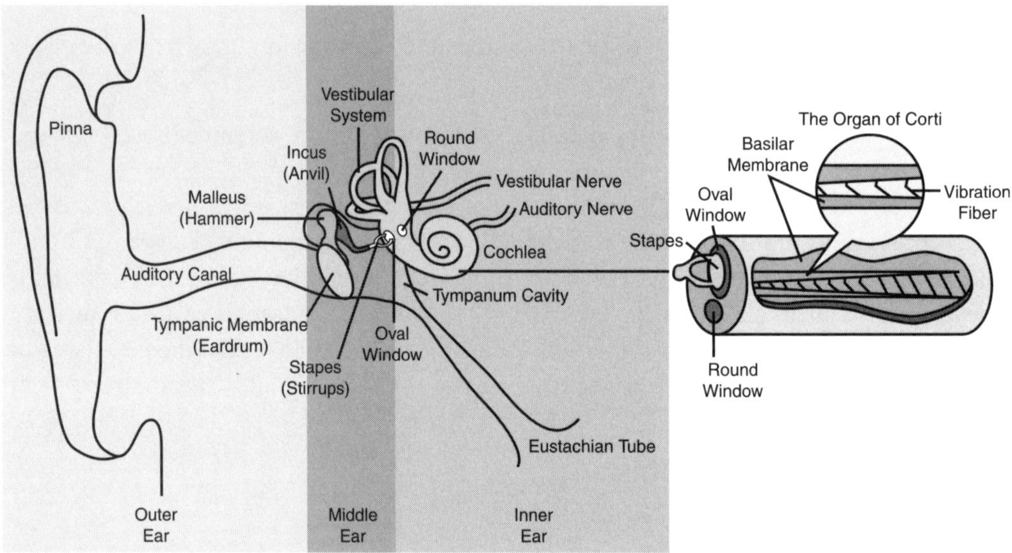

Figure 3.14 The inside of the ear.

The outer ear is made up of the pinna (visible ear), which serves as a horn to receive acoustic energy and lead it into the auditory canal. The auditory canal is approximately a straight tube, about 0.7cm in diameter and 2.5cm long, closed at its inner end by a stretched membrane, the eardrum or tympanic membrane. This diaphragm is kept under slight tension by muscles known as the *tensor tympani* and *stapedius*, which are vibrated by pressure fluctuations of a sound wave in the external auditory canal.

Behind the eardrum is the cavity of the middle ear that contains three tiny bones or ossicles: the malleus (referred to as the hammer), the incus (anvil), and the stapes (stirrup). The bones act as a small vibrating lever to amplify the atmospheric pressure against the oval window. Vibrations of the membrane are transmitted to the hammer, through the anvil, and to the stirrup. The stirrup pushes against an opening, called the *oval window*, which connects the middle and inner ear. Pressure waves exerted at the oval window are approximately 20 times greater than the pressure exerted on the eardrum.

The middle ear is connected to the rear of the nasal cavity by the Eustachian tube. This tube is normally closed, sealing the cavity; however, during the process of yawning or swallowing, it opens to permit air to enter or leave, thus establishing equilibrium between the external and internal air pressures. When we experience pressure changes, such as during airplane travel, the loss of hearing that we experience until we swallow or yawn is caused by the pressure difference on both sides of the eardrum. If the Eustachian tube is blocked, for instance when we have a cold, the pressure change cannot be equalized, and the pain can be quite severe.

Movement of the stirrup in the oval window transmits pressure waves to the liquid filling the inner ear. The inner ear consists of a sensitive system of tubes embedded in the bone of the skull, known as the *labyrinth*. At the end of this labyrinth is the flexible round window that stretches and provides a place for the fluid to go as it is pushed and pulled by the oval window. The labyrinth is made up of two systems: the vestibular system, which is concerned with the sense of balance of the body, and the cochlea, a shell-like structure, the most sensitive part of the ear, and the place where the sound pressure waves are converted into electrical pulses that are sent to the brain.

Inside the cochlea is a small chamber that contains a liquid called *endolymph*. In this chamber is the organ of Corti, which was first heard on the legendary Doors recording of "Light My Fire." Just kidding; I wanted to make sure you were still following along. The organ of Corti has about 24,000 hairs or fibers arranged on its surface, rather like a row of harps. The bases of the hairs are connected to a network of nerves that convert the motion of the fibers into electrical impulses that go to the brain. It seems that certain regions are responsible for various frequencies. When the fibers are moved and the nerve endings fire a pulse to the brain, they must then recharge. The recharge time is the limiting factor in how high a frequency humans can hear, because it takes about 1/20,000 of a second for this occur.

Hearing Ranges

Humans are capable of hearing a frequency range from approximately 30 Hz to 16,000–20,000 Hz for normal ears. However, the ears' functions extend beyond that of an extremely sensitive microphone; they respond to sound and analyze sound into frequency components, acting as both narrow-band analyzers and discrete-frequency analyzers. In conjunction with the nervous system, the ears are able to detect sounds of particular frequencies in the presence of intense backgrounds of wide-band noise and identify the direction from which the sound is coming. It appears as though the ears operate as if they contain a set of continuous noise and selective band filters. The hearing mechanism is therefore the most intricate and delicate mechanical structure in the human body.

Prior to the age of 18, frequencies as high as 20 kHz can be heard by both men and women; most middle-aged people seldom can hear sound above 15 kHz, and in some cases the cut-off is below 10 kHz. The threshold for frequencies in the range below 1 kHz is generally independent of age. The loss of hearing can occur through simply getting older, but increasingly it is caused by exposure to high sound pressure levels. An alarming number of young people have substantial hearing loss caused by high sound levels from iPods and other personal music players.

The frequency range of maximum sensitivity of the ear is between 2,000 and 4,000 cycles per second (2 kHz to 4 kHz) for normal ears and is called the *presence range* of hearing. It is also the frequency range for speech.

What Is Flat?

The term *flat response* is often referred to as a key specification of audio equipment, such as speakers and microphones. It indicates that the device in question is capable of gathering (or reproducing) sounds accurately along the entire frequency spectrum. This is an important benchmark for equipment, as it provides a clear point of some comparison and a context for a variety of other specifications.

But what most people don't know is that our ears are not flat, and their sensitivity changes depending on how loud the sound is. Put another way, equal intensity of differing frequencies is heard at different loudness levels. For example, as you can see on the audibility curve (see Figure 3.15), a pure tone with a frequency of 1 kHz and intensity level of 20 dB (SPL) is audible, while a pure tone of 100 Hz at the same intensity is below the threshold of audibility. This shows

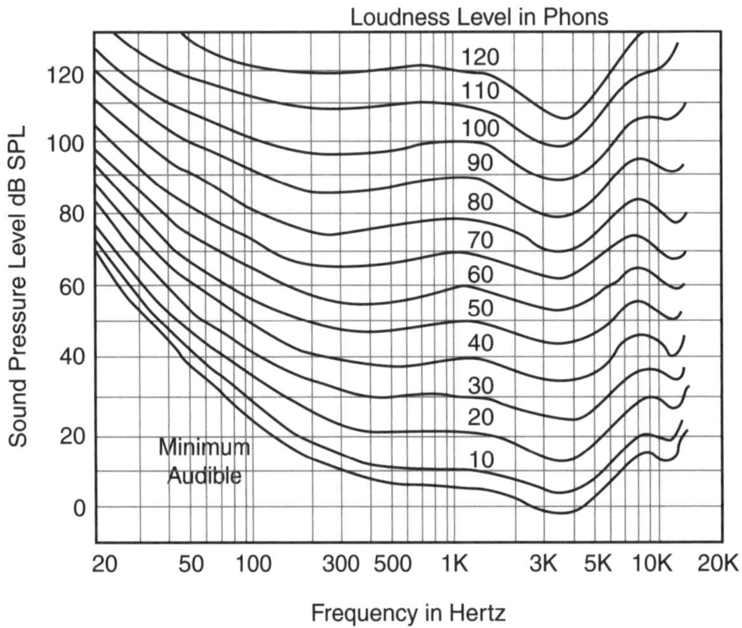

Figure 3.15 Equal loudness curves.

that the loudness of a tone is directly related to both intensity and frequency. This nonlinear response of the ear to differing levels of different frequencies was measured and graphed in the 1930s by the research team of Fletcher-Munson. The Fletcher-Munson equal loudness contours illustrate the average ear's sensitivity to different frequencies at different levels.

The relevance of this data to audio mixing or listening conditions in general is that the apparent loudness of different frequencies (low frequencies in particular) of our program material will rise as the overall monitoring level increases, and thus a false impression of low- and high-frequency balance will be created if all monitoring is done at the same level. Thus, when mixing, you should monitor at the level at which most consumers might listen (roughly taken as the level at which two people can converse in front of the speakers, approximately 85 dB [SPL]).When mixing music, the engineer should occasionally listen at both loud and soft levels, as well as a reasonable listening level, so that the balance can achieve a good compromise. Large increases in volume will produce an apparent increase in the level of low frequencies. Conversely, lowering the level to a more comfortable listening level will result in a seeming lack of low frequencies. Loudness switches are common on many consumer amplifiers in order to compensate for the loss of bass when listening at low levels.

Hearing Damage

As the intensity of the acoustic wave is increased, the sound becomes louder and eventually results in a tickling sensation instead of a sensation of hearing. This level, known as the *threshold of feeling* (see Figure 3.16), has a value of about 120 dB (SPL) between 200 Hz and 10 kHz. At approximately 140 dB (SPL), this tickling sensation changes to the threshold of pain. Exposure for even short periods of time to an intensity of between 140 dB and 160 dB (SPL) can and will lead to permanent hearing damage. Depending on the person, prolonged periods of exposure to sound levels far below this point can also lead to permanent hearing damage. Finally, exposure to intensities greater than 160 dB (SPL) will result in immediate damage to the hearing mechanism.

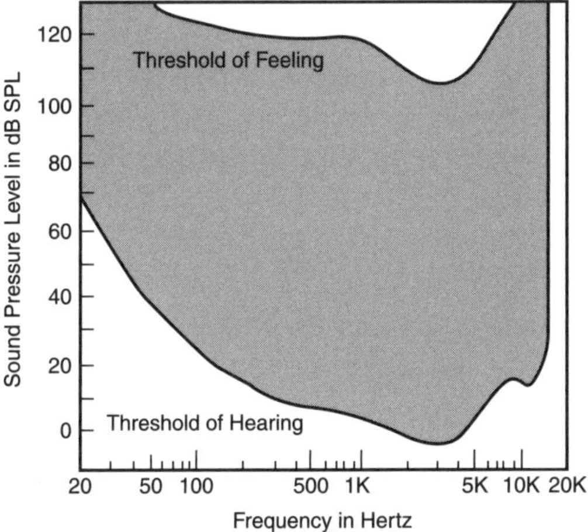

Figure 3.16 Frequency-dependent threshold of hearing and feeling.

When someone is subjected to high levels of sound, the hearing mechanism will generate a form of harmonic distortion. For example, a loud 1-kHz tone will be heard as a combination of 1 kHz, 2 kHz, 3 kHz, and so on. This also means sounds played at a high level will have a different tone (timbre) than when played back at a lower level.

Hearing damage has occurred when there is ringing in the ears. This condition is called *tinnitus*. When hearing loss occurs, it not only affects the frequency response, but also the ability to discriminate among sounds. For instance, those who have hearing loss are often able to hear someone standing next to them in a quiet room, but are unable to distinguish a conversation meant for them in a noisy room. It is also fatiguing to distinguish the conversation from someone nearby from the background in a noisy restaurant or bar.

Temporary threshold shift (TTS) commonly occurs when someone is exposed to loud music for a period of time. The ear becomes less sensitive and looses high-frequency response, but for most people this shift is only temporary, and their normal hearing returns by the next day or so. Have you ever started up your car in the morning after a night of clubbing and been surprised at how loud the sound system is? You probably cranked it the night before because you were experiencing some TTS. However, a lifetime of high sound pressure level environments can have a cumulative effect and cause permanent damage.

Hearing Delay and Directionality

In the 1940s, German doctor Helmut Haas wrote a thesis that identified that the ear cannot hear an extremely short time difference between a direct signal and its delayed "reflection." At a time distance equal to half a wavelength, phase cancellation will occur. (More on this in Chapter 4.) As the delay time increases, the delayed sound will move further and further away in time from the un-delayed sound. A few wavelengths away in time, the delay increases into the Haas zone, and the reflections begin to reinforce the un-delayed sound, but they are not yet delayed long enough to be perceived as distinct sounds. The delayed sound will constructively combine, for the most part, to reinforce, thicken, or seemingly double the sound. The longest imperceptible delay (for the average person) is around 35 milliseconds (ms) for a sound that changes very little over the course of time, such as violin or organ sustains. About 3 to 7 ms is the shortest perceptible delay on percussive sounds with lots of attack and no sustain—for instance, the sound when you strike a wood block.

A pan control on a recording console positions a sound in the stereo mix by making the sound louder on one channel than on the other. If the sound is equally loud in both channels, it will seem to be positioned in the center of the stereo mix. The difference in intensity between sounds reaching the two ears is one of the ways in which humans perceive direction and is the primary method at higher frequencies. The head is large enough to block short wavelengths of higher frequencies from about 1 kHz. Though the heads on some rock-and-roll legends (in their mind) can block much lower frequencies.

At lower frequencies, intensity differences between the ears are less apparent. While listening to a bass without turning your head, if you alternately stick a finger in one ear and then the other, you'll notice that the intensity of the sound remains pretty much the same. At lower frequencies the wave is so long that it easily wraps around a head that cannot block the intensity of the sound wave. For this reason, it seems that at lower frequencies, the brain uses differences in the phase of a sound wave as it goes past each ear to sense the direction of a bass sound.Our brain uses one other trick to sense a sound's origin, called *precedence*. The brain is able to determine which ear is the first to hear an event. Even if a sound has identical phase and is equally loud in both ears, if the signal is delayed to one ear, it will seem to be coming from the undelayed side. Some music producers use delay differences between the left and right channels instead of panning to position a signal in a stereo mix. Delays for positioning are frequently used in 5.1 mixing. The disadvantage of using delay to create direction is that the summed output of all the channels may lack monophonic compatibility.

Masking

We have all experienced difficulty hearing and/or understanding speech or music in the presence of loud background sounds. Under these circumstances, we refer to the desired sound or signal as being *masked* by the background. The most commonly experienced masking sound is noise that possesses a continuous broadband frequency spectrum. For example, in a radio or telephone, the interference may be caused by ordinary room noise at either the transmitting or the receiving end. Background music in a restaurant is used to mask the conversations at each table from anyone sitting at another table, and in elevators it masks the disconcerting sound of cables and chains clanging, but it also makes it more difficult for people to hear one another in conversation.

Within music, the greatest masking effect occurs when the frequencies are close to each other. For example, a 2-kHz tone will mask a softer 1.5-kHz tone but will have little effect on the audibility of a quiet 800-Hz tone. Harmonic frequencies can also cause masking. For example, a 500-Hz tone with a strong 1-kHz harmonic could mask a 900-Hz tone. Also, in general, stronger low frequencies will mask weaker high frequencies due to their greater energy component, and distortions (for example, heavy guitar) will cause masking of other sounds.

This masking phenomenon is one reason why in large sessions, an instrument will sound quite different when its mic is soloed, compared to how it will sound in the combined mix. An instrument that sounds fine by itself can be completely hidden or changed in character by louder instruments with similar timbre, requiring equalization or changes in mic selection or placement to make the instruments separate and sound different enough to overcome the masking.

When getting sounds, don't get too hung up on how a single microphone sounds on a given instrument, but how it sounds when all the mics that are being used on that sound are also on. Also, how does the sound of the track you're doing now work with what's already been recorded? A great recording is made up of individual great sounds, but also how all those sounds combine. To create clean, clear, open-sounding recordings, always be mindful of the effects of masking.

Windows of Uncertainty

You've been mixing for several hours. The mix has been hard work because everyone has an opinion about how his or her instrument sounds and how loud it is in the mix. The bass player keeps asking you to add more bass. You push up the bass fader, and it's a little louder, the producer next to you agrees. From the back of the room, the bass player has turned into a maniac and is yelling that no one is paying attention to him, and he's leaving. He wanted more bass and was ignored, and so he storms out. What happened? You did raise the bass, and you and the producer heard it, but the bass player didn't hear it. Before writing him off as deaf, think about this.

Our perception of what we hear is not precise or absolute. Something we heard yesterday may sound quite different today. And, of course, such uncertainty will be different from one person to the next. It is described as hearing's *window of uncertainty*, and on that day, the bass player's uncertainty regarding loudness change was greater than yours or the producer's. He really didn't hear the bass get louder. This window of uncertainty encompasses several parameters. For instance, our ears have continual uncertainties at different loudnesses. One person might raise a volume control and think that there has been a perceivable change, but someone else might not hear that small change. How long does someone need to hear any given sound before he's able to know what that sound is? How much does a frequency have to change before we recognize it as a pitch change or as a note out of tune? How long do you need to hear a change before you perceive it?

These windows of uncertainty vary from person to person. Whether the difference is a few volts, milliseconds, or frequencies within a range, everyone has a different window of uncertainty that will vary with loudness and the listener's fatigue. For instance, when a pure 100- to 200-Hz tone with a sinusoidal waveform is played for observers at two different loudnesses (moderate and then high), the majority of observers believe that the louder sound has a lower pitch than the softer sound.

For most people, the pitch of a tone is generally independent of its loudness in the frequency range between 1 kHz and 5 kHz, which is also where the ear is most sensitive. For musical tones—for example, violins, guitar, and so on—these changes are not as appreciable; however, they are still noticeable. This is one reason why musicians can find it hard to tune their instruments while listening through headphones. The headphones often produce higher sound pressure levels than may be expected. A surprising number of times, I've recorded a bass that seemed in tune one day but sounded out of tune the next.

An understanding of hearing must include what we think we hear. A surprising number of control-room arguments occur over "I'm in tune" and "No, you're not." Or "I can't hear the words," "We turned it up," "I don't care; sounds the same to me." Or "I want more delay on my guitar," "You got 30 ms," "That's bull, man; I can't hear it." I suspect many times at the heart of these misunderstandings is the difference in what we think we hear. The average musician couldn't give a toss about a window of uncertainty of pitch or loudness, or of delay, particularly when he is raising issues, but such insight by the engineer as to what may be happening could lead to a resolution that returns calm to the session and results in a mix acceptable to all.

When I started recording, I just wanted to do it. What was sound? It was what I could hear. How well could I hear? Good enough for people to like the sounds that I got. What more did I need to know? Some of the first serious recording I did was at a studio owned by a guy who made devices to test and measure the hearing of babies. He got me interested in what sound was and how we hear. It was life-changing because it started to give me a framework for why I did what I did. No band ever asked what a sound wave was or how I heard, but I was a better engineer for it. On a practical level, it seemed that once I understood how hearing worked, I was able to get better sounds quicker. An understanding of phase and reverberation was equally important, and in the next chapter we'll explore what happens when sound hits a wall (or anything else).

4 Polarity, Phase Cancellation, and Reverb

Polarity, phase cancellation, and the acoustics of a space have been placed together in this chapter because they are all about what happens to sound in a space. We begin with *polarity*, a term that identifies the difference between the extremes or poles of an electronic circuit. With regard to the practicality of transducers—microphones and speakers—it describes a relationship when airborne sound energy is converted to electronic energy. For example when sound strikes the diaphragm, a peak of sound pressure will push the diaphragm inward, while a trough will pull it outward. When this happens, it should generate an electrical wave that is first positive or upward-going, and then negative or downward-going. So another way of looking at it is that polarity is very much allied to phase. Real and relative phase were described briefly in Chapter 2.

Sound travels a direct path as well as a multitude of indirect reflected paths from the source to a microphone. Differences in all the sound paths means that sound leaving the source arrives at the microphone over a period of time because of the numerous reflections. All of these various waves combine, with certain frequencies reinforced and other frequencies cancelling. This is called *phase cancellation*, and it can create pretty ugly sounds when multiple mics are used for stereo or 5.1 recording, or when they are on a single sound source (such as drums). This chapter will explore how phase cancellation happens and what can be done to control it. At the same time, phase cancellation and reinforcement contribute greatly to the sound of reverb, and depending on the acoustics of the space, this can be a good thing...or not.

Understanding polarity, phase cancellation, and reverb is essential when using microphones and will be invaluable when you are sorting out numerous phase, polarity, and reverb problems that can occur.

Polarity

Recall that a sound wave in air is a series of compressions and rarefactions of air molecules that move away from the sound source until the energy dissipates. When a compression passes the diaphragm, it moves inward and should generate a positive voltage. Figure 4.1 shows that the microphone is wired to the mic preamp with the "correct" electronic phase relationship to the acoustic event. In Figure 4.2, the microphone wires to the mic preamp are reversed and electrically 180 degrees out of phase with the acoustic event.

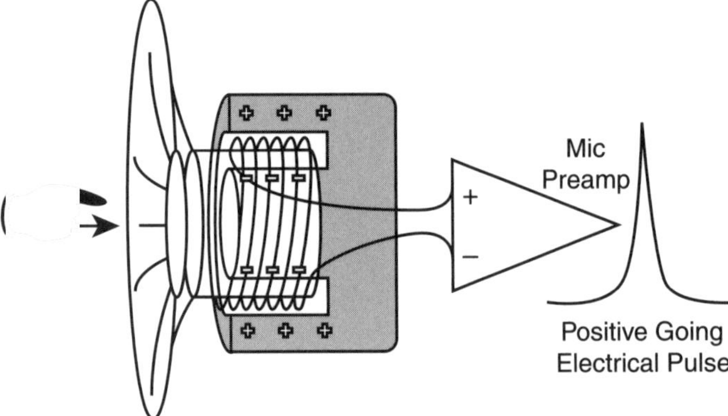

Figure 4.1 The diaphragm moving inward will generate a positive voltage if the wires are connected correctly.

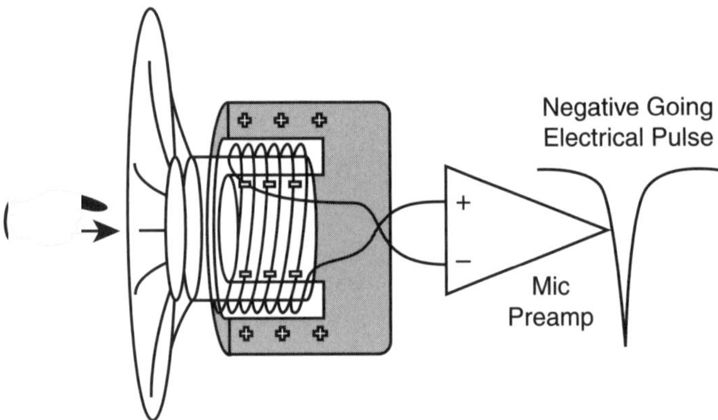

Figure 4.2 The diaphragm moving inward will generate a negative voltage if the wires are reversed and out of phase.

Correct polarity in relation to an acoustic event is relatively subtle and is generally inconsequential until more than one microphone is used at the same time. It is essential that all the mics in any given collection are the same polarity; otherwise, when two or more of them are placed on the same instrument, such as a drum kit, their combined "mono" output will exhibit severe phase cancellation. Stereo imaging is also affected when a pair of microphones is out of phase.

And so you say, "Don't all manufacturers wire up their microphones the same?"Not necessarily. Historically, different manufacturers have adopted different phase standards. On a practical level, it's a matter of two wires in the connector. Some have Pin 2 of a three-pin microphone connector as the hot or positive side; others have Pin 3 as the hot side (see Figure 4.3).

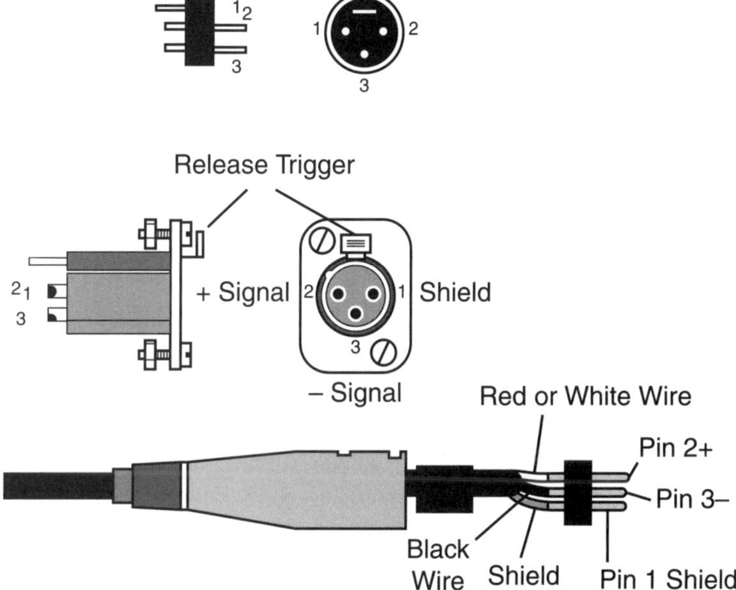

Figure 4.3 Three-pin mic cable connector and wiring.

What matters most is that all the microphones in your collection have the same polarity, and that whenever you get a new mic, you check to ensure it's the same as all the ones you already have. The next section will show you how to ensure that all microphones in your collection have the same polarity.

Verifying Correct Polarity

There are a few ways to determine the polarity of a mic. If you have a digital workstation that has a very accurate wave analysis, record the mic with a source such as a kick drum and then look at the waveform display in your DAW. The direction of the leading edge of the sound wave should be travelling upward, and all the microphones you test should do the same. If one does not, it's likely out of phase.

Another, more analog approach will audibly identify polarity problems.

1. Make sure that all mic cables and speaker wires are correctly wired and not accidentally reversed. Check the cables with a volt-ohm meter and verify that Pin 1 of the female connector goes to 1 on the male connector, 2 to 2, 3 to 3, and so on.

2. Plug in one cardioid or omni microphone and position it in front of a kick drum. Hook it up so its sound is coming through a speaker that has a visible cone. Have someone pump the drum pedal while you observe the speaker and see whether it goes in or out. If the phase of the speaker and all the wire along the way is correct, the speaker should

appear to move outward at the beginning of each beat. Now make that mic the standard for comparison of all the others (and excuse the drummer).

3. Sit at the mixing desk, mute the speakers, put on headphones, plug the standard microphone into an input, and raise the output so it can be heard right between the ears when you talk into it.
4. Mute the standard mic, but don't change the levels. In another channel, plug in and raise one of the microphones being tested so that it sounds identical in level to the first one.
5. Turn on both of them, hold them together, and talk into them both. If their combined output sounds hollow and heavily filtered, they are out of phase with each other. If, when they are both on, it gets louder, then they are in phase with one another.
6. If three or four in a row are wrong, then the standard mic may be wrong, and you should go back and recheck the mic, cable, and speaker wires in your kick drum test. There may be a connector wired incorrectly.
7. To change the mic's polarity, open up the connector in the microphone, unsolder Pins 2 and 3, reverse them, and re-solder. (Do not change the wires in the cables.)

Will reversing the polarity void a warrantee? It depends very much on the manufacturer and how good you are at soldering microphone connectors. If you've purchased a new microphone, and it's out of phase with all the other mics you own, I would suggest taking it back to the store where you bought it and having them do the same test against other mics they have in the shop. You might even test a couple of your other mics against a few in the shop. It would be good to know whether your set is in or out of phase with new stock.

If you have a large collection of mics that have an opposite polarity to the ones in the shop, but yours are all the same polarity, you may choose to live with it, but if you rent or borrow mics, you might want to change yours so they have the same polarity as those you casually use.

A demonstration of how to do the aforementioned polarity test is included in the DVD *Shaping Your Sound with Microphones, Mixers, and Multitrack Recording* (Hal Leonard, 2002).

If you're not confident about soldering a connector, you should learn how to do it. There are a number of short tutorials on how to solder a connector on YouTube.

It's probably worth suggesting a few tools you'll need for checking polarity, cables, and soldering. You'll need a small-wattage soldering iron (40 watts—higher power will burn insulation and parts), wire strippers/cutters, small long-nose pliers, and a small electronic vise to hold the connectors when you're working on them. The one in the picture has a magnifier. A blade screw driver small enough for cable connector screws, a small crescent wrench, a small Philips screw driver and a set of jeweler screw drivers. You should also invest in an inexpensive volt-ohm meter to test cables, connectors, speakers, batteries, power supplies, and such, from left to right, top to bottom (see Figure 4.4).

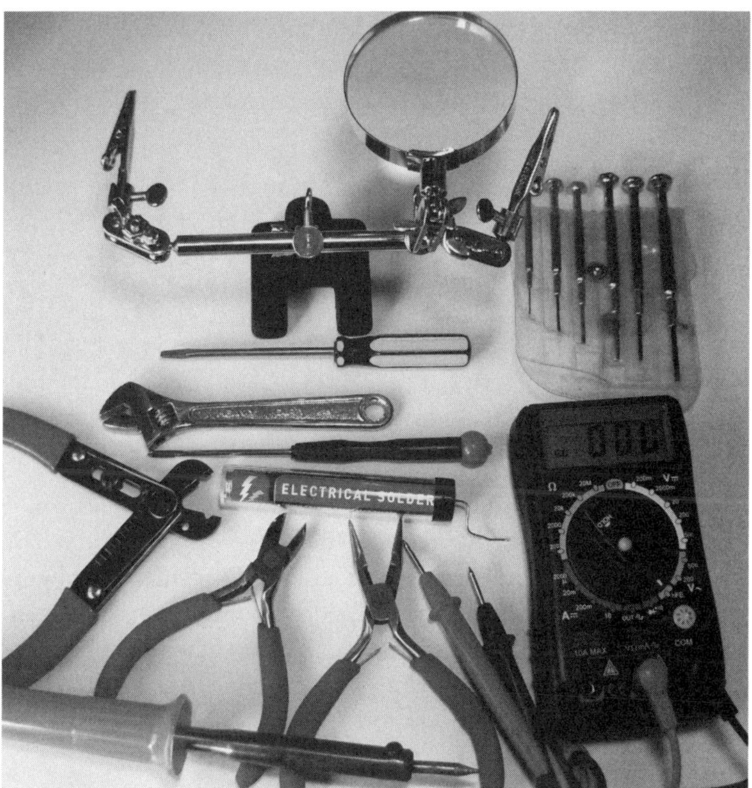

Figure 4.4 The basic tools for simple electronic testing and repair.

Bidirectional microphones have no defined polarity. A positive acoustic push on one side of the capsule will generate a positive electrical pulse. However, the same positive acoustic event on the other side of the capsule will push the diaphragm in the opposite direction, creating a negative electrical pulse. One side of the bidirectional microphone is the positive polarity half of the figure-eight pattern, and the other side is the negative polarity half of the pattern.

Usually the side on which the bidirectional mic has its logo will be the positive polarity side. On selectable pattern mics, the side that is "live" in the cardioid position usually has the positive polarity orientation. It's important to know which side has the positive orientation so that when they are used in groups, they can be correctly positioned with a common orientation; otherwise, common information entering two mics of opposite orientation will have a certain amount of cancellation when their outputs are combined.

Polarity Reversal Switches

There are times when it is desirable to reverse the polarity of a mic due to certain positioning or placement. For instance, some people like to place a microphone below the snare drum as well as above it. When the stick hits the snare, as the head of the snare goes downward, the mic above the snare will move outward, but the mic diaphragm below the snare will respond inward. Though both mics are picking up the same snare, when their signals are combined, there will be significant phase cancellation. In this case, a better sound might be achieved by reversing the polarity of the bottom microphones.

Some engineers will use two or three mics on a guitar amp, for instance, and get the sound they're looking for by varying the phase relationship of the mics before combining the mics to one track. When mixing in a DAW, it also not uncommon for engineers to delay a DI track, for instance, with the miked signal track to align the phase.

Another example when phase reversal may be useful is when doubling the same part in an overdub. You can create a different texture by reversing the polarity of the mic(s) that were used on the first track. The resulting sound of the combined tracks will be a little richer because the two tracks are ever so slightly different from one another. (More on DI, or direct injection, in Chapter 6.)

All professional mixing desks have phase reversal switches. For boards that don't, a short phase reversal cable can be made (or mounted in a small box) that reverses Pins 2 and 3 on one end. Phase reversal cables should be clearly marked to prevent them from being used by accident. (I always painted mine orange.) This cable can also be used as a temporary solution for a "visiting" out-of-phase microphone, but I would urge anyone who has several mics to make sure that all of their mics have the same polarity so it's one less thing to think about when you're setting up a session.

Acoustic Phase Cancellation (or Comb Filtering)

When sound travels to a microphone, it will take several different paths: a direct route (D1), and a reflected one (D2+D3, and so on). See Figure 4.5. Because the sound takes different amounts of time to travel the various paths, there will be slight delays between the direct sound and the multiple reflections. This also means that the sound waves arrive at the microphone at different phases of the same sound. (Refer to Chapter 2 on phase.)

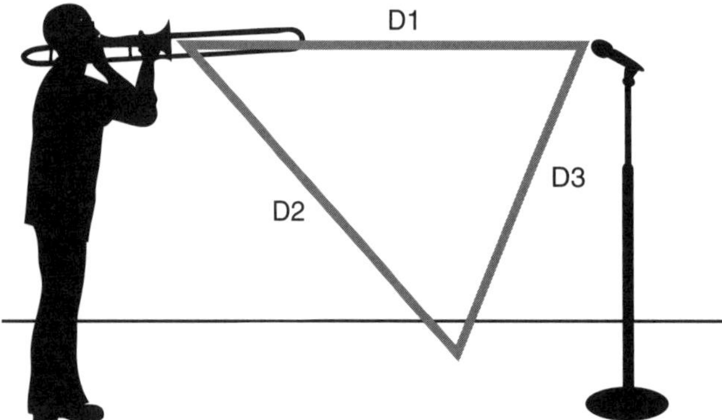

Figure 4.5 The distance difference between reflected and direct sound will create comb filtering. The frequencies affected have wavelengths equal to multiples of twice the distance difference.

Phase cancellation will be greatest when the reflected sound is a half wavelength after the undelayed signal. See Figure 4.6; Waves A and B are identical. The wave in Figure 4.6 could be any frequency. Wave B has been delayed just long enough (distance D) so that it is 180 degrees out of phase with Wave A. When they are equally combined, the waves illustrated (in Figure 4.6) will cancel. Then, further wave cancellation will occur to a lesser degree at one and a half wavelengths, two and a half wavelengths, and so on, with each dip in the sound creating teeth like a comb (see Figure 4.7). The resulting audio will sound similar to a phaser effect that is not sweeping. Longer reflections can also cause cancellation, though to a proportionately lesser degree, as the time difference increases between the direct and reflected sound waves, and they are increasingly dissimilar. The shorter the delay, the higher the frequency of the first and deepest "tooth" in the comb of cancellation. This is called *comb filtering*, so named due to the comb-like appearance of the graph that's created when the response curve is plotted.

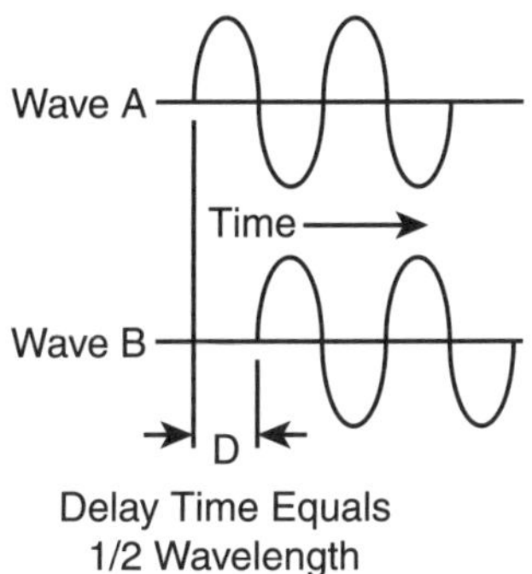

Figure 4.6 Waves A and B cancel one another when they are combined.

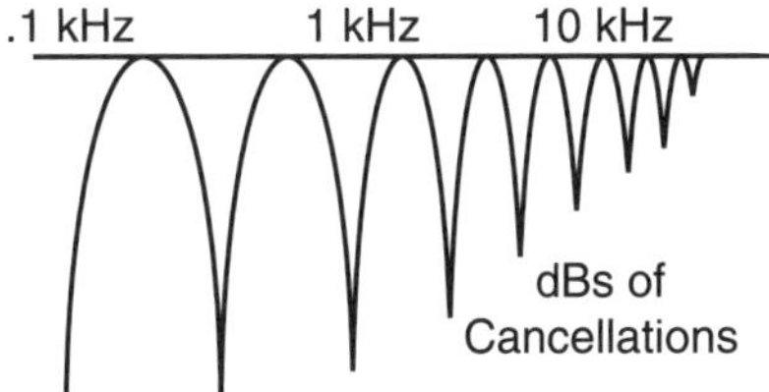

Figure 4.7 The effect of comb filtering on a full-bandwidth signal.

A Multiple-Mic Problem

A single microphone near a reflective surface can have comb-filtering problems, but the phenomenon becomes more likely when two or more microphones that are picking up a common sound source are combined. It's unavoidable and happens all the time. Such complex interaction can enhance the sound or adversely affect it, depending on variables such as distances, type of mic and pattern, and the instrument. All the acoustic variables of the recording space contribute to the consequence of reflection. Miking a set of drums with mics on both sides of the kick drum, all five tom-toms, the snare top and bottom, and separate mics on every cymbal will guarantee substantial amounts of comb filtering.

So the tradeoff is that close multi-miking gives an "in your face" sound, but it comes with some degree of (good or bad) phase cancellation. Some engineers take the view that the fewest number of mics used on a drum set can produce the clearest sound. It's a matter of taste and production style—and, of course, just how good the drums and drummer are.

The most noticeable comb filtering occurs if the sound source moves, as a cymbal does when it's struck (see Figure 4.8). When the cymbal is stationary, distances D1 and D2 remain constant. When the cymbal is struck, distance D1 gets shorter and D2 gets longer. When the cymbal rocks back, D1 gets longer and D2 is shortened, and so on. The acoustic phasing continues until the cymbal stops swaying. This causes the acoustic comb filtering to sweep with the rocking cymbals (see Figure 4.9).

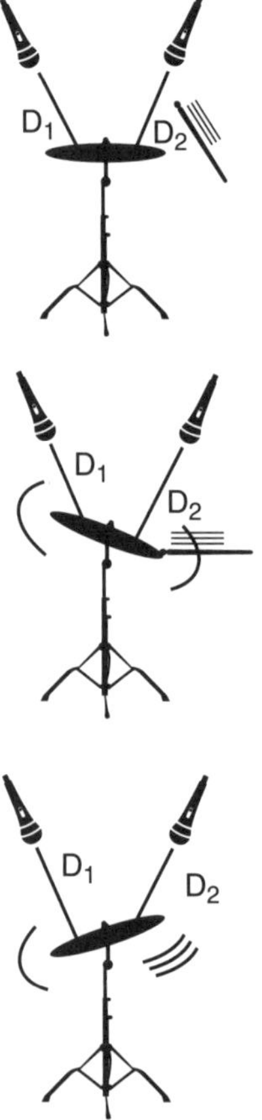

Figure 4.8 When the cymbal is struck, it sways back and forth. The distances between the mics and the cymbal are constantly changing until the cymbal stops vibrating. This will cause sweeping comb filtering when the two microphones are mixed together.

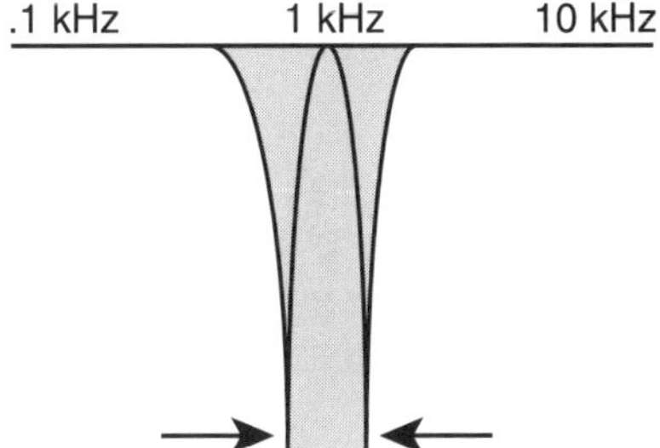

Figure 4.9 A typical example of the frequency range affected by sweeping comb filtering.

Acoustic phase cancellation in a combined pair of overhead mics on the drums is most apparent when the mics are heard in mono. The greater the number of reflective surfaces, and the closer they are to the microphones and cymbals, the more apparent and severe the sweeping comb filtering. It is a common problem when drums are recorded in a booth surrounded by glass. Unless the drum booth has amazing acoustics, and you're looking for a compressed sound, my feeling is that the best drum sounds are recorded with the drums in the middle of a large space, so reflecting walls are farther away. The drum set will have a much more open and live sound. I usually isolate the guitar amp in the booth.

The 3-to-1 rule has been around since I started recording. It's a surefire way to avoid comb filtering when two or more mics pick up the same sound (at about the same level but at different distances) and are mixed together. The mics should be separated by at least three times the distance the mics are from their source (see Figure 4.10). I've included the 3–to-1 rule in here because

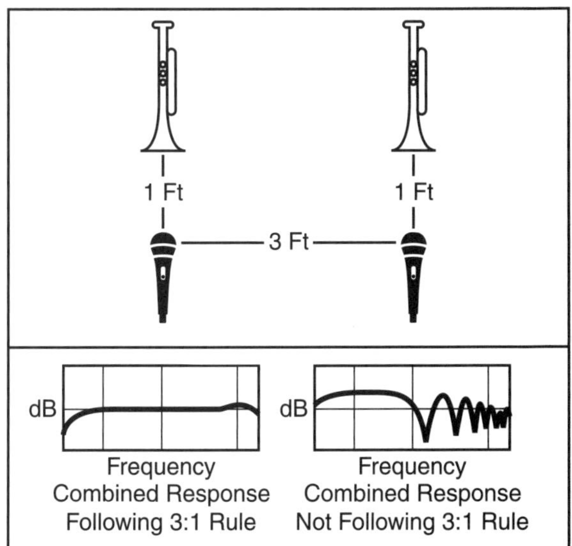

Figure 4.10 The 3-to-1 rule.

someone will undoubtedly mention it as a way to reduce comb filtering. In fact it works well, and it can be useful if you have 25 feet to stretch a horn section out in a line. In practice, though, 3 to 1 is pretty impossible when you've got 10 microphones on a set of drums.

So, the 3-to-1 rule is worth knowing and sometimes useful, but since, in many instances, you won't be able to apply it all that many times, you should assume that any time you use multiple microphones on the same sound, there is likely to be some phase cancellation.

Testing for Comb Filtering

Checking for comb filtering is pretty simple and should be done before anything is recorded, because comb filtering can't be fixed in the mix. After preamp and channel levels are set and a reasonable stereo balance is achieved, take, for instance, the pair of overheads and all the other drum mics and pan them to one speaker (in other words, listen to everything in mono). Some consoles have a master mono switch that simplifies this procedure. Have the drummer hit all the cymbals and drums. If comb filtering (phasing) is apparent, move one of the overhead microphones an inch or two and try it again until the cancellation is not apparent. While a drum set is the most likely candidate to have a comb-filtering problem, faithfully check the mono sound of any multi-mic setup, even if it is only a stereo pair on a guitar or a piano.

The acid test for a comb-filtering problem is how all the mics on the same instrument sound when they are combined to mono. As a rule, when I have a lot of microphones on the same sound, I'll pan them to one speaker, then switch off the mics in various combinations and listen for whether any of the combinations make the sound better or worse.

When the sound source does not move, such as a piano, the comb filtering won't sweep and will be considerably less apparent; nonetheless, on a given instrument or group of instruments, any pair of mics might sound better electronically out of phase with one another. A problem will most often appear as a low-frequency hollowness when the two microphones are combined. Pan an equal amount of each of a stereo pair to one speaker and hear how it sounds when the two signals are combined while reversing the phase of either one of the mics. It does no good to reverse both of them at the same time because that puts them back in phase with each other. There are times when the preferred sound of the piano will be with one of the two microphones out of phase with the other. The apparent center and general imaging may sound better by reversing the polarity of one of the stereo pair. Once the best sounding polarity relationship has been determined, reposition the stereo pair to the left and right monitor speakers.

PZMs and Eliminating Comb Filtering Pressure-zone microphones are designed to eliminate comb filtering that occurs when a microphone simultaneously picks up direct and reflective sound. The PZM's capsule faces and nearly touches a large barrier (see Figure 4.11). The gap between the PZM capsule and the barrier plate is just a sliver, and the capsule is very small.

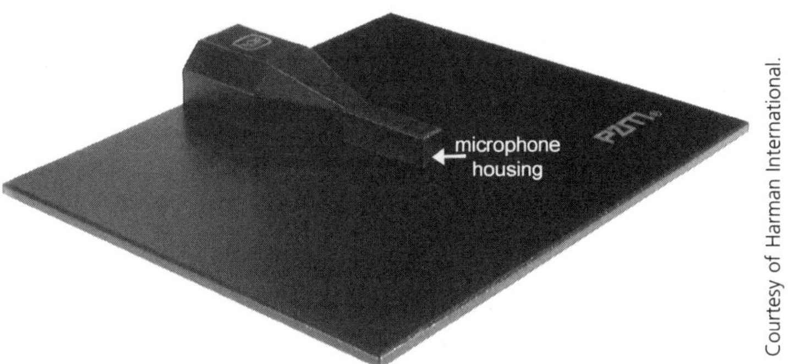

Figure 4.11 The classic Crown PZM-30D. The mic faces downward in the housing, almost touching the flat surface.

Typically the PZM is positioned on a wall or other large flat surface so that the direct sound travels the same distance as the early reflected sound. Thus, there is no comb filtering caused by differences in sound path distances (see Figure 4.12). Using a PZM, the sound travels to the boundary of the room where it is picked up. No sound can go beyond this boundary to reflect off a wall back into a microphone.

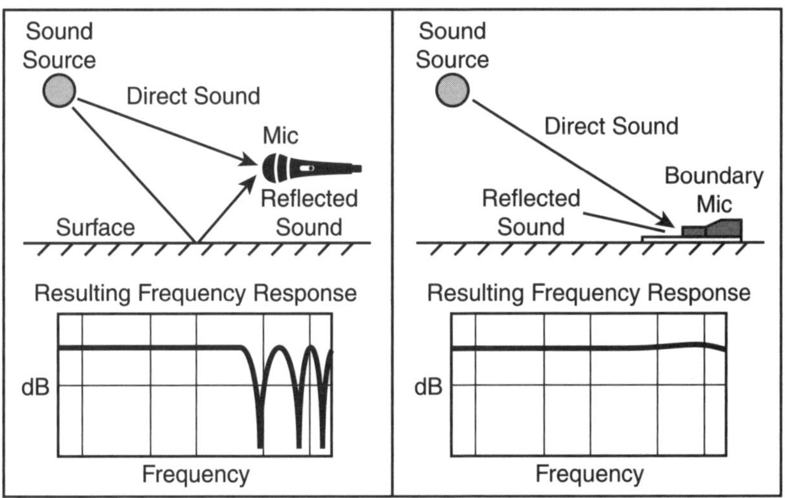

Figure 4.12 A PZM reduces the effect of reflection and multiple sound paths to the microphone. It is also referred to as a boundary pickup.

If a PZM mic is attached to a stand, it will exhibit the same comb-filtering problems as any other mic. PZMs must be mounted on a large barrier, such as a wall, a conference table, or a big piece of rigid Plexiglas. The bigger the barrier, the better the low-frequency response. PZMs are nondirectional and will pick up everything in a room. If the room is not good acoustically or is full of extraneous noise, a PZM will pick up all of that, too.

PZMs are terrible for PA because their nondirectional design makes them very prone to feedback. Some manufacturers have brought out what are described as *directional* PZMs, but this is rather misleading because as soon as the mic becomes directional and moves away from its wall boundary, it stops picking up what is described as a *phase-coherent pressure zone*.

On the other hand, if the room sounds good and the music does too, a PZM can work well. A pair of them placed at different points on the walls might be a good choice for making acoustic stereo recordings in a good-sounding hall.

Some people attach PZMs to the inside of a raised piano lid that acts as the barrier. For choir and orchestra recordings, a pair of PZMs works well on two large pieces of Plexiglas (6 to 8 feet by 6 to 8 feet) about 10 to 15 feet apart, hung on an angle from the ceiling. The two Plexiglas panels should be about 15 or 20 feet in front of the choir or orchestra.

Phase cancellation and reinforcement due to sound reflection ties in nicely as a starting point for a brief description of reverberation. Although digital boxes with an infinite number of possibilities can add reverb to the (live or recorded) sound coming through a microphone, experienced sound engineers will normally prefer spaces with great acoustics to make their recordings. The space is an integral part of the sound. A great-sounding space makes any instrument or vocal sound better, and that comes through the microphone. It also makes the musician feel better about how it sounds, so he performs better.

Adding a reverb effect to a "dead" sound (a sound with no natural reverb) will not create the same sound as if the instrument or vocal is performed in a good-sounding space. In Chapters 11 through 14, I will often mention acoustic techniques when miking. The remainder of this chapter will provide background to what I'll be talking about when you get to those chapters.

Echoes and Reverberations

Echoes and reverberations are the reason why any given room sounds as it does. Three factors are the principal contributors—the volume of the interior space, the dimensions, and the shape and materials of the walls, ceilings, and floors. These factors determine the acoustics of that space.

Acousticians (and effect processors) define reverb as the amount of time it takes for the reverberant sound to decay from its loudest point to when it is 60 dB below that point (see Figure 4.13). It is often identified as *RT60*. The RT60 reverb decay is a broadband decay with all frequencies having the same duration. In natural or acoustical reverb, the low frequencies tend to linger longer then the higher frequencies that are more readily dissipated due to absorption and phase cancellation. In a recording, this tends to cause the sound to have a nondescript, low-frequency rumble. Figure 4.14 shows different RT60 suggestions for different types of performances. Such information would be used by acousticians in the design of these spaces.

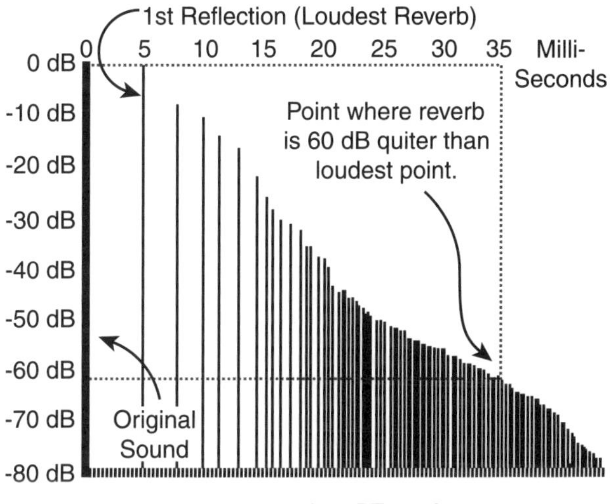

Figure 4.13 RT60.

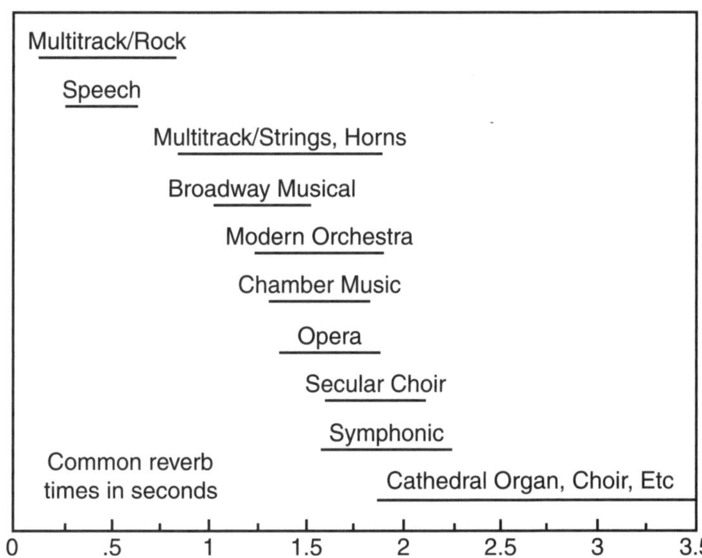

Figure 4.14 Typical reverb times for various sound environments and styles of music.

Essentially, the bigger the volume, the harder the wall surfaces, the greater the reverb that's likely to occur. And in general, the more random the wall angles, the longer the shortest distance between two opposing room boundaries, and the higher the ceiling, the more likely the reverb will decay evenly and sound good (see Figure 4.15). There are always exceptions, but I think that's a good short answer to the complexities of a good reverb. Some music will sound better in bigger rooms with more reverb, and other music will sound better if the room is less reverberant.

Choice and amount of reverb is a matter of taste of the production team and style of the music and production.

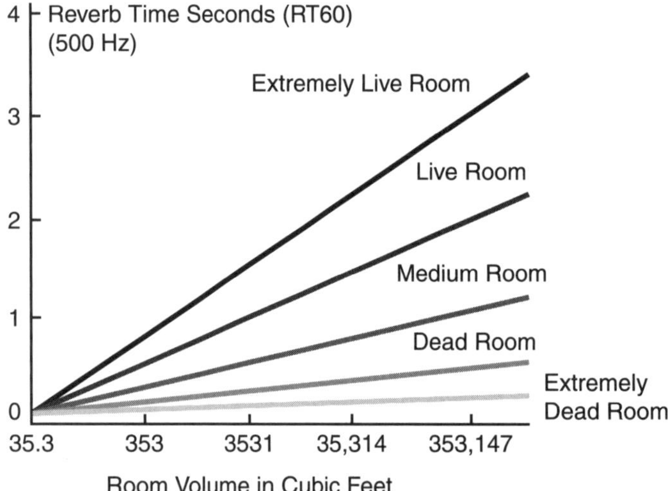

Figure 4.15 Room volume versus reverb time of different types of rooms.

Echo and reverb are often used interchangeably, but they are quite different. Echoes are sound reflections that are clearly identifiable, distinct, and often regular in their occurrence (see Figure 4.16). Reverb will most often have some echoes as a part of its initial sound, but the distinct reflections will soon become so dense with random reflections that individual reflections are indistinct.

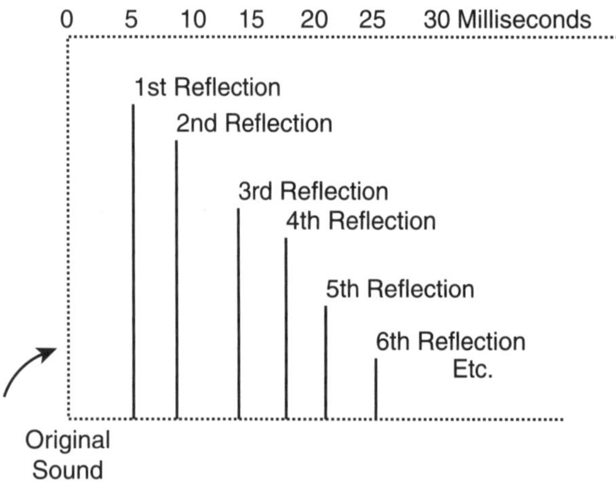

Figure 4.16 Echo has distinct reflections.

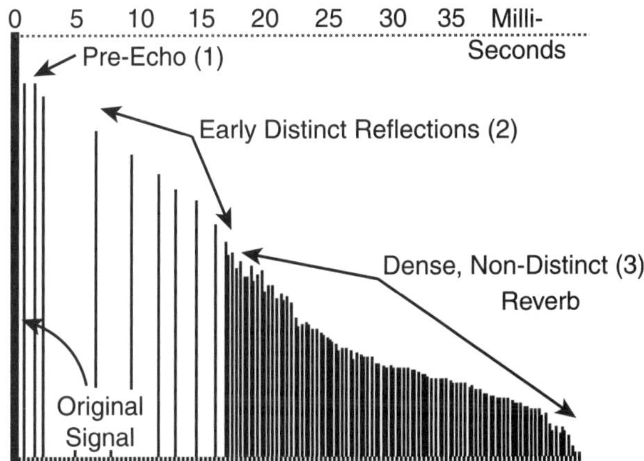

(1) Pre-echoes come from the stage floor, backdrop, and wings.
(2) Echoes come from the room's nearest hard surfaces.
(3) Non-distinct reverb builds as the number of returning reflections increases in number.

Figure 4.17 Reverb.

Pre-Delay

If you are near a sound source (or a microphone is near a sound source) in a reverberant environment, a certain amount of time will pass between when the direct or dry (no reverb) signal is heard and the beginning of reverb occurs. This period of time is called the *pre-delay*. The length of the pre-delay establishes how big the room is and the position of the listener in the room in relation to the source. Within this pre-delay period, between the direct signal and the beginning of the reflections from the nearest reflective walls, there are often *pre-echoes* that are generally within the Haas Zone (see Chapter 3) and are the result of reflections from hard surfaces very close to the sound source. For instance, when sitting in the third row listening to a band playing onstage, you might hear the very first reflections off the stage floor, which is between the source of the sound and you, followed by those off the proscenium. Next would come the reflections off the PA stacks, and then those off the back of the stage. These pre-echo delays precede the reverb. Then finally, the auditorium reverb would begin as the sound bounces off the nearest walls and ceiling and then the far walls, the balconies, and so on (see Figure 4.17).

Recall that early reflections of reverb, which are essentially short delays that are 30 milliseconds or less after the initial sound, will tend to reinforce the sound. Extremely short early reflections (up to about 5 to 15 milliseconds) will cause comb filtering or phase cancellation. These interactions can be constructive and/or destructive, depending on the frequency, sometimes adversely affecting the sound, while at other times enriching certain harmonics and overtones. Both could be happening simultaneously, enhancing some frequencies of the sound while detracting from others.

The First Delay Device On a historical note, the first delay device was used at racetracks soon after the invention of amplification in the late '20s. In those first installations, the speakers on the opposite side of the track were reproducing the same signal that was going to the grandstands. On the far side of the track, intelligibility was a real problem because the speakers facing the grandstand would reflect back to the opposite side of the track and arrive there sometime after the direct sound from the far speakers. When proposed, the solution probably incited gales of laughter. A large sewer pipe was buried from the grandstand to the far side of the track. The sound going to the grandstand speakers was also fed to a speaker system inside the pipe at the grandstand end. At the other end of the pipe was a microphone that fed the (heavily equalized) amplifiers driving the speakers on the far side of the track. The amount of time it took the sound to travel through the delay pipe was the same as the reflected sound from the grandstand, so the far side of the field heard the PA slightly after the grandstand, but in sync with the sound reflected off the grandstand and with considerably improved clarity.

In Chapters 11 through 14, I will at times describe things that you might do to alter the acoustics of a space to get the best sound. But every room is different, and the key to knowing what to do in an acoustic environment is acquiring a memory of how reverb sounds in all sorts of places. Become a good listener of space. Look for it anywhere you might be and anywhere you might go. Listen to the reverb and remember what it sounds like for the places you've been. Listen for the separation that exists in reverb, where the early reflections are coming from, what frequencies linger longer, and so on. Go out to parking garages, canyons, giant open pipes, and so on, and make some noise. (To the annoyance of my wife, I usually do a single hand clap, though as I've gotten older, I do refrain from this behavior in churches and such, but I just couldn't pass up a clap in the Taj Mahal.) These sonic excursions place you actively within the space. You're no longer just passing through. But even if you're there in silence, you can hear it. In real space, even if you don't excite it by clapping or making a sharp sound, you can feel the volume of a large space. You can hear its size. You can close your eyes and listen to that room in silence and hear the space about you, and when you move to another point in the space, the experience of the sonic surroundings will also change. Though the space remains the same, your perception of it will change with your positioning within it. When you're sitting in the middle of a vacant cathedral, your ears can feel and place the space. When you are surrounded by a quiet physical space, you can feel the ambience around you.

Paul Horn in the Taj Mahal The legendary flautist Paul Horn bribed a guard so that he could stay all night in the Taj Mahal and play his flute. He had a small tape recorder with him. The recording he made became so famous that the Indian government gave him permission to do a second series of recordings. He spoke about the experience. "The room came back to me like a thousand angel choirs. Actually, what I was doing, I sat there deep down in the tomb and listened to the room. I answered it. I made music together with it. Much more than my flute, the room was the instrument on which I played."

In this chapter I've covered phases and reflections of sound. And maybe, in a way, we've ended the chapter with the phases and reflections of life as we explore and remember each of our individual journeys through reverberant space. May yours be as rich as that of Paul Horn. If you become a good listener of space, I'm sure your memories of some of those spaces will be as rich as his. Of most importance, you will be a better sound engineer for it.

In the next chapter, we will look at microphone impedance and the difference between high and low impedance. We'll also look at how modern condenser microphones are powered through the same cable that carries the sound to the mixing desk.

5 Impedance and Balance

If this chapter looks boring, and you just want to get to the good stuff in Chapter 11 and beyond, I understand. But the next time you raise a microphone fader and find all sorts of hum and radio transmissions, you might want to come back to this chapter. This chapter also explains why using a long cord from the guitar and bass to the amp or mixing desk will tend to cause a loss of attack and high frequencies in the signal, but there is a solution. The chapter ends with an explanation of how condenser microphones are powered through the same cord that the audio signal travels by what is called *phantom power*.

High and Low Impedance

Impedance is primarily of importance where transducers connect to the input and output of a sound system—that is to say, between the microphones and preamps, guitars/bass pickups and amps, and between the power amps and the speakers. Knowing something about impedance is important because incorrectly connecting things at these junctions can radically affect the sound. Microphone, guitar, and speaker leads play important parts in impedance issues.

Impedance is a common specification in audio equipment or any other type of equipment that has an alternating, or AC, signal passing through it. Alternating current means a signal that is made up of waves or cycles—for example, mains power is alternating, as is an audio signal, while DC (direct current) does not alternate (see Figure 5.1). Impedance and resistance (the resistance of a circuit to a non-alternating signal, such as that from a battery power supply) both use the ohm as the unit of measurement. Impedance is referred to as Z, while DC resistance

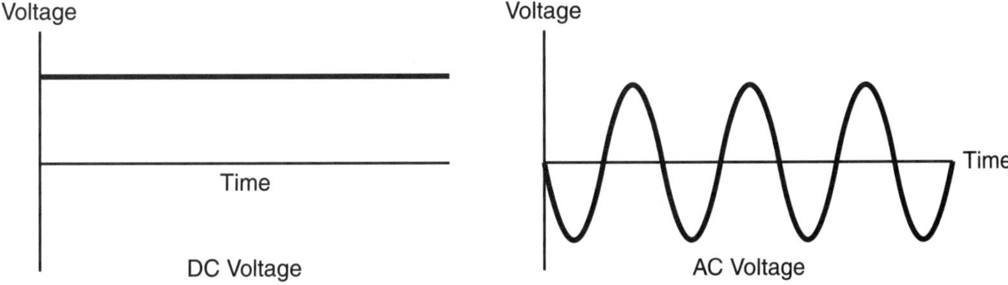

Figure 5.1 Graphical representation of the difference between AC and DC voltage.

uses the ohm symbol (Ω). Impedance is most commonly used when referring to the input and output of an electronic circuit, the output of a microphone, and the input of a speaker.

DC resistance can be measured with a simple volt-ohm meter, but impedance is more difficult to measure because the impedance will vary depending on the frequencies passing through the circuit. Impedance tends to be clumped into high or low impedance. Low impedance is 600 ohms or less, with microphones and most modern equipment having an output impedance from 50 to 600 ohms. High impedance is 7,000 to 15,000 ohms (or above) with most modern equipment having an input impedance of 20,000+ ohms.

A device with a low-impedance output can be connected to a high-impedance input and will generally work. For instance, by using the right cable, a low-impedance microphone can be plugged into a guitar amp, but many will sound better if they are plugged into the low-impedance input of a microphone preamp. However, if a high-impedance output device, such as many guitars or basses, is directly connected to a low-impedance input, such as a microphone input, the input impedance will be so low that the signal will be shorted out, and what signal does get through will be distorted. The guitar pickup simply generates a signal that is too weak to withstand the load of a low-impedance input. Guitar and bass pickups are the most common, and they are virtually the only high-impedance devices used in recording today. There are many modern guitar and bass pickup designs that are low impedance, but the sound of high-impedance pickups is unique, so they are still popular. For this reason, the input of a guitar amp is very high impedance.

To connect a guitar directly to a mic preamp, a direct box is inserted between the guitar and the desk so the high-impedance guitar output is converted into a low-impedance output. (More on direct boxes in Chapter 6, "Hum 101, DIs, and Related Transducers.")

For almost all other electronic devices, outputs have very low impedance (50 ohms or less), and inputs are high impedance (+10K ohms). In modern design, input impedance does not affect the outputs to which they are connected.

Coming back to high-impedance guitar and bass pickups and guitar cords, the longer the wire from the instrument to the amplifier input, the greater the loss of high frequencies. Also, transient response is severely degraded.

Why does this happen? An electronic signal is like water in that electrons will always flow from a place of higher potential to a place of lower potential (like water does). The electrons (and water) will seek out the path of least resistance from the positive terminal to the negative terminal of a device's output.

In most cables, the insulation between the wires doesn't work as well at higher frequencies as it does at lower ones. This frequency-dependant "resistance" is called *capacitative reactance* (see Figure 5.2). The capacitative reactance of a guitar cord—or, for that matter, any similar cable—is the same for both high- and low-impedance systems, but with a high-impedance output running through a long cable, the path of least resistance for the high-frequency portion of the audio

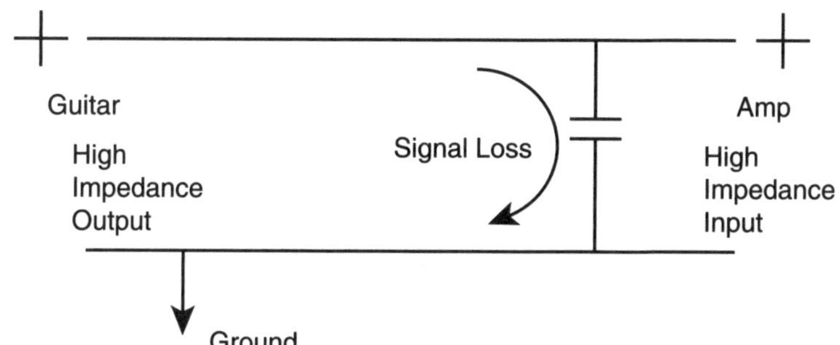

Figure 5.2 At higher audio frequencies, the resistance of the insulation between the ground and the signal wire in a long high-impedance cable is lower than the input of the guitar amp. This causes the signal to the amp to sound dull and lose attack.

signal will be across the two wires in the cable and is lost before it can reach the input of the device to which the wire is connected. Turning up the treble control on the amp will mostly increase the noise because the high-frequency signal will have been shorted out before it reaches the amp. In brief, the higher the impedance of the amplifier input and the longer the length of the cord between the guitar and amp, the greater the amount of high-frequency loss.

To reduce the loss of high frequencies when recording, use the shortest possible non-stretchy cord between the guitar and the amp. If a guitar signal has some distance to travel (such as into the control room), it should be connected with a short cord to a direct box that converts the signal to low impedance so that little of the high frequency is lost in the journey to the input. More on direct inject boxes (DIs) in Chapter 6.

On the other hand, the cable from a low-impedance output microphone can be quite long, without any degradation of the signal, because the input impedance of the preamp it's plugged into is so much lower than the capacitative resistance in the wire. Which is to say, the input device is the path of least resistance for the signal.

Balanced and Unbalanced Connections

A balanced connection has two wires that carry the signal, plus a magnetic shield that surrounds both wires and is connected to ground. A balanced connection reduces the possibility that external radio waves and hum will be amplified. Balanced connections are commonly used between a microphone and a microphone preamp, and in professional studios where there are long distances between interconnected equipment and/or lots of radio waves radiating from all the gear and transmission towers. A balanced connection is more than the cabling. Both the output device (such as a microphone) and the connecting input device (such as a mic preamp) must also be balanced. The lower the signal level (such as a microphone) and the longer the cable, the more likely that a balanced signal path will be needed.

A balanced microphone preamplifier has two input connections, neither of which is directly connected to the ground of the amplifier (see Figure 5.3). This type of amplifier is also referred

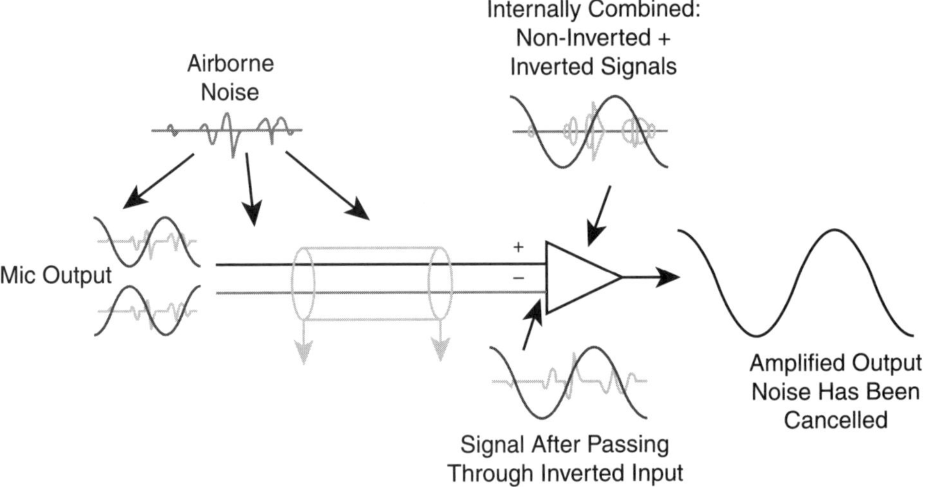

Figure 5.3 A balanced signal cable has two signal wires and a shield. A balanced input has two inputs and shield/ground. There is a high degree of rejection of external radio interference and hum that is common to both inputs—this is called common mode rejection.

to as a *differential* amplifier because it only amplifies the difference between the two wires and it rejects any signal that is common to both signal wires. For instance, radio waves that enter the mic cable and are picked up by both internal cable wires will be common to both wires and rejected by the inputs of the mic preamplifier. However, the alternating signal between the two signal wires from the mic (let's say) will be amplified. In other words, the signal pushes and pulls as it oscillates between the two signal wires.

Balanced amplifiers have a specification called *common mode rejection*, which defines (in dB) an amplifier's ability to amplify a differential signal while rejecting any signal common to both signal wires. The shield in a balanced system is the first line of defense in blocking airborne signals, with the differential signal wires eliminating what gets through the grounded shield. In other words, in a balanced system that has good common mode rejection, most of the noise rejection is done because the two signal wires are next to each other (and usually twisted together so the wires average their thickness and lengths), so that if any noise gets in, it does so equally and never creates a difference between the wires. The noise is common to both and rejected by the differential input.

On the other hand, an unbalanced connection uses the shield to complete the circuit connection. Unbalanced connections work well as long as the cable length is reasonably short, the signal level is high (commonly referred to as *line level*), and the environment does not have high levels of magnetic radiation or radio frequency interference. Unbalanced connections are also referred to as *single-ended* systems. An unbalanced system is most common and least expensive. It is used in all home consumer equipment. Single-ended systems have a common ground all through the circuit and are used throughout almost all electronic devices, including the input and output connections of the device (see Figure 5.4).

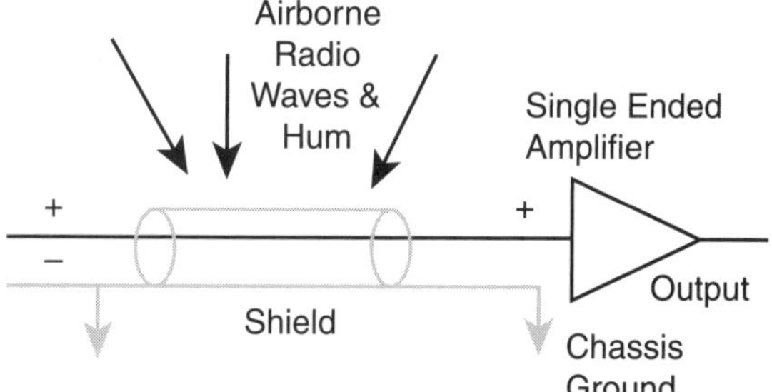

Figure 5.4 Unbalanced signal wire and an input with one input and ground. Most susceptible to external radio interference and hum. Potentially noisy, particularly when high gain is required, due to this interference.

Connecting Low-Z Mics to High-Z Preamps

Low-cost PA gear and guitar amps usually do not have an input with a three-pin XLR mic connector. Other than condenser mics that require "phantom" power supplies, low-impedance, balanced microphones can be connected to these unbalanced inputs in one of two ways. If the cable distance is longer than 10 to 15 feet, an external input transformer should be used so that common mode rejection is maintained and any radio or magnetic interference is rejected. If the cable is short and/or high-powered radio signals or magnetic waves are not a factor, an input transformer may not be necessary, and you may only need an FLA23 (see Figure 5.5).

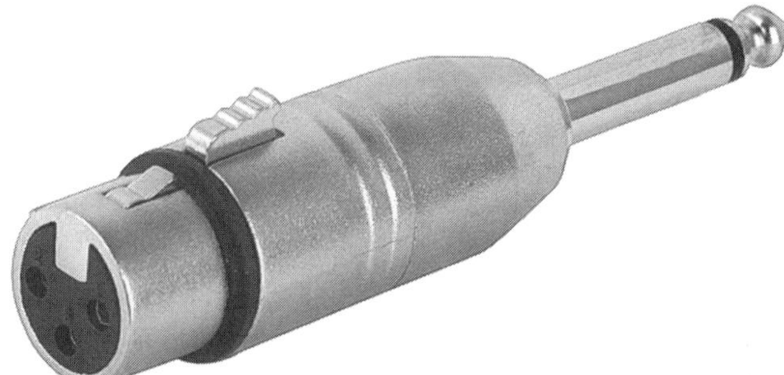

Figure 5.5 FLA23 XLR to guitar jack adapter.

Or if you're handy with soldering and you have experience making cables, you can construct one that will do the job. Use a three-pin female XLR at one end and a 1/4-inch standard phone plug at the other. Connect Pin 2 of the XLR to the tip of the phone plug, and connect Pins 1 and 3 to the shield of the plug (see Figure 5.6). If the mic has very low output, an input transformer will help to step up (or boost) the signal, but most mics have sufficient output to be plugged directly into an unbalanced mic input.

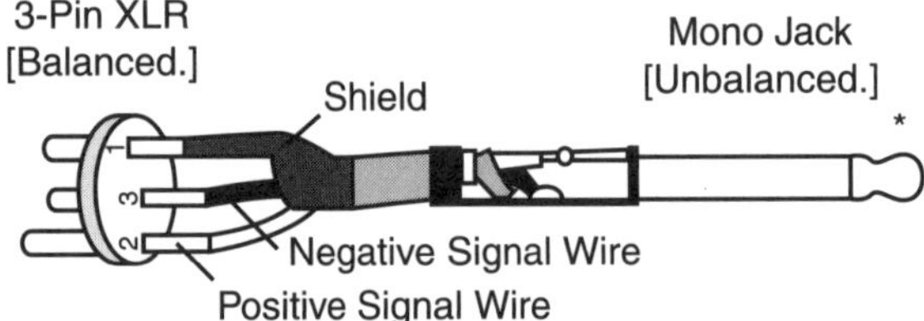

Figure 5.6 Solder the positive (pin 2) wire of the XLR to the tip of the guitar jack. At the guitar jack, twist the shield and the negative wire together and solder to the ground/shield of the guitar jack.

Phantom-Powered Mics and Balanced Systems

As explained in Chapter 2, a condenser microphone requires a power source for its internal preamplifier and, in many cases, to charge the condenser capsule itself. The majority of "solid state" condenser mics use phantom power, and some location microphones can be battery-powered. Most mixing consoles have the phantom power supply built into them, but external supplies are available. Phantom power got its name because no additional wires are required. The supply power from the console to the condenser mic goes through the same balanced wires that take the audio from the microphone to the console.

Phantom power has been around since the late '60s, when transistor amplifiers replaced tubes in condenser mics. The positive side of the phantom power's direct current supply (commonly +48 volt [DC]) is connected to both of the balanced audio lines, and the ground of the supply is connected to the cable shield. At the microphone end, the internal preamp uses a balanced output (often a transformer), which isolates the audio signal from the phantom power (see Figure 5.7). Because a

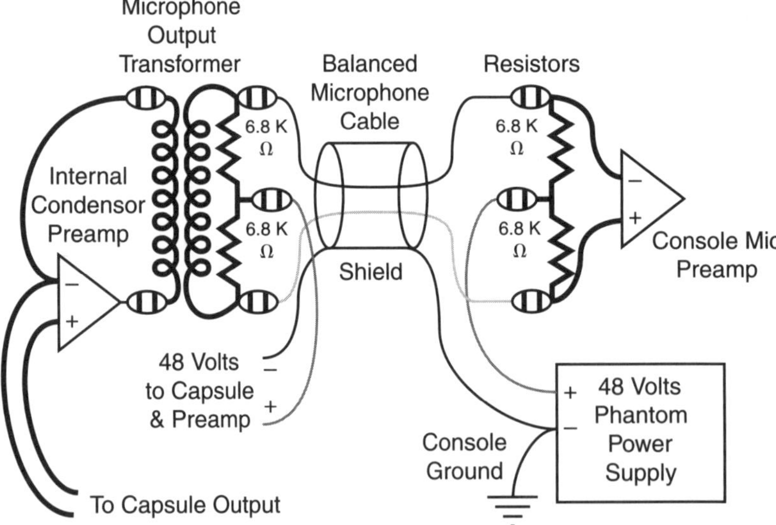

Figure 5.7 This drawing shows a microphone with a transformer output, but many microphones use an IC to achieve the same results. Phantom power applied to both signal wires is rejected by the balanced mic preamp, while the alternating audio from the mic is amplified.

balanced microphone generates a differential signal, and the balanced amplifier only amplifies the differential or difference between the two inputs, the +48 volts on both of the signal lines is rejected by the mic preamp while the audio, which oscillates between the two balanced lines, is amplified.

Phantom power should only be activated for condenser microphones. If it is mistakenly applied to certain other types of microphones, the sound can be affected, and in some cases it can permanently change the microphone's characteristics. If there are any faults in the cables, it is also possible for the phantom power to blow up certain ribbon mics. So, it's a good idea to only have it on when it's needed. Mixing desks with a single button that activates the phantom power to all inputs should be modified by installing separate switches on each input or by permanently disconnecting the power from a few of the inputs.

Dodgy Cords and Phantom Power A common source of noise when using a phantom-powered microphone is the cable. It is essential that the base of the shield pin is tightly screwed to the connector housing. If the base is loose, other microphones will work just fine, but microphones requiring phantom power will be affected by the intermittent connection between the pin and the housing.

I'm willing to admit that impedance and balanced and unbalanced cabling is a bit hard going. But it's pretty important stuff to know when you've got six people all ready to record, and you're still trying to figure out how get rid of the sound of a fire department radio dispatcher from one of your microphones, or the hum from the bass just can't be ignored. The rest of the book will be easier going, and we are quickly approaching subjects that are a lot more interesting. The next chapter covers other types of transducers, such as direct boxes, how they work, and how to build one.

6 Hum 101, DIs, and Related Transducers

The best sound can be destroyed by hum. Hum that wasn't there before the musicians arrived, and is now as loud and clear as an elephant in the room. Many sessions invariably begin by sorting out hum. This chapter looks at the origin of hum and goes on to explain how to eliminate it. Invariably this will include in one way or another the use of direct boxes.

This chapter takes a close look at what a direct box (often referred to as a *DI*, for *direct inject*) is and how it converts the guitar signal into a balanced, low-impedance signal that can be connected to a console mic-preamp. It also explains a direct box's other function of eliminating hum. The chapter also looks at guitar pickups and contact pickups, and it contains a brief section on wireless systems. Pickups and DIs are essentially the primary alternative to a microphone.

Electrical Power Transmission 101 Hum happens because of the way electric power works. All electrical power sources, from a battery to a power station, have two terminals—one is positive, and the other is negative. Electrons flowing from one to the other release the potential power of the battery or the power station. The electrical potential begins to be used as soon as a light bulb, a city, or a guitar amp is connected to the power.

In the case of the battery, chemicals inside the battery generate and store an excess of electrons at one of the terminals and there is a shortage of electrons at the other terminal. The flow of the electrons between the two terminals through the light bulb (or whatever) will power it until all the excess electrons have been dissipated and an equilibrium of electrons has been reached between the two terminals. The flow of electrons in all batteries is in one direction and is called *direct current* (DC) (see Figure 6.1). Electrons will always flow through the path of least resistance, so if a wire is directly connected between the two terminals (see Figure 6.2), the electrons will quickly flow until the battery is dead, and little of the battery's power will pass through the light bulb. The straight wire has less resistance to the flow of electrons than the light bulb.

In the case of electricity coming from a power station, the electrons are always being replenished. Also, unlike the battery, the electrons do not travel in one direction, but the current alternates in its flow (AC). At the generating plant, one of the terminals is buried

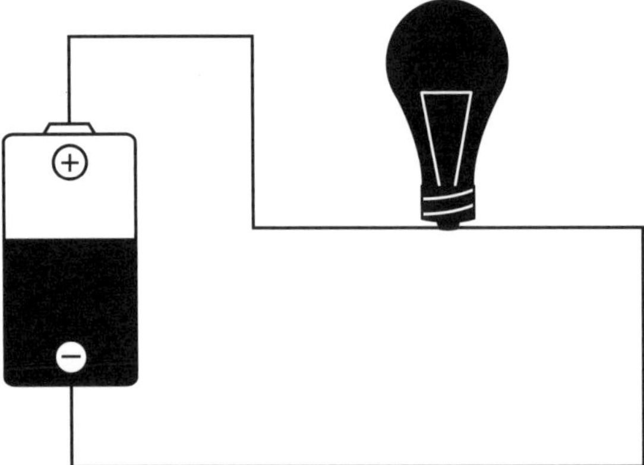

Figure 6.1 Direct current from a battery powering a light. The light filament has a few dozen ohms of resistance. It is the resistance to the flow of electrons through the filament that causes it to get hot and glow. The light will glow until the electrons stored in the battery have reached equilibrium between the positive and negative terminals.

Figure 6.2 The same as Figure 6.1, but now there is a wire in parallel with the light. The wire has almost no resistance, as opposed to the light that does have resistance. The electrons will always flow through the path of least resistance, so nearly all of them will go through the wire and not the light. Because there is no resistance to their journey, they will do this very quickly, and the terminals will reach electronic equilibrium almost immediately. The wire has created a "dead short," and the light will not glow.

in the ground, and the other terminal goes out through the power grid. The planet Earth is used as a common connection for the flow of electrons.

In any device, there is also an earth or ground, which is a common connection for the entire circuit and it is ultimately connected to the real earth so the electricity can flow from its highest potential to its lowest through the device. If the device has a metal housing, it, too, will be connected to earth to ensure that if someone touches the frame (or chassis), he won't get shocked, or if the circuit fails, it will blow a fuse.

But in any building there is a lot of wire between the wall outlet and the meter box which is also near where the ground wire really reaches Earth. (In most small buildings, that's through a water pipe where it enters the earth.) If the distance from where the gear is plugged into a grounded mains receptacle is a ways away from where the ground wire actually goes to Earth ground, there will be a measurable resistance (from the wire) to the flow of electrons. The greater the resistance in that ground wire, the more likely it is you'll have some hum or other noise in your system. The ground connection at the wall, and where your gear is plugged in, is actually slightly "above" the real ground where the water pipe is.

To explain it another way, voltage is a difference in electrical potential, and current is what flows from a point of higher potential electrons to a lower one, called earth or ground. There are two reasons for *earthing* a device. First, safety: If the device malfunctions, 110 volts (or higher in many other countries—up to 240V in Australia) may be shorted to the chassis. If there is no earth connection, when you touch the chassis or anything metal on the device, the current will flow through *you* to the earth. In most cases this ground will be the plug into or out the device (in our case most commonly a guitar amp). Whether this electrifying experience kills you will depend on how much current is also available in the mains power, the strength of your heart, and how wet you and your shoes are, because this changes the resistance of your body. The lower the resistance of your body, the more current will travel through you to ground. But if an earth wire is connected to the device and its chassis, the current flows through the ground wire and not you! This should cause the device's fuse (or the building's fuse) to blow, thus indicating that the device has a serious problem.

Certain devices do not need an earth wire connected (such as hair dryers, effect pedal power packs, and so on) because they are designed in such a way that it is impossible for the main voltage to reach the outer case.

The second reason why an earth connection is essential is that audio cables and equipment need the shielding of all the interconnecting cables to ground. Without proper shield and chassis grounding, whatever radio waves are out there are amplified.

Getting a Good Earth Anything that is above true earth is physically as well as electrically above ground by a few ohms of resistance. Good conductivity, through, for instance, a big copper wire straight to a corrosion-free clamp to a metal water pipe is acceptable ground for purposes of mains power and is usually what you've got connected to the ground pin of all the AC wall outlets in your building. As mentioned earlier, since the ground at the wall is connected through lots of wire to the water pipe, there are usually a few ohms of resistance between wall ground and the water pipe. That slight amount of resistance can cause a current flow through the ground and can become a source of hum or some other elusive electrical noise. The best studio ground starts with a large-diameter multi-stranded copper cable that goes from the mixing desk power supply down to real earth. An area of several feet is dug up to about a foot deep. Then in the hole a layer of dampened clay covered by moist sand and salt is covered with a heavy copper grid. Then the copper wire running from the studio is unbraided and spread out like a root system and welded (or clamped) to the copper grid. Then more salt and sand bury it. Then you will have an excellent earth ground.Those devices that handle the lowest signal, have the greatest gain, or use the most power, such as the mixing desk and all the power amps, should be connected directly to this earth ground.

Why does any of this matter?? Go with me here, because it's the source of all hum.

Hummmmm ... and Fixing It

Let me give a common example of when hum appears before I explain what a ground loop is and how to fix it.

You're recording a keyboard. You're going to mike the amp, and you'd like to also record a direct line out from the amp. All your mics sound fine, and there is no hum. The amp is also hum-free. When you plug into the direct line out of the amp, the amp now has a nasty hum (usually 60 Hz, or a harmonic of it), as does the signal coming into the mixing desk. What you're hearing is the sound of the mains power travelling through two paths to ground. This is called a *ground* or *earth loop* caused by double grounding (see Figure 6.3).

The ground connection for the mixing desk goes to the mains power meter and earth ground, as does the ground connection for all the power outlets where the amp is connected. The lengths of the two runs of ground wire are different as each weaves a separate way through the interior of the walls and floors. This means the ground in the wall outlets in the studio is slightly different than the ones in the control room. When the ground of the mixing desk is also connected to the ground of the amp, each device now has two different paths to ground. The difference in the resistance of paths causes current to flow between them as well as directly to the earth ground. While the current is low, once it is amplified by the high gain of the amp and the mic preamp, it is heard as hum.

There's always a certain degree of double grounding or ground loops, but such conditions should be avoided. The more ground loops you have, the more noise and hum, but it will be most objectionable when it gets into a signal that requires a lot of gain. The rule is to strive for a single path to ground.

Instead of directly connecting the amp to the mixing desk, using a direct box will eliminate the loop. A direct box will also have a ground lift switch that will either connect or "isolate" the earth ground between the two devices. When the ground is lifted, the audio signal

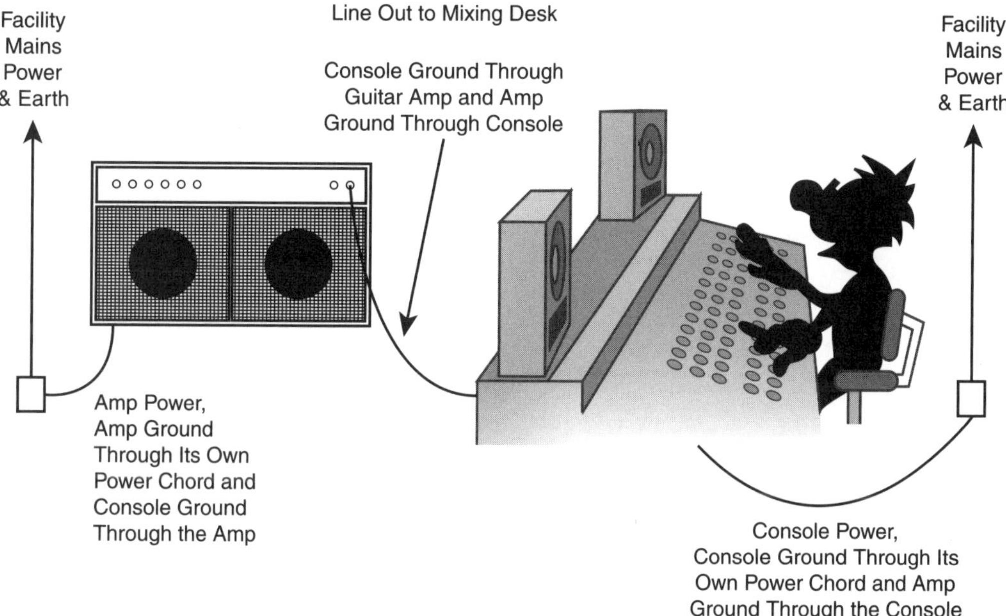

Figure 6.3 A ground loop and the often-resulting hum are generated when there are two paths to the mains power ground. In this example, the loop is completed when the ground of the amp is connected to the mixing desk via the audio cable. The mixing desk is connected to ground through two different power points – one directly and the other through the amp.

passes through the box, but the mains power systems remain electronically and electrically isolated.

If a guitar or bass amplifier is connected to the instrument as well as a direct signal going to the console, the ground probably should be lifted (disconnected) because the amplifier (and bass or guitar) will probably be picking up the electrical ground through the amplifier's power cord. On the other hand, the ground should be connected when, for instance, a bass is plugged into a direct box and no instrument amplifier is involved; otherwise, the bass will not be grounded, and there will be significant hum.

Dangers of Lifting Ground

I have seen on a few occasions that when ground lifting is not available, someone will remove the ground pin on a three-pin adapter so the amp plug is isolated from earth. As a short-term studio solution, that may be fine, but don't ever break the ground pin off a three-pin power cord to reduce the hum because there is a possibility that the power fuse won't blow if there is a short in the device. People have died from this. Scenario: The guitar player has his hands on the guitar (that is plugged into the amp that has a power short and a broken ground pin). He grabs the strings (that are also connected to the amp chassis, which is not connected to ground), and then his lips touch the microphone (which is connected to ground through the PA), and it blows him right off the stage. Definitely a hard act to follow.

Exploding DIs: There's Nothing to Be Afraid Of—We're Professionals Once everything is connected, flip the ground switch on and off to determine the best position for minimum hum. When you flip the switch, quickly pull your hand away from the box. Though it has only happened to me twice in my life, if the amplifier has a short to its chassis and its ground pin has been cut off, when the ground lift switch completes the circuit from the amplifier's chassis to a proper earth ground, the ground lift switch will get jolted with several amps of current and will literally blow up. The box will jump off the floor, flames will come out, and your heart rate will definitely go up. (What a rush!) It's unlikely you'll get shocked since you're not completing the circuit (the mic cable is), but it's a pretty bad way to start a session. If this should happen, the direct box will probably need to be replaced, and the amplifier should not be used until it is fixed.

Eliminating Other Noise (Electromagnetic and Computer Signals)

If there is hum or buzz that is associated with computer devices, hard disk recorders, screen radiation, and so on, then an isolation transformer or direct box can magnetically couple the audio signal while maintaining ground isolation between the mixing desk and the computer. (How transformers work is a sidebar later in this chapter.) For computer output in particular I use small isolation transformers that can be found in most car stereo and electronic supply shops (see Figure 6.4). This approach is also used in stage box splitters where the mic has to go to a house PA and stage monitor mixer or a recording truck. These isolation transformers have two (possibly three) isolated outputs.

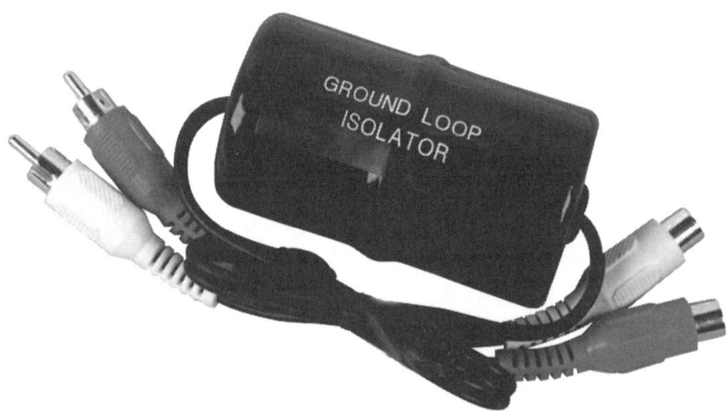

Figure 6.4 Basic line-level stereo signal isolator.

Also, hum and RF will come out of any box that is using nearly dead batteries. Keep the batteries new, or better yet, use an AC adapter. Hum will also occur if the AC adapter does not put out the correct voltage or does not have sufficient current (which is identified in amps of current) for the device being used. For instance, a small multitrack draws a fair amount of current. Another thing to remember is that all the AC adapters should be plugged into the same power strip and kept away from the audio cables that will pick up hum radiating from the supplies.

Hum and buzz can also come from static discharge or electrostatic interference in the electrical system of many types of neon and fluorescent lighting. Fluorescent lights must have their transformers outside of the acoustical space, or their noise will be heard. The problem is worse when the lamps are wearing out. The flickering radiates quite a strong discharging field and creates all kinds of clicks, pops, and so on. The solution is to avoid using fluorescents.

A radiated field can also be generated by certain designs of incandescent light dimmers. The hum may not exist at one dimmer setting while becoming quite severe at another setting, or it might get worse as more light fixtures are connected to the same dimmer. There are dimmers available that do work fine in studios; be sure yours do.

Direct Boxes

Direct boxes (also referred to as a *DIs*) are used to directly connect a 1/4-inch (7.6-cm) unbalanced high-impedance signal (guitar or bass) to a low-impedance balanced microphone input. They are also often used to connect an unbalanced output, such as a keyboard, to a balanced input, such as a microphone input. Most direct boxes have high-to-low impedance transformers inside of them that magnetically transfer the signal magnetically from the input winding (the primary) to the output winding (the secondary). Many engineers (and musicians) feel the sound of a bass plugged into a transformer-type direct box is better than if it is plugged straight into the high-impedance input provided in some mixing desks or a "transformerless" direct box. Some guitar and bass pickups prefer to see the "loading" effect of the transformer.

Most direct boxes have two 1/4-inch (7.6-cm) jacks that are wired together and that connect to the high-impedance input of the transformer (see Figure 6.5). The output of the transformer goes to a low-impedance three-pin microphone connector. If the instrument's signal needs to go into the console as well as into an instrument amplifier, the instrument cord goes into the direct box, and another cord goes between the other 1/4-inch (7.6-cm) jack and the amplifier (see Figure 6.6).

How Transformers Work A transformer converts AC power at a certain voltage level to AC power at a different voltage, and/or converts impedance from high to low, and/or converts a balanced signal to an unbalanced one or vice versa.

A transformer has a ferromagnetic core (often iron) that has multiple coils, or windings, of wire wrapped around the core. In a direct box there are two different coils—one is a high-impedance winding, and the other is a low-impedance winding. (The differences are

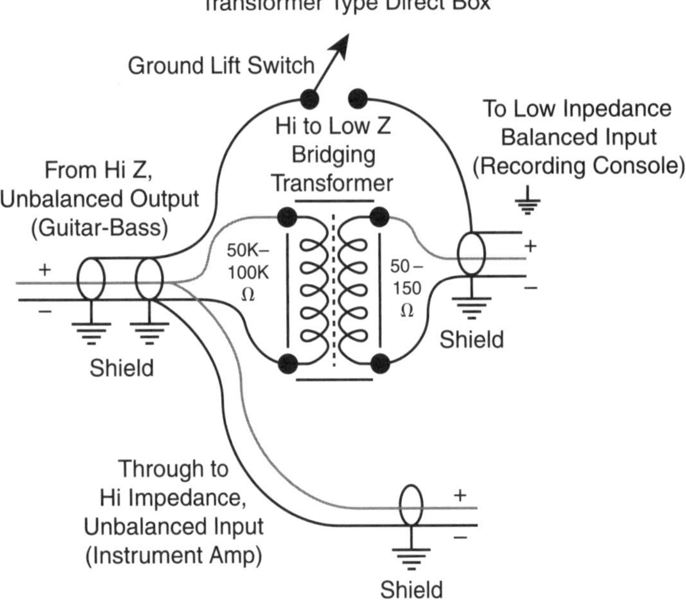

Figure 6.5 Transformer-type direct insert device (direct box).

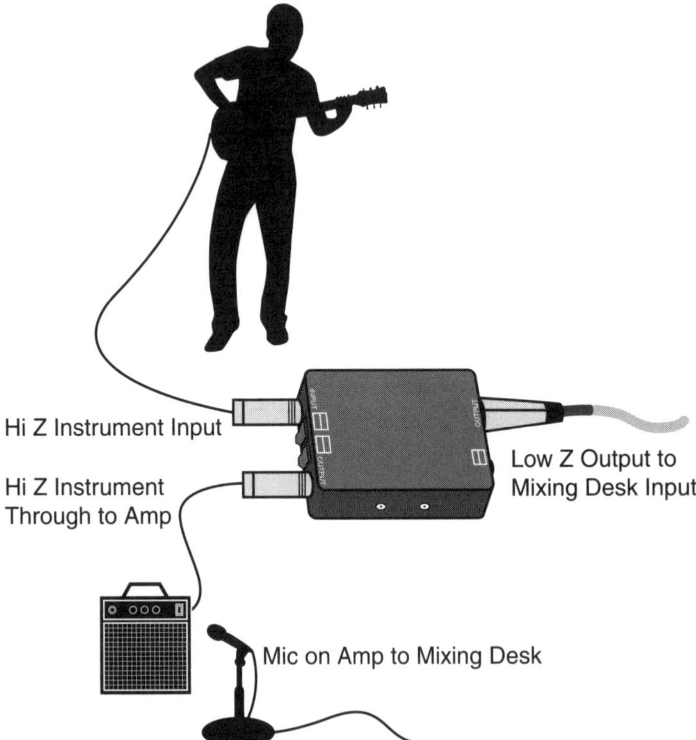

Figure 6.6 Whirlwind Director transformer DI in action. Switches on side—one is the ground lift switch, and the other is a pad to reduce the input signal if a line-level keyboard is connected to the direct box.

wire diameter, metal composition, coil design, and length of the wire.) The alternating current in the input coil causes alternating magnetic lines of force to blossom outward around the core and the second winding. When the alternating signal changes direction with each audio cycle, the lines of force collapse and then blossom outward again, but in the opposite polarity. Because the constantly changing lines of magnetic force are continuously crossing the wires of the second winding, an alternating current is generated in the second winding that duplicates the signal in the first (see Figure 6.7).

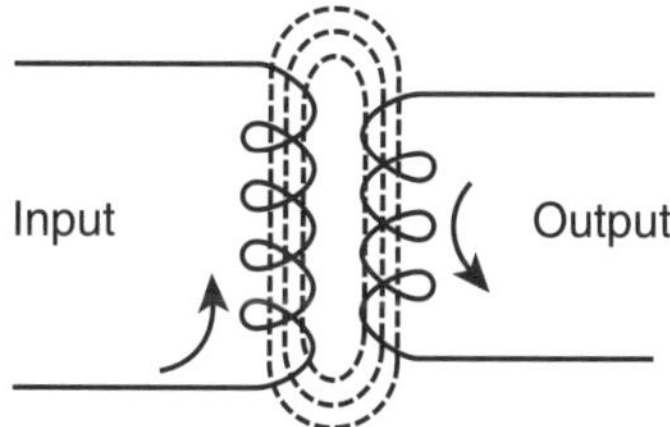

Figure 6.7 As the current in the input coil (called the primary) alternates, the magnetic field (called the flux) blossoms and retracts through the output coil (called the secondary). When the field does this, it generates in the output coil a signal that is the same as the input signal. Coils within transformers are not electrically connected but are magnetically connected, thus an alternating signal (such as audio) can pass through while maintaining isolation between grounds.

Transformers provide a means to magnetically connect two alternating signal devices without connecting them electrically. In the early days of electronics, transformers were used between each stage of amplification because the high voltage of vacuum-tube circuits made it impossible for them to be directly connected as they are in modern low-voltage circuit design. Transformers are also used in power supplies to convert mains power (110V to 240V) to 9V or whatever the device may need.

Transformers are often used to provide the balanced input for a mic preamp or line output for a mixing console, the balanced output of a microphone and of course in a direct box.

Transformers do have a tendency to reduce the transient response of a signal passing through them and alter the sound in other subtle ways. On the other hand, these very characteristics may be highly desirable for a certain sound. Cheaper transformers will also tend to lose high-frequency response. With transformers you pretty much get what you pay for.

Transformerless (also described as *active*) direct boxes are a better choice if a direct box is used for connecting a keyboard or drum machine to a balanced input. An active direct box has an internal amplifier that converts the Hi-Z signal to Low-Z and balances the output. They are sonically more transparent than transformers and have better transient and high-frequency response compared to most transformer-type direct boxes. There are many transformerless direct boxes on the market, but few provide a ground isolation function. Transformerless direct boxes require power, so the best of them will operate with phantom power. Having to worry about batteries in a direct box can be a real pain.

Most classic guitars and basses have outputs that should be turned up completely when going into a direct box. But both types of direct boxes can be overloaded and distort, so if, for instance, the signal from the keyboard is coming from a headphone level output, or the guitar, bass, or electric violin has an internal preamp, you might see whether reducing the instrument's output gives you a better signal.

Often a guitar or bass player will want a direct sound (using a DI) and a miked amp sound. Sometimes, when the two are combined, they cancel substantially because the two signals are out of phase with each other. In going through all the amplification circuits in the signal path, the electronics have reversed the relative polarity of the speaker amp compared to the direct signal coming from the instrument. To correct the problem, reverse the polarity of either of the signals—the direct box or the microphone. If you use a digital audio workstation, you can also align the two signals by delay shifting one against the other to get them in sync.

Wireless Microphones

Wireless transmitters can be used with nearly any type of microphone or guitar/bass pickup (keeping in mind that condenser mics need power supplies). In a recording studio environment, wireless systems are seldom used because it is generally simpler to plug in a wire than to worry about batteries. But they are essential in live performance, which also means they are used on concert recording.

The advantage of wireless mics and instruments is clear: There are no cords to trip over. And, as previously mentioned in Chapter 5, there is no typical top-end loss. A short cord goes to the transmitter, and a short low-impedance line runs from the receiver to the mixer or amp. See Figure 6.8.

Over the last few years, high-tech wireless systems have come a long way. It's not unusual for a dozen or more wireless microphones, guitars, and stage monitor headphone systems (also called *foldback*) to be operating at the same time during high-tech rock shows (dozens are used in live theater). Though taxi and emergency radio signals getting into a wireless stage system are now rare, this does occasionally happen. This is due to one or more of the wireless systems using the same channel as taxicabs, ambulances, and such. Also, as the battery in the transmitter becomes weak, radio interference is more likely, as are wireless dropouts, a loss of dynamic range, and distortion on peaks. Most designs will operate for eight to ten hours on a battery, but the best advice is to change or recharge the battery often.

In general, there are two types of transmitters—body-pack or belt-pack transmitters that may be worn on the body or that clip to the user's belt, respectively. For instrument applications,

Figure 6.8 Shure wireless microphone setup.

a body-pack transmitter is often clipped to a guitar strap or attached directly to an instrument, such as a trumpet or saxophone. Body packs can also be used for lavaliere or tie-clip microphones for lecturers or stage actors and headpiece microphones for singer/dancers and aerobics instructors. Handheld mics have the transmitter built into the handle of the mic, and usually a variety of interchangeable microphone capsules are available. All wireless transmitters require a battery (usually a 9-volt alkaline type) to operate.

The mic or an instrument cord is plugged into the transmitter that has an internal antenna or a short stub sticking out from the bottom. The strength of the radio signal is limited by government regulations. The distance that the signal can effectively travel varies with the location. The range is generally from 100 feet to more than 1,000 feet. Wireless systems work best in line of sight of the receiver. If there are walls and girders between the transmitter and the receiver, radio echoes and reflections off the building may cause signal dropout or a dead spot. When this occurs, in some systems there will be static during the dropout.

The receiver picks up the radio signal from the transmitter and changes it back into an audio signal. The receiver output is essentially a standard mic signal and can be connected to a typical microphone input. Many receivers have a gain control so the output can also be connected to a line input. In a PA application, the receiver might be on the stage and connected to the mixing desk through the stage box into which all the other mics are plugged.

Wireless receivers can have a single receiving antenna, similar to an FM radio. Single-antenna receivers work well in many applications but are sometimes subject to momentary dropouts if the transmitter moves around the room. The best wireless systems use *diversity* receivers with two receiving antennas. The receiver uses the antenna with the clearest signal and will switch to the other if and when the active one becomes unstable. In some systems the receiver will mix the two. A diversity system minimizes dropouts because it is most unlikely that two dead spots will simultaneously occur on both paths.

Each wireless in a particular location must operate on a different frequency; otherwise, they will interfere with each other. Different brands have different ways of handling this. In some cases you have to order each device with a different fixed frequency. In other cases, the transmitters and receivers can be switched to different frequencies. A third approach is that different internal frequency plug-ins are available. It's not necessary to have all the same brand if you're using multiple wirelesses, but you will need to keep track of the frequencies of transmission so that all of them have different transmission frequencies.

Guitar Pickups

Guitar pickups are also transducers because they change string vibrations into electrical signals. Each pickup design has a unique sound, and each one sounds different depending on the guitar it's in, how it's adjusted, what kind of strings are used, and so on.

They can also pick up resonance from the body of the guitar, which adds to the unique sound of that instrument. Some do this much more than others, and this can be a problem. When connecting a guitar directly into a mixing desk (usually through a DI box), the sound in the room where the guitar is played will frequently be amplified. The guitar will sympathetically resonate to the sounds in the room—for instance, from the monitor speakers. The problem is worse if the guitar is run through a compressor, causing low-level noise to be amplified with the compressed sustains. This leakage is particularly objectionable because it sounds quite alien due to the sound characteristics of the pickups.

For example, suppose you're recording a guitar in your living room or a control room. Because the guitar is directly connected to the mixer, you figure the noise in the room won't get into the recording. The rough vocal is playing back, or a bad guitar part that you're using as a guide. Or, in the case of recording in your living room, your kids are running around. On playback, if you solo the part you've just added, you'll find in with the new part is a metallic-sounding rendition of the bad guitar and vocals, or your kids screaming at each other. In general, hollow-body guitars will pick up more external sound then solid bodies will.

Types of Pickups

A guitar pickup is a very simple electromagnetic device. The output signal is generated in the pickup winding when the steel strings vibrate through the lines of magnetic flux. This then causes a change in the magnetic field surrounding the coil of wire, and a signal is generated in the coil (see Figure 6.9).

There are two types commonly used—*single coil* and *humbuckers*. The single-coil pickup comes in Fender Telecaster- or Stratocaster-style guitars (see Figure 6.10). The pickup usually has six permanent magnets, with several thousand turns of fine copper wire wound around them.

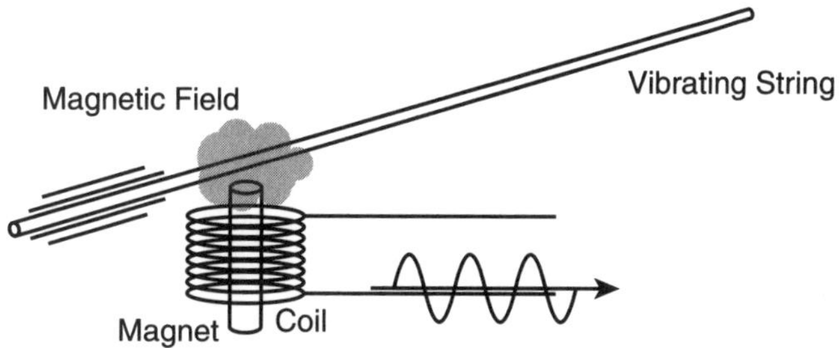

Figure 6.9 One of many coils and magnets in a pickup.

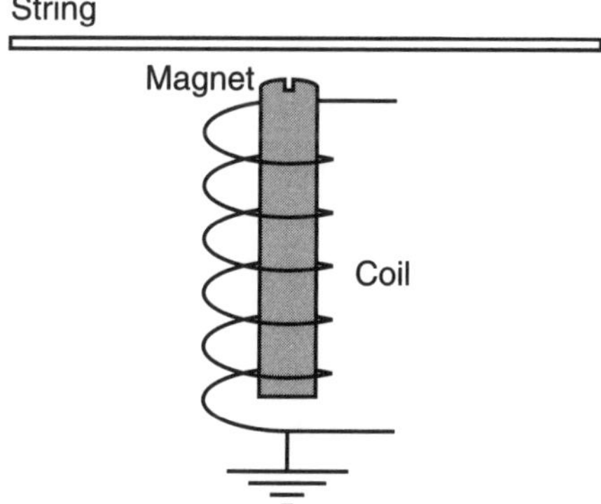

Figure 6.10 Single-coil pickup: When the string vibrates, it sympathetically changes the magnetic flux around the coil, and a signal is generated in the single winding.

Unfortunately, single-coil pickups are equally effective at picking up stray 50- or 60-Hz fields radiated by AC mains and other equipment.

The humbucker was invented to reduce hum. (You probably figured that out from the name.) Figure 6.11 is what they look like; note one row has screw adjustments while the other row does not. Keep in mind that the signal is generated by the interaction of the strings vibrating in the pickup's magnet field and the coil, but the hum is generated by only the coil. The humbucker has two single-coil pickups placed side by side, and both are connected in series (see Figure 6.12). Both coils pick up the same amount of string vibration and background hum, so if they were simply added together, the same amount of hum and noise would be generated as in a single coil. But of course, then it wouldn't be called a humbucker. The humbucker usually has a single permanent magnet and two sets of pole pieces. The North pole touches the base of one set of pole pieces, and the South pole touches the other set, and the two coils are electrically reversed. When the two coils are combined, the signal from the vibrating strings is generated as though it were a single coil, but since the polarity of the windings is reversed, the hum is reduced to almost zero. In practice, there will still be a small amount of hum, because the two coils are very rarely identical.

Figure 6.11 Seymour Duncan humbucker pickup.

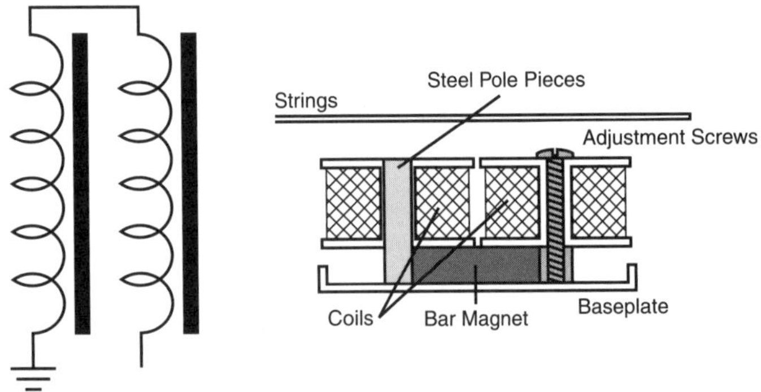

Figure 6.12 The most common humbucker design has two coils wired in series so that external electromagnetic waves are rejected, but the vibration of the string is amplified.

So why doesn't everyone use humbuckers? Like so many other things about sound, single coils sound a certain way that many people love.

Contact Pickups

Many modern acoustic guitars come with acoustic pickups that are far more natural sounding than older designs of a few years ago. For those that don't, they can be fitted with a contact pickup. A contact pickup is also called a *contact mic*. However, it doesn't respond to airborne sound but to mechanical vibrations of the instrument to which it is attached. They are most commonly used on acoustic guitars, but they can be used on anything that has a soundboard or vibrating surface, including violins, bouzouki, mandolins (see Figure 6.13), windows, or a wall. Essentially the contact pickup has a flat surface an inch or so square (though a few are several inches long) that is firmly attached to the vibrating surface of the instrument. When the soundboard vibrates, the pickup's surface does too. A few contact pickups are similar in design to dynamic or condenser microphones, but the vast majority of contact pickups use a piezo-electric crystal to generate a signal.

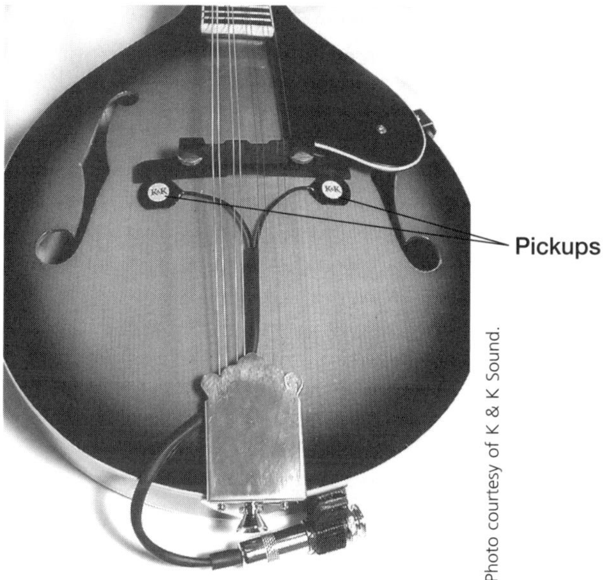

Figure 6.13 Mandolin Twin piezo contact pickup.

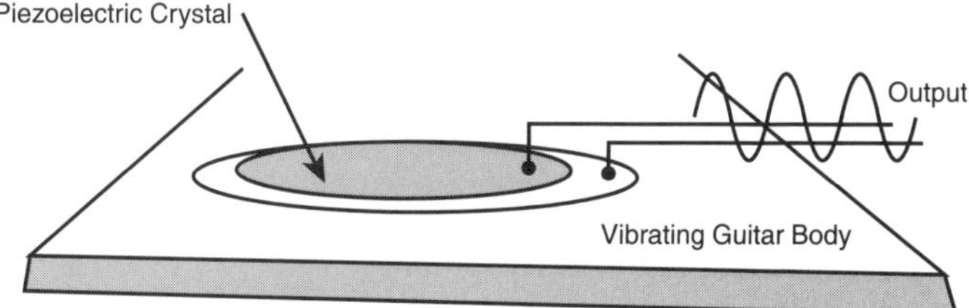

Figure 6.14 A piezo-electric pickup with its sliver of crystal. The instrument body flexes and twists the crystal that in turn generates an alternating signal.

Piezo-electric crystals, as sound pickups, have been around for decades and were/are commonly used in low-cost phono cartridges. Piezo-electric crystal material has a unique behavior. It generates a voltage when it is slightly twisted or placed under subtle stress (see Figure 6.14). A wafer of crystal is attached to the rear of the pickup's surface. Two wires are connected to both sides (or ends) of the crystal, and as the contact surface vibrates, the crystal is sympathetically stressed and twisted, and a comparable signal is generated. Piezos are very high impedance, and many come with a preamp so the lead from the pickup can be kept very short.

A contact mic can be attached to the body of an instrument by glue, sticky putty, rubber cement, or pretty much any adhesive, provided it remains flexible. If you're attaching it to someone else's instrument, be very sure that the adhesive can be pulled off without leaving any mark or damage whatsoever.

The sound quality coming from a contact mic will vary greatly depending on the design and its placement on the instrument. Some contact mics tend to sound metallic and a bit brittle but pick up the string attack very well. The blend of this sound and a mic on the instrument can create an interesting electric/acoustic sound. On the other hand, sometimes they will generate a lower range of the instrument's sound. However, they will miss the acoustics provided by the space in which the instrument is played—but, of course, that also means they will have good isolation from all the other instruments that might be playing in the same space. There is a bit of trial and error in initially finding the sweet spot for the contact's placement, so be prepared to take some time to find the best place(s) for the pickup(s).

While there is good isolation with a contact mic, in a loud PA environment or if plugged into a loud guitar amp, the contact mic will pick it up. Under these conditions, contact mics can go into feedback or sound boomy.

Contemporary music will always have guitars, bass, and every imaginable type of keyboard. This chapter has looked at how those instruments connect into a recording or PA system. Probably the most useful section of this chapter explains hum and how to get rid of it. In the next chapter, we will look at those things that often make the difference between good-quality sound and sound that also has noise and distortion. We'll look at mic pads, mic stands, and shock mounts.

7 Accessories and Necessary Hardware

In life it is so often the little things that make the biggest difference in the end. This is definitely the case with stands, pads, booms, windscreens, and shock mounts, not to mention sandbags, gobos, and decouplers. You may not know what some of those things are or what they are used for, but they will make a significant difference in taking your microphone technique from average to professional. Some of these things tend to gather at the bottom of the mic drawer. And some of them might be costly, but if you're handy, you can make them for next to nothing. These items are used all the time in recording and will improve the quality of your sound, reduce the amount of extraneous noise that might enter the mic, and provide a means to fine-tune the acoustic sound around the instrument you're miking.

Microphone Pads

Most microphones are designed to handle a wide dynamic range of signals before distorting. Most have a much broader range than the average microphone preamp. Sometimes the mic will put out so much signal that the preamplifier input will overload even when it is adjusted for minimum gain. For this reason, it is sometimes necessary to reduce the signal going into the preamp input.

A *microphone pad* is a resistive network that introduces a loss to the microphone's output before the signal enters the preamp. Figure 7.1 shows one type of design called an H pad. A well-designed pad lowers the signal passing through the circuit while maintaining a correct impedance match between the output of the microphone and the input of the mic preamp (as does this circuit). Unfortunately, this design cannot be used with a phantom-powered condenser microphone, since it will lower the voltage being supplied to the mic.

Whether a pad is needed depends on what's being recorded, what mic is being used, how and where the instrument is being miked, the gain of the preamp, and the typical output level of the mic. For a violin or wind chimes, a pad will probably not be needed, but for a drum, a blasting guitar, or a trumpet, it probably will. If you have no pad, pulling the microphone back from the sound source will, of course, reduce the sound pressure entering the mic, and in a pinch, I've done it. But it's not my preference, because if I want a close sound, I won't get it if the mic is pulled back. It will sound different. Asking someone to sing or play softer is equally bad form.

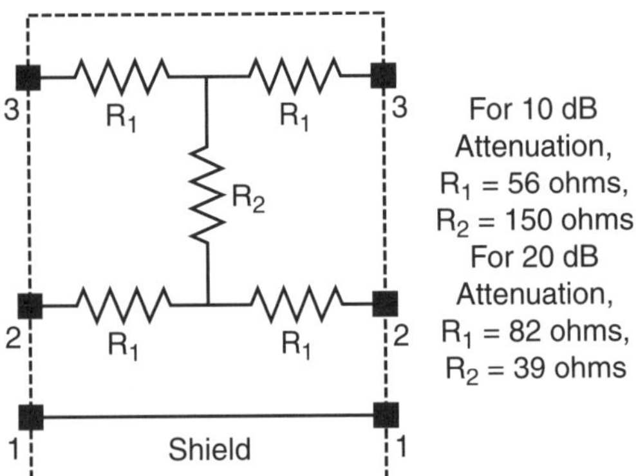

Figure 7.1 An H pad circuit for a balanced mic. This design maintains the same impedance for both input and out. It cannot be used when phantom power is needed for the microphone.

Where's the Pad?

Most mixing desks have an internal switchable pad on each channel electronically located right before the mic preamp input. Less expensive mixers and most self-contained multitracks seldom have pads. If the mixing desk doesn't have them, inline external pads can be used. These are cigar-sized tubes or small boxes with microphone connectors at both ends (see Figure 7.2). An external pad connects between the microphone and the input of the mixing desk. External pads are available with 5, 10, 15, 20, or 30 dB of loss, and some are selectable. If you're handy with a soldering iron, you can build you own pad in a small box or a piece of pipe with mic connectors at each end. Use the information in Figure 7.1. (Hint: If you build your own, be sure to buy low-noise metal film resistors.)

Figure 7.2 The Shure A15AS Switchable Inline Attenuator reduces the level of any balanced microphone or line-level signal by 15, 20, or 25 dB. The A15AS allows phantom power to pass through from the mixer to the microphone, so it can be used with condenser microphones.

A condenser mic's capsule will often put out a stronger signal than the microphone's internal preamp can handle, so it will have a selectable pad built right into the microphone (see Figure 7.3). On some condenser models, the pad is a separate part that resembles a small, short pipe. The capsule is unscrewed from the preamp, and the pad is then threaded between the capsule and the preamp. On microphones that use screw-on pads and other attachments, if you get oil from your fingers on the contacts, it will cause tarnishing, create a bad connection, and change the sound performance.

Figure 7.3 Internal pad on a RØDE NT2-A.

Microphone Stands

The stand and boom are what hold the microphone in position. Avoid cheap, unstable stands. It is critical that the various fittings and adjustments are sturdy enough to hold up over the long term. The hardware for changing the stand's tilt, boom extension, and height should be reliable and easy to adjust. The most common failures on stand hardware are stripped threads and worn-out locking spacers. The locking spacers are washers that are squeezed against the boom and stand extensions by the height and tilt adjustment levers. These washers are neither obvious nor visible, but they are critical to the long-term reliability of a stand.

The design of the washers, how they are compressed, and the availability of replacements are important considerations when buying stands. Loose and worn-out fittings mean that the microphone will lose its position through the course of the session. It is seriously annoying to position all the mikes, and then find halfway through a session that a few of them have shifted because they wouldn't hold their position. Even if the stand has nothing wrong with it, the fittings will loosen, so you should check a stand periodically and tighten all the bolts, nuts, and wobbly wheels. Otherwise, when you mike a set of drums, the sympathetic rattles in the stands will be picked up through the mic. Or, even worse, the mike will suddenly come crashing down into the body of somebody's prized guitar. Lastly, it is very uncool to use gaffer tape to "fix" a mic-stand adjustment problem. It makes the stand next to unusable because it can't be adjusted, and no matter what gear you might have, it gives the impression that your equipment is falling apart.

How many stands you need depends on the size of the studio and the type of recordings that are being made. For basic recording, you need at least a couple of small stands and one large one. Obviously, not many stands are needed if vocals and an occasional guitar are the only live sounds that are ever recorded.

There are many different manufacturers of mic stands. The price range is wide, but the difference in quality is not obvious. The cheapest won't hold up; the most expensive are worth it but for many are also a luxury. Make sure that the legs can be locked in place and don't close up when the stand is picked up and moved. Be sure all the pivots, clutches, and lock nuts (like on

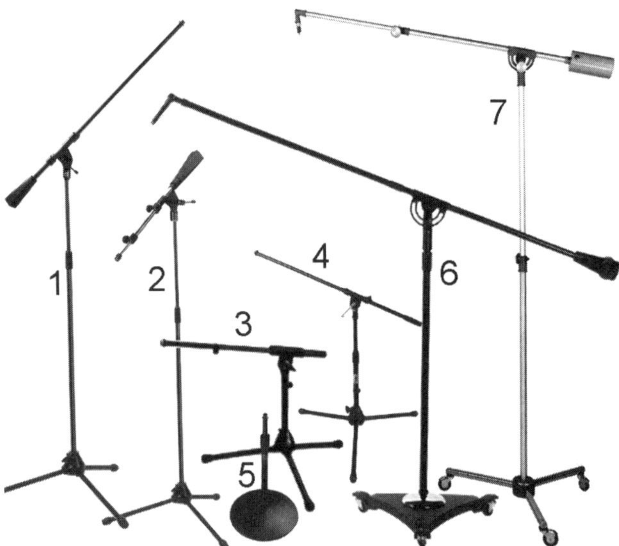

Figure 7.4 Common microphone stands.

the counterweights, or wheels) are well made to last. Be sure that nothing rattles (such as the extension tubes). Above all else, make sure the adjustment mechanisms are easy to loosen and tighten, and once positioned they don't suddenly let go.

Figure 7.4 shows a number of different stands (not to scale). These scales are:

1. A very typical stand with a fixed-length boom. The height extends 3 to 5½ feet, with a 3-foot (or so) boom. Major studios have a couple dozen of these. A smaller rock studio would have 10 or so.
2. These stands have an extension inside the boom. Some studios have a combination of the #1 stands and these. If you had eight to ten of #1 stands, you might consider two to four of these.
3. This is a short stand with an extender boom. The extended height is 1 to 2 feet. This stand is very useful on snare and amps sitting on the floor. It's useful on cello and string bass. A large studio would have four to six of these. A rock studio would find two or three useful. The advantage of the extension boom is that it's more compact, hence you get in close without having the rest of a full-length boom extending backward.
4. This stand does the same job as #3, but it has a fixed-length boom. It, too, has a height of 1 to 2 feet.
5. This stand is ideal for kick drum or if you need a mic under a snare drum. It has a height of 1 foot or so (you can also get them at ½-foot height). A big studio might have two to three of them. A rock studio might have one.

6. This is a common studio stand. It extends from 4 to 6 feet high and has sufficient size to handle a 4½- to 5-foot boom. Large studios will have several of these. A rock studio will have two or three for drum overheads, room mics, and vocals.
7. This is a Starbird stand, first designed and manufactured by George Starbird right after World War II. Most are still in use. Manley Labs acquired the right to make them a few years ago. Major studios might have several, and a rock studio might have one or none. They are large, heavy, and ideal for heavy microphones. The height will extend 8 feet, as will the boom horizontally, which means if you go fully vertical, it will go up to nearly 16 feet. If you have the room, having one for vocals will impress.

If you only need one stand, it's preferable to get a large boom so that the base can be positioned far enough away from tapping feet. The best stand for vocals will have the base 2 or 3 feet away from where the microphone is actually positioned, with the microphone hanging downward from the stand. Large, heavy bases with wide-set legs are best for recording. Many times a stand will exhibit sympathetic mechanical vibrations from nearby foot tapping, bass kick drum, or floor or riser movement. Once again, be sure that the boom, counterweight, and height extension are sufficiently tightened so that the microphone doesn't come crashing down on the floor, a musician's head, or an instrument.

It is a very good idea to make or buy a few sandbags that you can easily place on the stand base (or in some cases, the rear of the boom) for added stability, so even if the boom is overextended, it won't tip over. While a mic stand that is properly built, then selected and positioned for a certain microphone and purpose, won't need a sandbag, I've also seen (many times) an over-balanced stand come crashing down on something. So, I usually put bags on any stand I think is even slightly extended and will straddle the bag over the stand with one end drooping onto the floor. I prefer a canvas bag that's about a foot or so long that has a heavy plastic liner filled with sand. Don't overpack them, or they tend not to sit well on the base, and during the session the vibrations will shake them out of position.

In a large studio or where microphones are moved between stands, a quick-change release is one way to avoid the constant search for the "right" holder and in the long term prevent microphone threads from becoming stripped. The Atlas LO-2 (see Figure 7.5) is a spring-loaded, quick-release microphone stand connector that has been made by Atlas Sound for decades. The male part stays on the stand while the female part stays with the mic so it can be easily interchanged. Because microphones will gather dust if they are left out, the LO-2 makes it easier to take a mic down and put it away whenever it isn't being used. They're available online from a number of retailers for less than $20. The cheapest one I found was $13. (Caution: Be sure the quick-release spring lock has engaged into the "keyhole" before walking away from the mic and stand. If the mic is hanging downward and is not secure, its weight will pull it off the stand and down to the floor or possibly though the body of somebody's Stradivarius. Also, for the more expensive and/or heaviest of microphones, I would probably not use the LO-2.)

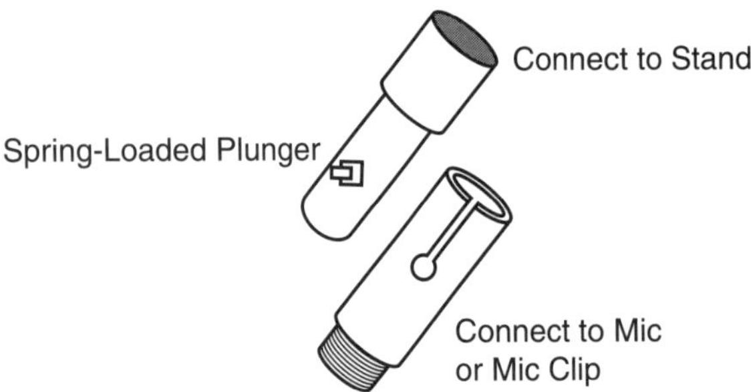

Figure 7.5 LO-2 quick-release mic stand connector.

In general, what you need in a stand for live or recording work is about the same. I suppose the biggest difference is that you're more likely to have one or two larger stands for recording, and you probably want a stand or two with a solid round base instead of a tripod base. A round base is easier to cluster together when you have many mics in the same area, for instance on drums.

Reconditioning Mic Stands On most mic stands, at the end of the height extension shaft is a rubber ring that keeps the shaft stable and moving smoothly and creates a vacuum so the extension doesn't come crashing down as soon as you loosen it. On older stands, this rubber ring will wear out, and the shaft will start to clang around inside. The inside of the tube can also become dirty and cause the extension to seize up. Pull out the extension and clean the interior of the tube and rubber gasket with a rag and rubber cleaner. If the rubber ring is too far gone, it can be ordered separately and replaced. Don't use conventional multipurpose oil to re-lubricate the tube. Use horn-valve oil; otherwise, the rubber will quickly decompose and seize up the extension tube. Also, take the time to tighten the various bolts and nuts holding the stand together, the counterweight, and the boom pivot.

Windscreens

Windscreens are essential any time you're recording outside and it's a windy day. Most people have seen a news scene or a movie/TV set where someone is swinging a handheld boom with a large, fuzzy "blimp" at one end (see Figures 7.6 and 7.7). Inside the blimp is a shotgun microphone, and the blimp keeps wind noise out of the microphone. Blimps come in a variety of designs. A shotgun microphone is held in the middle of the blimp by an elastic suspension.

Heavy-duty windscreens are built into all handheld PA mics (see Figure 7.8), and they are there to reduce not only wind noise, but also the percussive pops that occur when a vocalist has the mic right up against his mouth. In outdoor conditions an additional windscreen may be placed

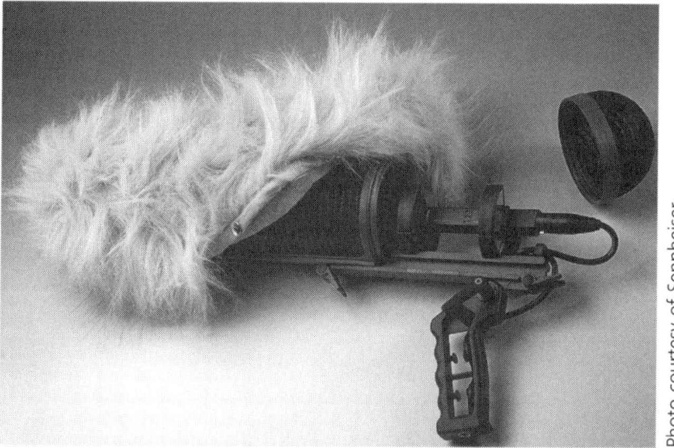

Photo courtesy of Sennheiser.

Figure 7.6 The components of a Sennheiser "blimp."

Photo courtesy of Angelo Galeano.

Figure 7.7 A "blimp" at the end of a Galeano Lab boom. Blimps are used in screen production and operated by a boom swinger.

over the internal windscreen. If you use a PA-type microphone for recording, if it has a "ball-style" windscreen, such as the Shure SM58, you might find the sound is better if you screw off the windscreen. If left on in the studio, this type of windscreen will tend to reduce the transients and the brightness of the sound.

Figure 7.8 Shure SM58 internal windscreen partially exposed below an external windscreen.

Windscreens are also needed for most vocal recording, but they are seldom the heavy-duty type you find in a PA mic because the vocalist is usually a few inches or more away from the mic, and the mic is not necessarily in direct line with the vocalist's mouth. A light foam windscreen often comes with a studio mic, but it's common practice to use external windscreens that are positioned a couple of inches in front of the mic (see Figures 7.9 and 7.10).

Though commercial external windscreens are available, you can make one from pantyhose that is stretched over an 8-inch loop at one end of a straightened coat-hanger wire. Position the loop about 6 inches in front of the mic and attach the other end to the mic stand.

Figure 7.9 Neumann U 67 vocal mic setup with windscreen.

Figure 7.10 A windscreen assembly that provides a choice of windscreen.

When pops are a particular problem, pull the mic back from the vocalist and raise it, then tip it slightly downward toward the mouth so it's slightly off-axis to the direct attack of the voice and wind percussiveness.

Vocals aren't the only thing that can cause popping. A sound source that is extremely percussive can also cause problems. For example, shakers or maracas have such high-pressure transients that moving them back and forth toward the mic can cause the mic to sound as though it's being blown into. The solution is to try a windscreen, increase the distance between the mic and the instrument, or position the mic slightly off-axis to the direction of the sound source's movement.

Microphone Contagion Most old PA mics should be condemned by the Health Department. The windscreen is filled with contagious funk because people sing so closely into them and salivate all over them (yuck). After a couple of months of mic-munching, a heavily made-up singer can completely block a windscreen with lipstick. Most windscreens can be unscrewed from the mic and degreased and washed. Once the windscreen is dry, it can go back on the mic. Before replacing it, make sure none of the glue that holds the internal foam screen in place has let go; if it has, use a minimum of Super Glue to secure the screen to the housing. If the foam inner liner has rotted away, replace it and glue it in place. Be sure not to block any of the openings.

Shock Mounts and Floor Vibration

Unless your recording space has a thick concrete floor, it's likely that it vibrates when the speakers are pumping, or you're recording drums and amps, or a big truck shifts gears outside. When you record an acoustic guitar, the microphone will be turned up, so you might also hear footsteps from the room next door. If the floor moves, the stand will pick up the movement and so will the mic, resulting in its output having a noisy low end and sounding "boomy." The quieter the sound being miked, the more noticeable any type of mechanical vibration will be. This low-end rumble builds up as you add track after track, resulting in the mix having a lack of space and clarity. The sounds you've been going for will be clouded by this pervasive swamp of low-end rumble.

Vocal mics are usually built with internal isolators to minimize handling noise, and studio microphones often come with external vibration isolators called *shock mounts* (often sold as an accessory). The best of them look like two rings of elastic spider webs, with the mic suspended in the center of the two webs (see Figure 7.11). Unfortunately, they are fairly limited in how well they "decouple" the microphone from the stand.

Photo courtesy of Georg Neumann GmbH.

Figure 7.11 Larger microphones like the Neumann TLM 103 D digital microphone, particularly when they are used for vocals or at a distance from the sound source or in a room with a floor that vibrates, should be held in a suspension/shock assembly such as this.

Although I do know people who have poured several truckloads of concrete into their subflooring, not many people are going to do that. So here are a few doable isolation ideas that may work for you.

- Some studios attach stands with booms to the ceiling above the area where the drums are usually recorded. This also works if you have a certain place where you record vocals. It works best with lower ceilings that don't have any living area above them.
- For very quiet or vocal overdubs, a good way to isolate the microphone and stand is to set them on top of a block of mattress-type closed-cell foam rubber 3 feet square and 8 inches or so thick. (Sandbag the base if it seems precarious on the rubber.) Have someone make you a cloth bag with some cloth handles for the rubber block, and it can also be used as a "gobo." (See the upcoming "Gobos" section.) See Figure 7.12.

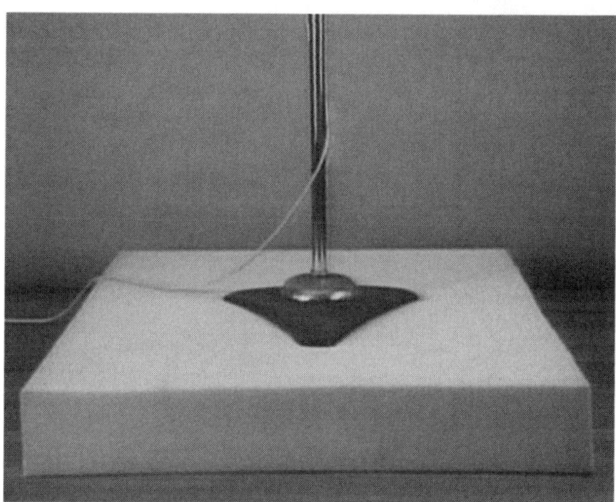

Figure 7.12 Rubber block stand isolation (can double as a gobo).

- I had to isolate eight pianos in eight rooms of a large wooden building. I came up with a simple decoupler design (see Figure 7.13). I took two 1-foot squares of ½-inch-thick plywood and put four rubber and cork air-conditioning decoupling blocks in between them. The decoupler blocks are 2 inches square and a ½-inch thick and are sold at any air-conditioning supply house. On their top and bottom, they have a rubber grid that runs in one direction on the top and in another on the bottom, with cork in between. Then I glued a 6-inch-square piece of plywood with a 3-inch-round hole to the top so that the piano wouldn't roll off the pads. One pad went under each wheel of the piano, and another without the top plywood piece went under the heel of the player so that the heel/pedal height remained the same. I used as little glue as possible to fix the decouplers to the plywood so that the flexibility of the rubber grid was not impaired. With the isolators installed, the mechanical transmission from the piano was substantially reduced. (Of course, the piano benches had to be raised slightly.)

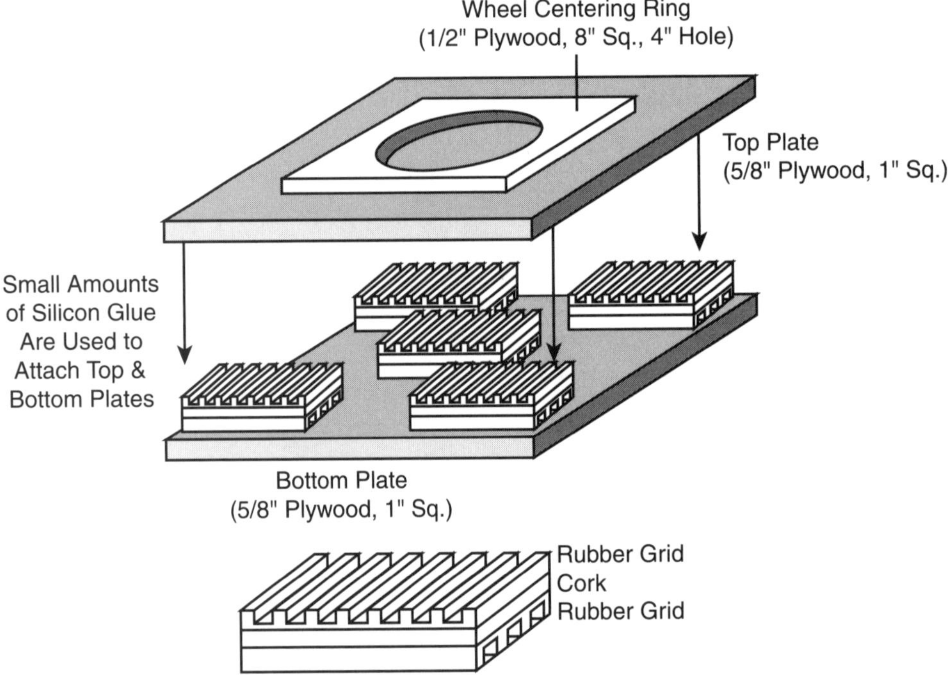

Figure 7.13 Plans for a piano decoupler.

- Set the guitar amp or bass amp in the middle of a large block of closed-cell foam rubber.
- Another idea is to make something that looks like a baby jumper. Attach four steel cables from the ceiling or a simple timber or metal frame. Attach the four cables to one end of four heavy-duty springs and attach the springs to a wooden platform large enough to accommodate the amp. The amp sets on the platform with the springs decoupling it from the floor. The springs should be attached with turn buckles so that the height can be adjusted. The platform should be built with a speaker in mind, so the selection of the springs takes into account the weight and allows for a certain amount of stretch, but not too much stretch to where it loses springiness. Light foam rubber should be shoved into the interior of the spring to reduce higher-frequency vibration.
- If you have a floor that moves but is nonetheless well built, you might build a small isolation floor. If you have the room, make a 4-inch raised floor. A floor that's 10 feet by 10 feet is very usable. Start with a base of ½-inch plywood or exterior-grade compressed chipboard on top of a ½-inch sheet of sound board. Attach to the wood base a frame made from 2×4s with additional timbers (about every 12 to 18 inches) running parallel to one of the sides, and

brace the corners. Then caulk all the joints and line it with heavy plastic. Fill it up with packed dirt or sand. Then glue and nail tongue-and-groove timber flooring diagonally across the top 2×4s. This will give you a recording floor that is extremely dense and large enough to record most things. Have on hand a removable piece of carpet if you have people standing on the floor, but the idea is to create a place where you can get early reflections without any floor movement. A similarly designed floor may be a good idea for a control room (if you have one), but you would allow for wiring troughs from the mixing desk, effects racks, and recorders.

- A cheap way to decouple offending vibrating bodies, such as speakers, is to stack up several layers of corrugated cardboard and set the speakers on top of the cardboard stack. For those disco DJs who use turntables, this is a surefire way to decouple a turntable and eliminate turntable feedback.

Gobos

The term *gobo* is studio slang for an acoustic separator, or "go between," that is positioned between two or more instruments—usually between drums and the rest of the rhythm section and/or between guitar amps. Tall ones are often used to create a sort of vocal booth for a singer. A gobo can be as simple as a large block of closed-cell foam rubber inside of a cloth bag with handle straps, which can also be used, as mentioned earlier, under an amp or microphone stand. Because of the nature of low-frequency waves, gobos are most effective at blocking absorptive frequencies above 400 Hz.

To be effective at stopping sound, a gobo needs to be dense, and the sides are almost always sound absorptive. They must be easy and flexible to move and assemble into whatever session setup configuration is required. They must be able to be pushed together without any gaps at the floor or the edges where they intersect. Lastly, they need to be stable and not prone to falling over. Bigger studios often have a few sizes, with the average being 3 to 4 feet square and 6 to 8 inches thick. I've worked in studios that had narrow ones and with ones that were 4 feet wide and almost floor-to-ceiling, with a window at the top so they could be built into a basic vocal booth.

There are many design approaches. Here is how I would approach building a gobo (see Figure 7.14). Start with a 1-inch by 6-inch wood frame. Inside the center of the gobo is a spine of a couple of layers of 5/8-inch gyprock or a sheet of 1-inch plywood with fibreglass or rockwool insulation batts on both sides of the center sheet. (Polyester lacks density.) The dense center should be sealed to the frame so there are no gaps. A durable cloth material is stretched and stapled to the frame. The best cloth material is something called *frontrunner*, which has a weave that won't sag over time. If I want to overstuff the sound absorption batting or just give the frontrunner more support, I'll attach a layer of chicken-coop wire mesh over the absorptive material before attaching the cloth. Then I finish it with some edging around the frame that covers up all the staples. Because the gobo is fairly heavy, it needs wheels that are attached to brackets attached to the bottom so they are set wide enough for the gobo to be stable. At the same time, to get the most benefit, the wheels shouldn't prevent the bottom from going to the floor or the edges from touching when next to another gobo. Also, the wheels shouldn't get in the way of setting up mics and instrument hardware or be a source of tripping. To get a good seal with the floor, put some carpet on the bottom of the gobo.

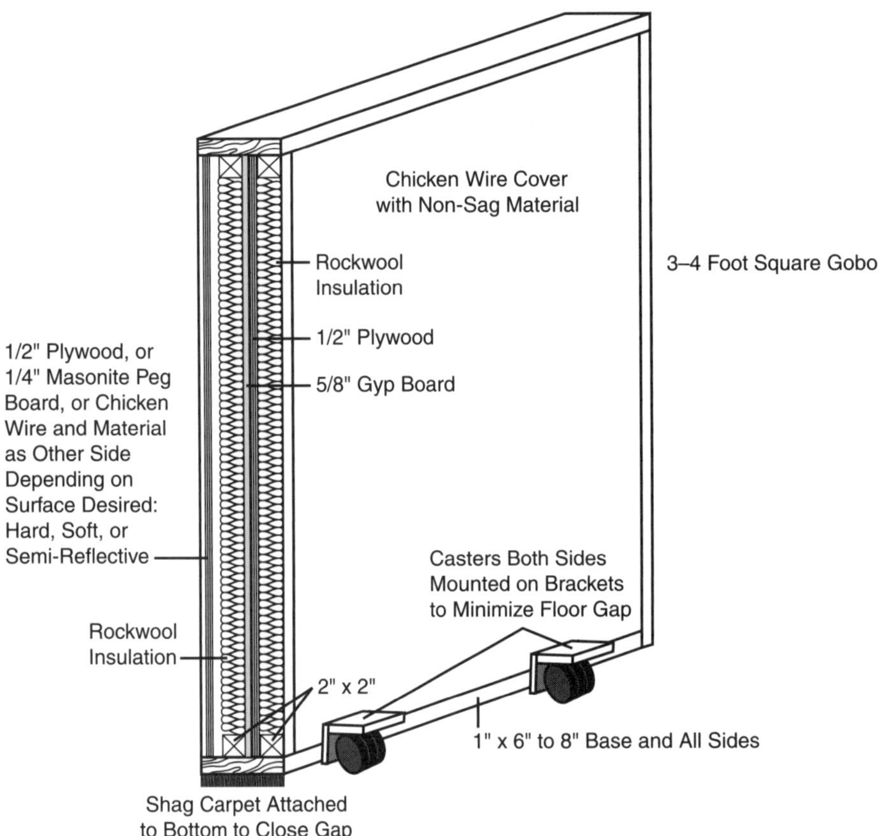

Figure 7.14 A design for a gobo.

Gobos can also be used to alter and enhance the acoustic environment around an instrument. For this purpose they can be made more versatile by having one side absorptive with the other side reflective (or semi-reflective). These portable surfaces close to different instruments create exceedingly early reflections and get some unusual sounds. Attach a reflective surface to the edge of the frame, but don't brace the internal side—you want the panel to flex with the low-frequency energy. By moving with the long low-frequency waves, it absorbs some of their energy, a bit like a shock absorber in a car. I've seen a variety of materials used as reflective surfaces for gobos; here are three:

- A sheet of thin wood panelling will reflect higher frequencies, while absorbing some of the low frequencies (because it flexes).
- Pegboard will also reflect high frequencies, while absorbing mid to low frequencies. The low frequency is absorbed by the flexing of the pegboard. Mid frequencies travel through the holes and are trapped inside the gobo, and high frequencies are reflected off the hard surface between the holes.
- I realize that most people don't have a large space and room for many gobos, but what we had at CBS studios is still worth a mention. A couple of gobos had a thin sheet of metal on one side. When we did horn and string dates, we would often position them 8 to 12 feet from the players, and the sound would be noticeably brighter.

Piano Bags

If you have an acoustic piano, and you record it along with other instruments, you might want to consider acquiring a piano bag to reduce the leakage into the piano. The bag is made of very heavy quilting and is made to go over the entire piano, all the way to the floor (see Figure 7.15). Conventional gobos around the piano will increase the isolation.

Photo courtesy of Instrument Covers, Salem, Oregon.

Figure 7.15 A studio piano bag made of extremely thick quilting. The bag is designed to enclose the entire piano with the lid open fully or partially. Flaps are also available for inserting booms for microphone placement.

If you know someone who's handy with an industrial upholstery sewing machine, you might be able to have a bag built for you. I had to make a few once, and I started by buying the heaviest quilts I could find. You can buy them from moving companies. The ones we built also had a flap that extended behind the pedals, so pretty much the entire soundboard of the piano was encased, with the exception of the keyboard and the pedals. Near where the lid opened were flaps with Velcro closers so mic booms could extend into the piano, and there was extra material across the lid so it could be opened in its low position. There are companies that make these bags, but all the ones I've seen were custom-made to suit the piano and the client's needs for miking and such. One company I am aware of is Instrument Covers, located in Salem, Oregon.

This chapter has explored an array of bits and bobs that are seldom the first things people think about in their quest to make great recordings. As I said at the beginning of this chapter, it is the little things that mean so much. Interestingly, many of the suggestions are things that don't cost a fortune to implement. One thing is certain; these devices and techniques will reduce noise and leakage in the sounds coming from your microphones. Your sounds will have clarity and brightness.

In the next chapter, we'll look at a variety of stereo techniques.

8 Stereo Microphone Techniques

In this chapter, we'll begin to use microphones and to apply the information that were presented in the first half of the book. This chapter will explore stereo recording in its many forms. For some types of recordings, it is amazing what you can achieve with two microphones if you know what to do with them. There are people who have made a career out of making recording with just two microphones, and many critically acclaimed recordings have been made that way (mostly in the orchestra/choir concert genre).

Stereo miking is also widely used throughout all multitrack production to record acoustic instruments and to capture the overall ambience of group performances.

Why Stereo Miking?

Stereo miking allows you to pick up sounds from two points in space, similar to the way our ears function. If we only had one ear in the middle of our forehead, we would only need one mic. The fact that our ears are on opposite sides of our heads, instead of right beside each other, means that sound reaches them at slightly different times and intensities. Those differences allow us to recognize what direction sounds are coming from. (Refer back to Chapter 3 if you missed it.) Capturing sounds via stereo miking and playing those sounds back through a two-speaker system lets you create the illusion of instruments, voices, or any other recorded sound existing within a simulated left-right stereo spectrum. The illusion is created by the difference in intensity, phase, and time of arrival of the sound entering the capsules of the two microphones.

Surround Surround sound is common in DVD releases and digital broadcast, with most TV and movie productions having Dolby 5.1 audio. Although on occasion there is a need to record 5.1 live, such as when recording environments for a film or possibly a live concert, surround sound is primarily created during the mixdown process from single mono and stereophonically recorded tracks. An excellent paper is available on mixing surround sound from the National Academy of Recording Arts and Sciences. See www.grammy.com/Recording_Academy/Producers_And_Engineers/Guidelines.

For most stereo recordings, a pair of identical microphones is used. In most cases these will be condenser microphones (a few stereo ribbon mics have been made), which have better sensitivity for picking up sound at a distance. A non-identical pair of mics can work for some stereo images, but it won't create an accurate stereo image. Some stereo microphones have two microphones in one body (see Figure 8.1). Depending on the model, each of the microphones may have selectable patterns that provide the option of XY, stereosonic, or MS placement (described later in this chapter). Professional stereo microphones allow one of the microphones to rotate on the body so that the angle between the two mics can be adjusted for the width of the sound source and to facilitate the various stereo techniques (see Figure 8.2). For instance, the front of an acoustic three-piece might be 10 feet, while the front of an orchestra could be 80 feet.

Photo courtesy of Georg Neumann GmbH.

Figure 8.1 The inside of the capsule housing for a Neumann 69 i.

The closer the microphones are to the sound source, the more specific points will be picked up in the sound's panorama. If the mics are too close, certain aspects of the sound will be accentuated, while others are lost. For instance, if the mics are too close to a choir, the three sopranos in the front row will stand out compared to the other 30 voices.

Photo courtesy of Georg Neumann GmbH.

Figure 8.2 Neumann USM 69 i stereo microphone. The USM 69 i stereo microphone has two separate dual-diaphragm capsules. These are mounted vertically and rotate against each other. The directional polar patterns can be selected separately for each capsule.

The farther the microphones are from the sound source, the more open the sound becomes—in other words, the greater the blend and texture of the sound source and the environment. However, if the mics are too far back, the sound will have too much reverb and will lack brightness, clarity, and definition. When the sound is coming from different height levels, as would be the case of a choir on stage risers, if the microphones are too high, the sound coming from the rear of the ensemble will be louder in the mics than the sound coming from the front.

For best placement on large ensembles, it is essential to have some rehearsal and experimentation. For a large orchestra, it might turn out that more than one stereo pair is needed and mixed together. For instance, it might require a pair at the front, picking up most of the sound; a pair a few feet above the middle section; and a pair above the small percussion at the rear. When there is no time for experimentation and only enough time to set up one stereo pair, a safe placement is slightly above and behind the conductor. This placement will hopefully pick up the balance created by the conductor.

When the Recorder Fails It is surprising the number of times I've been asked to record a choir or youth orchestra. I'll go out with a couple of mics, enough mic cable, a long power cord, a stereo recorder, and tight-fitting headphones (and I'll double-check that all the adapters, power supplies, and leads are there). In one instance, the recorder didn't work, so I quickly made up some adapter cables and plugged the mic leads into the audio input of a small digital video camera. Later, I loaded the video into my video-editing package, stripped the sound into a separate file, and exported it as a WAV file.

If you are recording a live performance, it's a good idea to ask the conductor to tell the audience to be as quiet as they can. If there is a rehearsal in the place where the recording will happen, go to it to find out whether there is much traffic sound or other exterior noise that may be picked up. The other thing to remember is that if a hall sounds pretty good when there is an audience, don't assume it will sound that way without an audience. Proper concert halls have upholstered seats that are acoustically equivalent to someone sitting in them. A community hall often has portable seats that are put away, and even if they are fixed, they tend to be more reflective than a human is. If they're fold-up metal chairs, they can have a distinctive metallic sound reflection. If this is a problem, ask all your singers or musicians to bring to the recording quilts that can be draped over all the chairs until you get the right amount of reverb. Winter jackets do surprisingly well, too. It will make a huge difference. Also, if there are dimmers on the house or stage lighting, have them run up and down in rehearsal to ensure that they don't generate hum when used.

XY Coincident Placement

For non-pop music (classical, jazz, and so on), many engineers use an XY coincident approach that has both microphones quite close together (see Figures 8.3 and 8.4). This technique minimizes comb filtering (refer to Chapter 4) and phase cancellation when the outputs from the mics are combined. The results of XY placement sound quite real on headphones but don't have the separation that people expect on stereo speakers.

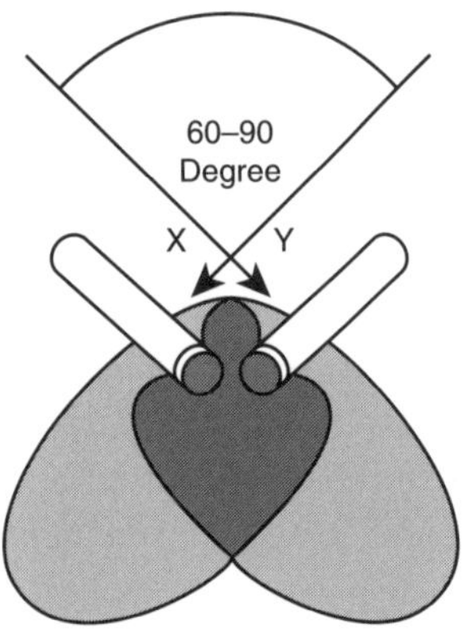

Figure 8.3 XY coincident stereo placement: The tips of the matched pair of cardioid mics almost touch at a 60- to 90-degree angle, at 45 degrees off-axis from the sound source.

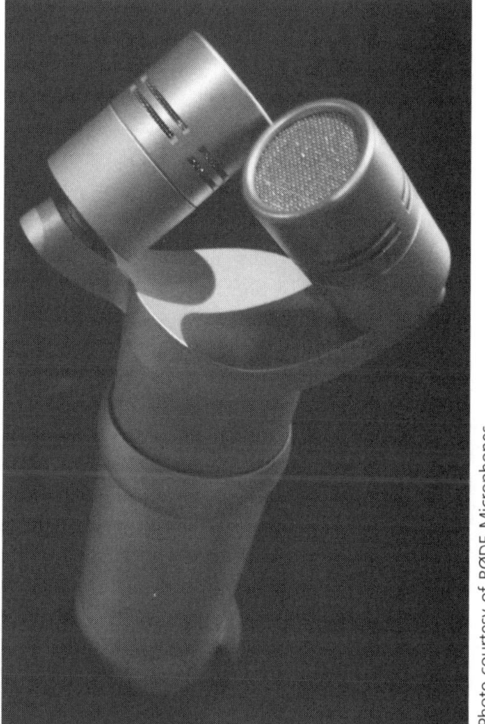

Photo courtesy of RØDE Microphones.

Figure 8.4 RØDE NT4 ½-inch condenser XY coincident stereo microphone.

The microphones in the pair are angled toward one another. Most of the time, cardioid microphones are used, with the capsules facing the sound at an angle somewhere between 45 and 60 degrees off-axis from the sound source. However, when a stereo recording made using XY placement is spread out over two separated speakers (as in home stereos), the resulting sound is not stereophonically dramatic. To achieve a more dramatic stereo separation, the mics should be farther apart, as in the AB configuration discussed in a moment. AB is my preference because I prefer a wide stereo panorama.

ORTF

The ORTF stereo placement technique was adopted by French Radio and uses two cardioid microphones spaced by 17 centimeters (roughly the same as ear spacing) and angled outward at 110 degrees. The Office de Radiodiffusion-Télévision Française (ORTF) was the French national agency that (between 1964 and 1974) provided public radio and television in France. This technique is much like XY, but there is a built-in space between the two mics, and they point outward rather then inward (see Figure 8.5). Although it does provide better separation than XY and fewer phase issues than a more widely spaced pair of microphones, it does not provide a wide stereo panorama.

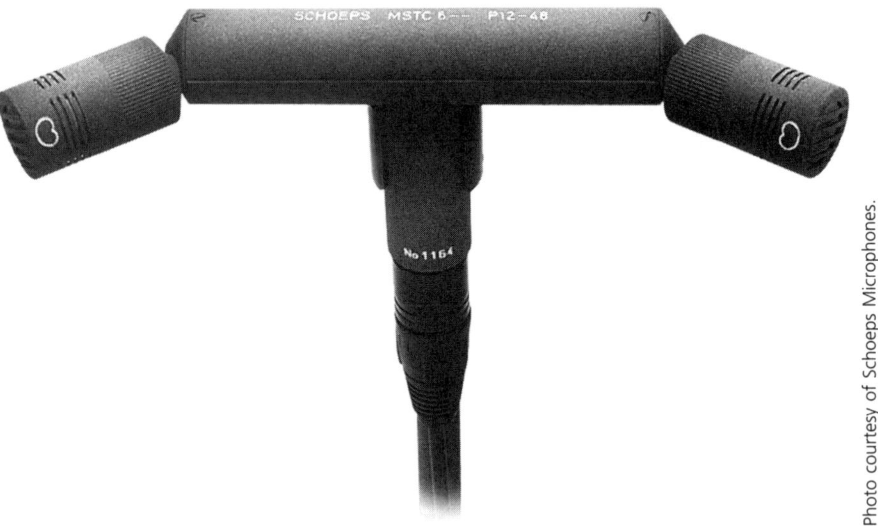

Photo courtesy of Schoeps Microphones.

Figure 8.5 An elegant approach to stereo miking, the Schoeps MSTC 64 U assembly with matched pair of MK 4 cardioid capsules.

Jecklin Disk Technique

A Jecklin disk is a sound-absorbing disk placed between two microphones to create an acoustic "shadow" from one microphone to the other. The technique was invented by Jürg Jecklin, the former chief sound engineer of Swiss Radio. He believed using the disk created a warmer and more natural stereo image. Many sound engineers agree. A matched pair of omnidirectional microphones is positioned on either side of a 12-inch solid circle of about 3/8-inch thickness. Covering both sides of the circle is a layer of sound-absorbing material (see Figure 8.6, which uses soft plastic foam). Different versions of the disk have used polyester insulation, wool blanketing, or other similar materials for the acoustically absorptive sides. The capsules of the microphones are above the surface of the disk just in the center, about a foot apart from each other and each pointing 20 degrees outside. Commercial versions of the Jecklin disk are available, but many people make their own.

Blumlein Pair

Another miking approach that's somewhat similar to XY placement is positioning two bidirectional microphones on top of one another at a 45- to 90-degree angle from the sound source. Both positive sides, also called *lobes*, must face the sound source, with the negative side facing the rear of the hall to pick up reflections (see Figure 8.7). Bidirectional microphones provide a more open sound and are particularly suitable for concert halls or other good-sounding spaces. This approach is called *a Blumlein pair* after the engineer who developed it. Pretty much any stereo ribbon mic, such as the Royer SF-12 (see Figure 8.8), will be able to do this right out of the box, as the two ribbons will be mounted 90 degrees off from each other.

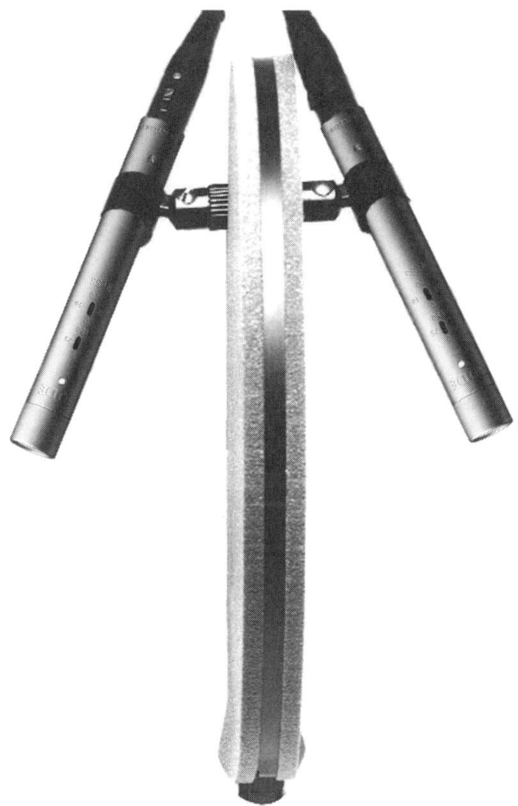

Figure 8.6 Jecklin setup with a pair of RØDE NT55 with (NT45 O) omni capsules.

Figure 8.7 Blumlein pair. Two bipolar mics positioned 90 degrees from one another and 45 degrees off-axis from the sound source.

Photo courtesy of Royer Labs.

Figure 8.8 Royer SF-12 stereo ribbon microphone.

AB Technique

Neither the XY nor the Blumlein pair miking technique creates that bigger-than-life sound that is expected in pop recordings. Most stereo pairs for rock and roll are separated by 2 to 3 feet or more. This miking approach is described as an *AB technique* (see Figure 8.9). For instance, for a pair of drum overheads, the distance between the mics may be 2 to 3 feet. This amount of separation gives an expanded stereo impression when reproduced on living room, home theatre, and car speakers. On headphones, however, the sound seems to originate at the top of the head, rather than in front of the listener. This happens because the distance between the stereo microphones is compressed, with the phase difference between the two channels confusing the perception of the sound. The brain is being told that our ears are separated by 3 feet or so. Needless to say, this is seldom the case, with the exception of those infamous rock-and-rollers who are "legends" in their own minds.

How far apart AB stereo mics should be placed and how close they should be to the sound source depends on the desired panoramic separation for the stereo image and the size and nature of the sound source. Much like a choir that is miked too close, an even transition of the stereo

Figure 8.9 AB stereo placement.

panorama in the acoustic field is lost if the mics are too close to the source. If the sound source is very wide (again, like a choir), the separation of the pair and their distance from the source must be carefully chosen. If they are too close to the middle, the sides are lost, and conversely, if they are at the extremes, the center will not come through. Complex setups may have groups of AB pairs that are appropriately blended and positioned in the overall mix.

But when it comes down to it, it's all about taste—yours or your client's. Experiment when you have the time, and you'll build up experience that will be invaluable when you have to mic something and you have no time.

Decca Tree

Most commonly used for orchestra recording, an expansion on the AB approach is a Decca Tree setup. The technique was developed in the early 1950s and first commercially used in 1954 by the engineers at Decca Records, London. One of the criticisms of the two-microphone, AB approach is a softness in the center of the stereo panorama, often described as a "hole in the middle." This lack of a hard center becomes worse when the ensemble being recorded is large. (In the case of the Decca engineers, they were recording the Mantovani Orchestra.) To create a strong stereo center, three omnidirectional microphones are used in a triangular pattern (see Figure 8.10). Originally, three Neumann M 50s were used, but other large- and medium-sized diaphragm condensers have been used. All three are mounted on a T frame at the top of a large stand. The left and right mics are roughly 5 to 8 feet apart, and the third is centered 3 to 4 feet in front of the other two. The exact dimensions will vary with the size of the room and the ensemble. The side mics are angled toward the outside boundaries of the ensemble and panned hard left and right, and the middle mic is panned center. As always, there are phase issues to consider, so listening in mono just to make sure there are no nasty surprises is suggested. If there is a problem, moving the distances slightly will remedy any obvious problems.

The stability of the center image is not only due to the additional microphone covering the center of the soundscape, but also because the center mic picks up the passing wave before it arrives at the two side mics. There are commercial Decca Tree frames available from AEA and others. Or, you can make one from pipe or something similar, fit it on a tall boom, and place it above and behind the conductor, angled downward slightly.

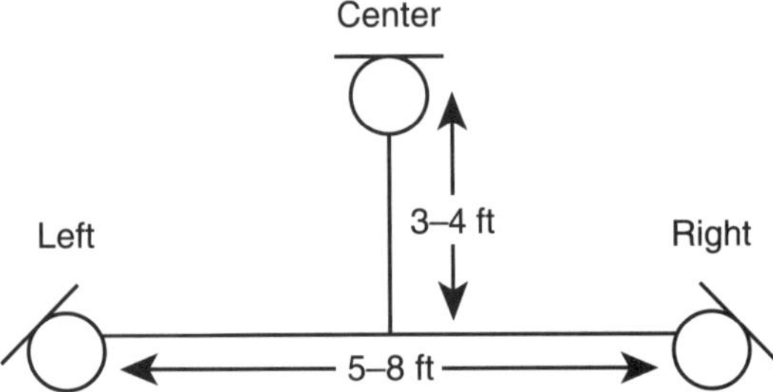

Figure 8.10 Decca Tree setup.

The MS (Mid-Side) Technique

Another classic approach to stereo miking is the *mid-side technique*, known as *MS*. There are mics specifically designed for MS recording, and many stereo mics, as previously mentioned, will operate in an MS configuration. Or, two mics can be used, provided the "side" mic is bidirectional (see Figure 8.11). (Traditionally the mid mic has a cardioid pattern, but good result can also be achieved with an omni or figure-eight pattern. And the best result is achieved if the two mics are similar, if not identical, capsule types.)

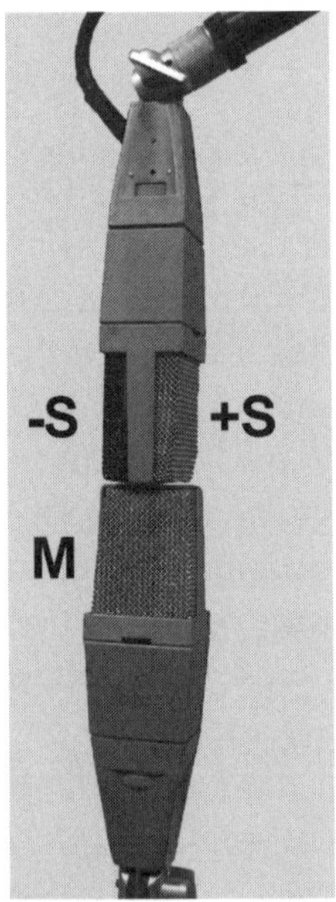

Figure 8.11 The bottom AKG 414 is set to cardioid and facing us and the sound source. The top 414 is set to bidirectional.

How does MS stereo work? Recall that a "bipolar" mic has both a positive and a negative polarity, as each of the two sides, or lobes, of the pattern are out of phase with one another.

The mid microphone (M) with the cardioid pattern (and a positive polarity) squarely faces the sound source. The side microphone (S), which is bidirectional (with its typical positive *and* negative polarity figure-eight pattern), is positioned at right angles to the mid microphone and the source (see Figure 8.12). In other words, it faces the "sides." The left/right stereo is created by mixing M+S for one side and M–S for the other side. The + indicates that the S microphone is in phase with the M microphone, and the – indicates that the S microphone is out of phase with the M microphone.

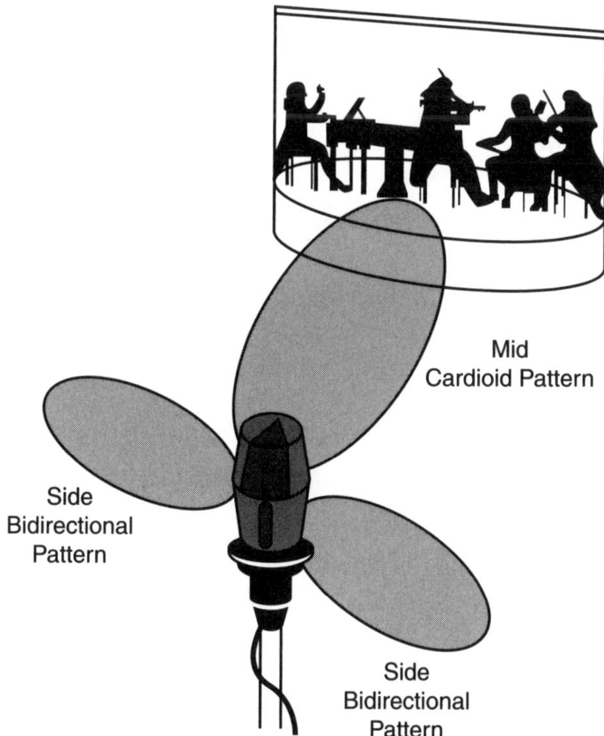

Figure 8.12 MS stereo placement.

When the polarity of the side mic remains in phase with the mid mic (in other words, M+S), the sound coming into the positive lobe will reinforce the sound entering the cardioid (that is, mid) mic where the two patterns overlap. Sound entering the negative lobe of the bidirectional mic will cause phase cancellation to the sound entering the mid mic where the two patterns overlap. So M+S creates one channel (see Figure 8.13).

By reversing the polarity of the bidirectional mic, those signals that were previously summed are now cancelled, and those that were cancelled are now summed (see Figure 8.14). Put another

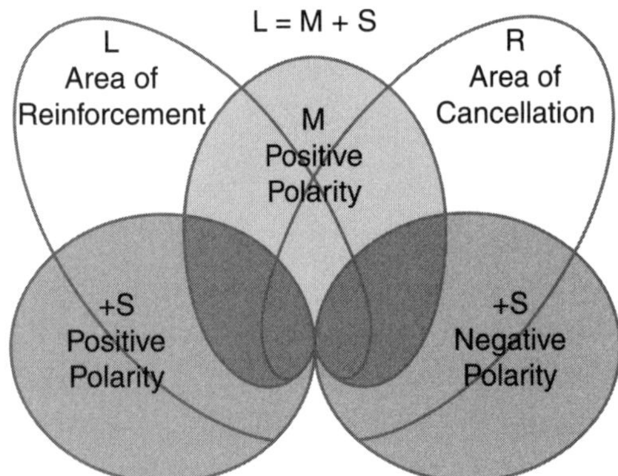

Figure 8.13 M+S.

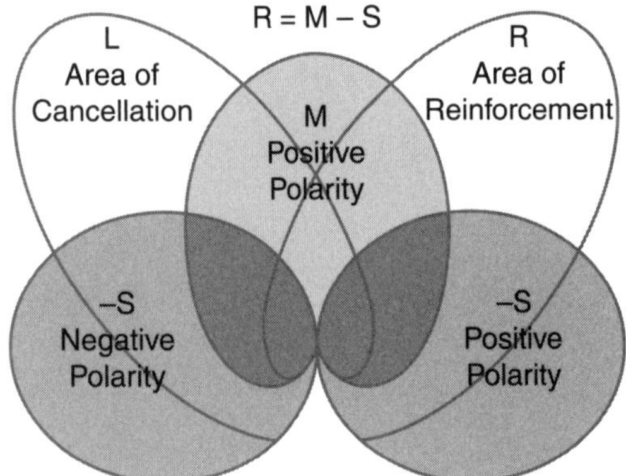

Figure 8.14 M–S.

way, the signal that was cancelled in the M+S channel is reinforced in the M–S channel. The symbolic equation is L=M+S (for the left side), while R=M−S (for the right side). This technique creates a very natural-sounding, though subtle, stereo image. If you listen to just the cardioid microphone on headphones, because it is panned to the center and a single microphone, it will sound monophonic and lack any stereo image. As the two "side" faders are raised into the mix, the mono sound will spread into a stereo panorama.

Implementing the MS Technique The cardioid microphone is plugged into a single input of the mixing desk and panned to the center. The bidirectional microphone is connected to two inputs of the mixing desk and panned hard left and right, with one of the two bidirectional inputs having its phase reversed.

The patching of the bidirectional mic can happen a couple of ways by patching the patchbay "mult" output of the line out of that channel to a second channel's line input.

MS matrix boxes are also available that take the bidirectional mic's output and split it to two outputs. If you're working in a DAW environment, you could also use a plug-in to matrix the M and S after the fact.

Raise the side faders. The stereo image will move from mono outward to stereo. The amount of side information that is added will control the width of the stereo image. A word of caution, however: If the output of the side microphone is greater in the mix than the mid microphone's output, the center will be poorly defined, and when combined to mono, it will drop in level.

The MS technique is frequently used for classical recording. Stereo recordings for television also use this technique, because mono compatibility is very good. Another advantage for television-production recording is that the degree of stereo separation can be determined in post-production, after the recording is made. On location, the mid mic is recorded on one channel of a stereo track and the side mic is recorded on the other channel. By keeping the mid and side separate, the stereo panorama can be adjusted to match the specific visual image. The mid mic can be used by itself for a standard mono audio track, or varying amounts of the side mic can be added to expand the stereo perspective A mic designed for this application is the Neumann RSM 191 (see Figure 8.15).

Photo courtesy of Georg Neumann GmbH.

Figure 8.15 Neumann RSM 191.

The MS technique does not create the exaggerated separation that some engineers want in pop recordings, but it is an excellent and natural-sounding technique for jazz, choirs, and orchestras, and many people do use the technique for stereo drum overheads. This approach has better phase coherency than XY, and it's nearly the best you can have for listening on headphones.

A Dummy Head

One interesting technique to record something for listening on headphones is to use a dummy head (or get a dummy to let you use his head) that has small microphones in the ears. There are stereo microphone systems that fit over the head like headphones, but instead of speakers covering each ear, there are microphones. Usually included with this system is a dummy head that resembles a wig mannequin that will attach to a microphone stand. When you listen on headphones to something that is recorded this way, you are definitely there (see Figure 8.16). It's particularly clever for recording dialogue or atmospheres for games, because many players use headphones, and a dummy-head setup really captures the clues of sonic directionality.

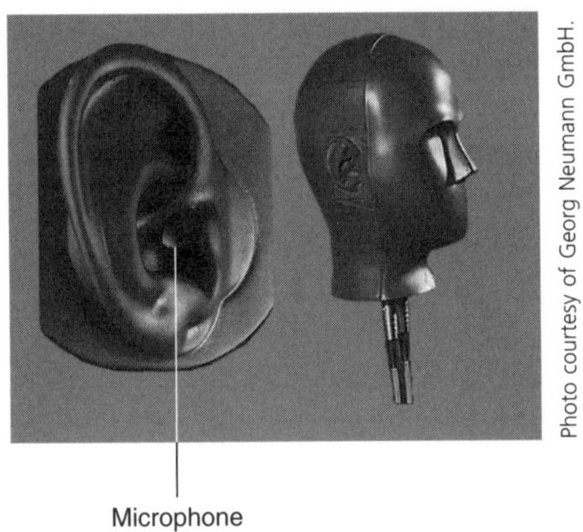

Photo courtesy of Georg Neumann GmbH.

Figure 8.16 The Neumann KU 100 has high-performance microphones inside each ear at a point near where the eardrum would be. The KU 100 is used for a wide range of industrial applications as well as music recording.

Making great-sounding recordings with just a stereo pair of microphones is a real skill. This chapter is but a starting point. Making good stereo recordings is central to great-sounding mixes because the complexity of a stereo recording of a sound source will seldom be matched by sending a mono track into a reverb processor.

In the next chapter, we move into the studio and begin to set up for a session.

The Telefunken 270 In the early 1980s, Dan Alexander took several worldwide trips to purchase tube microphones and other classic vintage recording equipment. The rarest,

Photo courtesy of Telefunken USA.

Figure 8.17 Telefunken Ela M 270.

and indeed truly unique, classic microphone was the original Telefunken Ela M 270 stereo microphone, serial number 101. Ultimately, TELEFUNKEN I USA obtained this microphone in order to re-create the design. Today, the original Ela M 270 resides at Blackbird Studios in Nashville, currently home of one of the most extensive collections of vintage recording equipment in the world.

Figure 8.17 shows an exact reproduction of the Ela M 270 made by TELEFUNKEN I USA. It is essentially a stereo version of the Ela M 251. The Ela M 251 is widely revered as a benchmark of high-fidelity recording technology, and the Ela M 270 offers the same exceptional sonic performance in a stereo package—perfectly suited for XY, MS, or Blumlein techniques. Each diaphragm of the Ela M 270 offers selectable cardioid, bidirectional, or omni polar patterns. Utilizing either output of the microphone yields essentially the performance of the Ela M 251.

---

9 The Recording Session

Unless you live in Hollywood, New York, London, or Nashville, recording studios that operate solely as commercial fee-for-service operations are now few and far between. In the beginning (the 1930s), studios were extensions of record labels, but when tape recorders were invented (in the 1950s), and rock and roll came into being, independent studios appeared. The labels continued to have their own studios, but an increasing number of artists wanted to record at the independents that were less corporate and would cater to the artist's whims. By the late '80s, many labels had closed their studios, and increasing numbers of independents were flourishing. But at the same time as their demise was beginning to take hold, successful musicians started making demos at home on semipro equipment (¼-inch 4-track, ½-inch 8-track, 1-inch 16-track). It wasn't as good as pro gear, but it was good for demos, and despite the quality issue, a surprising number of successful records were made on that generation of gear. Much of that gear went into home studios that were once two-car garages or basements. Many of them operated commercially as a second tier to the pro independents who found their demo businesses had dried up. In the '80s, a coalition of independent Hollywood studio owners petitioned the LA city council to shut down home studios that were operating as businesses in noncommercial residential zones.

With the appearance of the personal multitrack (porta-studios, ¼-inch 8-track, ½-inch 16-track) in the early '80s, both pro and semipro studios would soon lose more business. Again, the gear wasn't as good technically as the pro equipment, but how good did it need to be? It sounded pretty good, and if the song was pressed or cassettes were duplicated and sold, no one would care that it was made in the dining room. The big studios remained the place where people would go if they had a budget, because that was where the good engineers, good-sounding rooms, and good gear were. But over time, many commercial studios closed their doors because many of their clients had their own gear.

The emergence of sound engineering schools also meant that many could learn how to record without an apprenticeship at a commercial studio. Many times, students just wanted to learn how to record their own music. Was it better than the rare opportunity of assisting an experienced engineer for a couple of years before getting the opportunity to sit down at the mixing desk? No, but it was more formalized and structured, and that was good too. It was also part of the home recording/project studio movement.

The '90s brought MIDI, samplers, and sequencers that could make master-quality recordings pretty much anywhere, but live recording was still limited by hardware and storage issues. Since then, those hurdles have been overcome by all sorts of digital advances in processor and storage technology, plus the Internet has provided an explosion of free (or nearly free) software and information. Nearly everyone now has access to high-quality recording gear. A less obvious benefit is that unlike earlier generations of equipment and formats, standardized computer files can be easily and cheaply transferred from a home studio to a large studio and back again. Later generations of semiprofessional and personal multitracks were pretty good but were always difficult to try to bump up to 24-track 2-inch for further recording, or even to hook it up in a good mixdown suite.

Today, most musicians have at least a small recording setup at home. They will record a vocal or an acoustic guitar, and if they have a "studio" as well as a "control room" space, they may record drums or a four-piece band. But recording drums is a huge leap in equipment, facilities, and skill, so often when rhythm tracks are recorded or a project comes in that pays more, many will go to commercial studios. Doing these "casual" sessions with a lot of musicians you may not know on a tight budget and limited hours can be nerve-wracking, particularly if you don't do these sorts of sessions all the time. This chapter will help.

This chapter covers how to prepare for, set up, run, and tear down a session. At the end of the chapter I've also included a step-by-step outline. Much of it will be useful regardless of the size of the session, but the greater the number of players, the more useful this chapter will be. You might also find useful a NARAS download called "Session Documentation Examples" at www.grammy.com/Recording_Academy/Producers_And_Engineers/Guidelines.

Studio Floor Plan

Whether you're running a one-man shop or working at a multimillion-dollar recording facility, setting up a session starts with considering the space and equipment you have at your disposal. If you're regularly responsible for setting up sessions in your studio, particularly if you're running sessions that involve musicians other than yourself, you should keep on hand copies of your studio's floor plan to use as a sketchpad for planning the setup of each session. Sketching in the approximate placement of all instruments and microphones will help you keep things straight, and it will serve as a handy record should it ever become necessary to re-create the setup to match a previous session. The floor-plan form should have enough room to indicate which microphones are being used on which instruments, which inputs they are plugged into, how many headphones are needed, where the direct boxes will be, where the players will be positioned, and the position of any acoustic separators (gobos). These forms are, of course, essential for elaborate sessions, but even in simple sessions, it's helpful to keep notes about which microphones were used and how you positioned them. Such a plan is essential if more than one person is setting up the studio. On the other side of the floor plan could be the track sheet, with information about signal processing patches on specific tracks.

Larger Studio

What could you expect in a larger studio, and how might you approach a setup in one?

- A larger studio will usually have a booth or two for isolation of vocals and such, with the biggest studios having a drum booth and/or a "live" piano room. If it's a rhythm section (drums, bass, guitar) recording, I find relegating the drummer to a booth tends to make it more difficult for the band to lock into a groove (see Figure 9.1). On the other hand, if you've got drums as part of a much larger, more acoustic ensemble, you may find the booth for the drums is a much better way to control the sound (see Figure 9.2). On occasion, and depending on how loud the guitar amp might be, I will have the drummer in the main studio

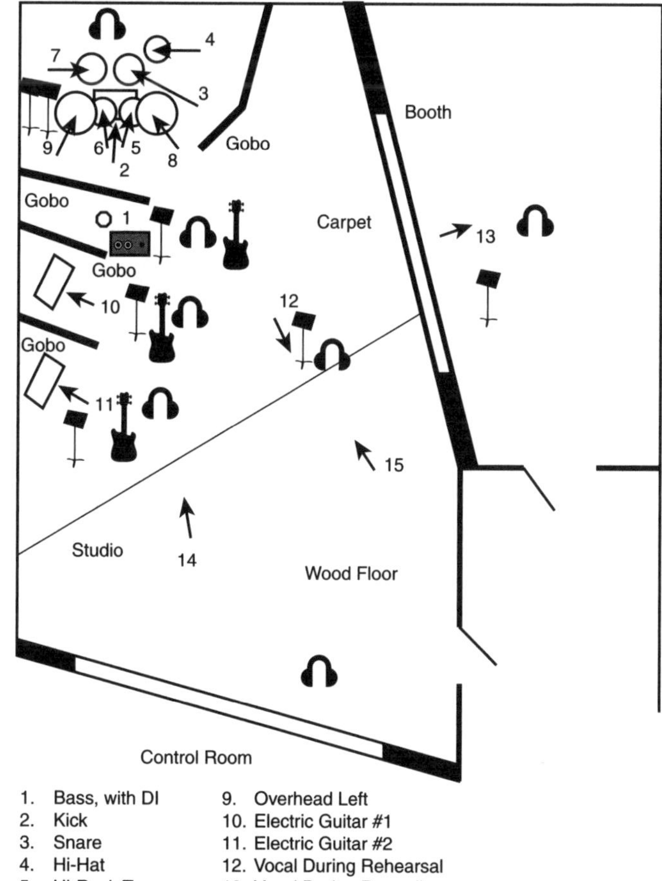

Figure 9.1 Setup for a four-piece band. Note the spare set of phones and two music stands for the drummer.

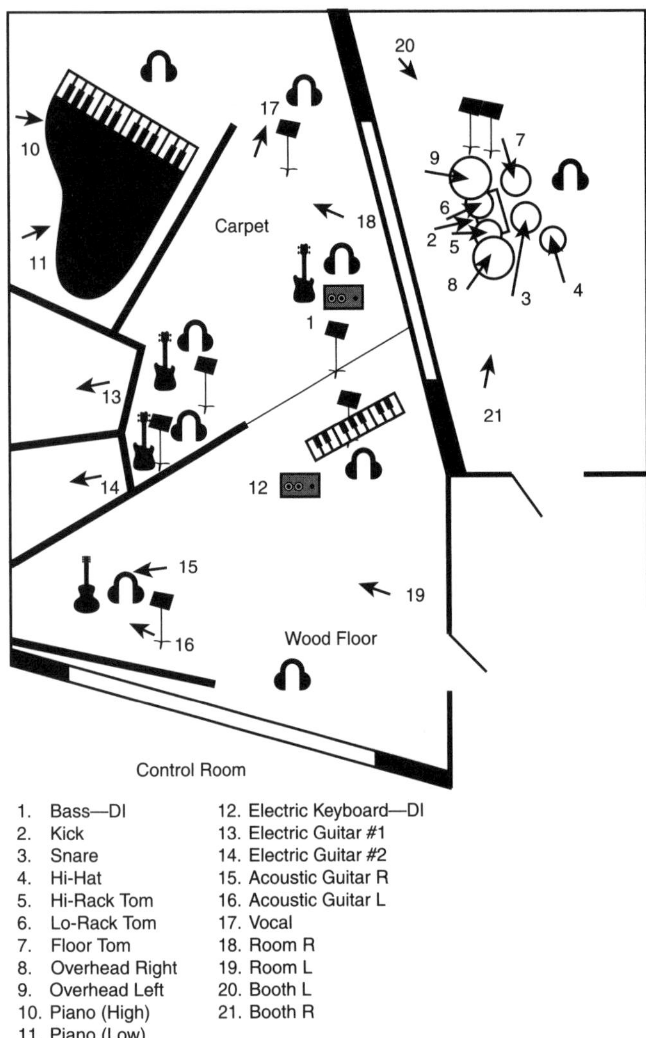

Figure 9.2 Setup for a more acoustic seven-piece band. The vocalist is near the piano player. Note the spare set of phones and two music stands for the drummer.

area and the electric guitar amp in the booth, with a cord from the guitar in the studio running into the booth.

- A bigger studio has a recording space and a control room, with most having a large window between them. Steer clear of setting up anything close to the window to avoid unwanted reflections from the glass.
- A larger studio may also have a drum area in the main area where the acoustics have been designed to absorb low rumble and enhance the higher percussion sounds. Near the drum area may also be an area where the bass would usually go and where there is extra bass

absorption in the walls. Most larger studios will also have a section of floor that is hardwood, and the rest will be carpet. Or they have a hardwood floor and carpets that are rolled out when the room needs to be a bit deader. A larger studio will usually have an array of gobos, and it's likely there may be ways to alter the acoustics through hinged wall panels that change the amount of reflection and absorption, as well as ceiling reflectors that can be tilted to change the angle of reflection (see Figure 9.3).

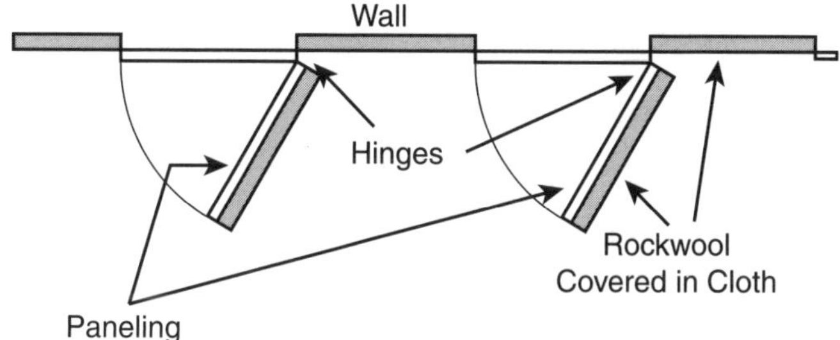

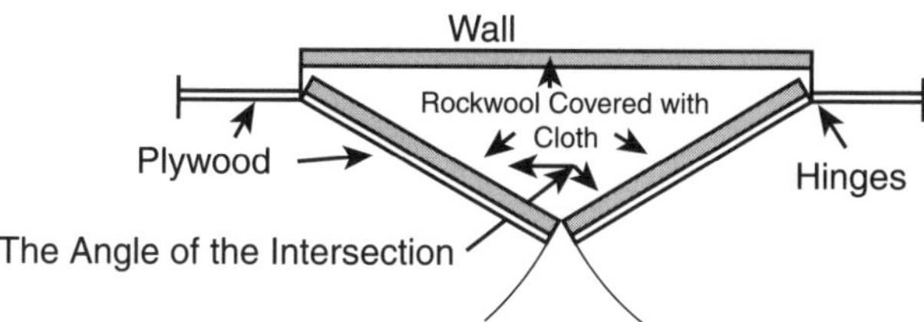

Figure 9.3 A basic approach to creating variable acoustic wall surfaces. The hinged panels can be 4 to 6 feet high and 2 to 3 feet wide. In the bottom drawing, when the absorptive surfaces are closed, they form a triangle that creates an angled reflective surface. The angle can be varied from not much of an angle to a substantial one. I suggest an inside angle of between 100 and 160 degrees. If there are several of these systems, use slightly different "closed" angles for each.

- There will be a large wall panel (possibly more than one) into which the microphones connect. Look closely at how the panel connectors are numbered (above or below the connector) and whether there are panels in different parts of the room (see Figure 9.4). The same panel may also have the headphone outputs, and in many cases the studio will have multiple headphone feeds. It's rare that you would plug a headphone directly into the wall panel; rather, the headphone output would go to a number of headphone-distribution boxes. Many studios will have dedicated headphone systems that allow each musician to control his own headphone mix.

- A bigger studio will have a greater selection of mics, most often stored in a cabinet, and a variety of stands. Most will have a place to put cases, and many will have a certain number of house instruments (piano, drums, amps, organ, and so on). If you plan to use the piano, be sure to let the studio know beforehand so the piano can be tuned if necessary. Be sure to reserve any special microphone or equipment you especially want to use.

Photo courtesy of Tabatha Hawk.

Figure 9.4 Typical microphone connector wall panel.

Smaller Studio

In a home studio, if the only thing that is ever going to use a microphone is the owner's vocal and/or acoustic guitar, then probably it will be recorded sitting or standing right near the computer. The most important thing will be to ensure that the space is as quiet as it can be. Buzzes from power supplies, fans, and squeaky chairs will be the subtle offenders that will need quieting.

If you have limited your recording setup to a single room, but you occasionally record a singer or even a band, you can get pretty good results from the living room and bathroom as long as you are well prepared. The real trick here is planning it while your partner is not around, and then getting the place back to the way it was before she gets home.

In order to have a good session with a five- to six-piece band, here is a guide of what you will probably need:

- A mixer with 16 inputs and as many outputs as you have recorder inputs. Unless you spend a lot of money, most computer-based recorders are limited to eight or fewer simultaneous-record inputs, and you'll need at least eight to keep from having to premix the drums to a couple of tracks. There are a few mixing desks that have a digital interface to the computer's software, but they are pretty pricey.

- A microphone snake (also called a *loom* or *multi-core*). This is a cable with many mic lines inside. At one end are female connectors (or a box with female connectors), and at the other end are male connectors that plug into your usual microphone inputs.
- Six to eight industrial extension cords that have quad receptacles at their ends.
- A power amp for the headphones. (The headphone amp in the mixer won't do, and the monitor amp can't be used at the same time for the headphones and the speakers.)
- A headphone-distribution system that has an outlet in the control room space so you can hear what the band is actually hearing. Then a long headphone lead out to a couple of headphone boxes near the band members. Rather than a single box of six or eight plugs, it's much better to have three or four boxes of three plugs so they can be spread out.
- As many headphones as musicians, plus a few extra. They all need to be identical; otherwise, they will all sound different and it will be impossible to keep everyone happy. They also need to have an impedance of at least 50 ohms, or the amplifier will have difficulty driving them all. Hook up the headphone cable to the 8-ohm output of the amplifier. All the headphones need to be tight fitting.
- A talkback system so you can talk from the console to the musicians in the other room. Most mixing desks will have a way of sending a talkback into a headphone feed. Many mixers will have a talkback button that turns off (or dims) the monitor feed when the TB is activated. If yours doesn't, and you're using a channel input for the talkback mic, be sure to turn off the talkback when not using it, and be sure the monitors are low when you do. Also be sure the TB mic is not in the monitor mix, or everyone will get a blast of feedback in their phones, which does not build confidence in your ability in the minds of those wearing the phones.
- A couple of roll-down 8-foot-square carpets, and two to three 4-feet-by-8-feet sheets of ¼-inch plywood so you can change the acoustics if you want. And you may have furniture that has cushions that can be used for gobos and drapes that can deaden down the room if required.
- Enough music stands if the musicians are reading a chart—at the very least, one stand for the singer or guitar player to have a place for the words or chords. Also, a pencil. If charts are on the agenda, you need sufficient light for the musicians to read the music. Don't laugh—it's amazing how many times I've seen a small studio freak out when they find out their cool lighting isn't bright enough for the musicians.
- A couple of stools and a few metal folding chairs. This is particularly essential for musicians who play in clusters. Rock musicians may be just fine with the existing furniture, but many instrumentalists prefer to have chairs with no arms and that support them. Musicians also have a tendency to lean back in chairs and rock on the back legs, so don't use plastic chairs or the dining room chairs your grandmother gave you when she died.

- Lastly, if you don't have line of sight, I can't stress how useful it is to have a video camera set up in the recording area and connected to a monitor in the control room so you can see what's going on with the musicians.

Again, a floor plan, even of the living room, is a good idea because it provides a reference when someone asks to record the same way.

The Session

If you're preparing for a session in which outside musicians will be coming into your studio, you should concentrate first on setting up the studio space where they will be working. After that, you can work on setting up the control room. The arriving musicians will be easier to deal with if their space is organized before they arrive. The microphones, music stands, headphones, power boxes, chairs, direct boxes, and so on should be in place and ready to go. If you're an assistant engineer setting up a session for an engineer other than yourself, be sure you know how the engineer wants the session set up and what microphones (as well as outboard gear, guitar amps, keyboards, and so on) will be required. Most mic collections are not unlimited, so you'll need to decide the best way to get the most out of the mics you have on hand. If the setup is well organized, the musicians will be able to bring in their instruments, set up in front of the mics, plug in, and record within a reasonable setup period. For a basic setup like the one shown in Figure 9.1, I usually allowed 40 to 50 minutes from when the musicians arrive to when we would be playing back a first recording. If the setup is more than a couple of instruments, start it at least an hour (if not more) before the musicians are expected. Scoring dates with dozens of union musicians will take hours to set up. I would suggest that if you have more than a five-piece (drums, bass, keyboard, and two guitars) coming in, you should organize an assistant for at least the setup phase. It saves so much time if you can have someone help test the microphones as you raise the faders and make sure each one is working. Also, during the first hour of the session, there will invariably be a headphone that doesn't work, a cable that's dodgy, or someone who wants something unexpected.

Stands, Lighting, and Seating

Begin your setup by positioning the gobos (if you have them) and then the mic stands. Set the stands to one side of where they will ultimately go so the musicians can bring in their amps and drums without knocking over the stands. If you plan on putting a block of rubber (as described in Chapter 7) under the amps, have that ready for them as well. Then place the mics on the stands. Be sure the counterweights are large enough to hold the mic, or use sandbags to keep the stand from falling over. Make sure the stands don't rattle or vibrate. Any mic on a boom should be raised (or retracted) so it won't be knocked over during setup. Don't leave any counterweight at head height. Coming up under a large counterweight can definitely put a pause in what you are doing right then. Put out power strips near those musicians who will need them. Keep any microphone power supplies or headphone-distribution boxes out of areas where there will be foot traffic to avoid the possibility of their being kicked. Even if the band won't need music stands for holding sheet music, you should set them out if for no other reason than to hold the headphones. (Otherwise they go on the floor, which is bad, or around the mic, which is worse—feedback.) Or make yourself a headphone holder out of an old mic stand, a wheel, and some large garage hooks. In the long run, a holder will save you money in repairs and replacement of headphones that would otherwise be chucked on the floor. If the musicians are reading sheet music, the conductor will stand in front of the musicians. If a podium is not available, he will need two stands side by side so he can lay out the entire chart. Most drummers will also want two stands so they don't have to worry about turning pages. Keep the music stands low and cover them with carpet (or some other padding) to avoid sound reflections and to prevent them from sympathetically vibrating. In sessions in which charts are being used, every stand should have a sharp pencil (medium soft) with a clean eraser, preferably long enough to hold and not chewed on. Don't buy cheap music stands. Look for proper orchestra stands, such as Manhasset stands. On eBay you can expect to pay $20 per stand, but I have seen better deals for used ones.

The lighting in most sessions should be subdued enough to be comfortable but bright enough to keep people from running into things. Bright lighting will be needed for string sections or other groups that must read music. Music stand (orchestra) lights are best, but only a few studios have them. Most studios just don't do many big dates, so the best solution is to suggest that the players bring their own music stands and lights. In such cases, power strips should be in place before the musicians arrive so they can just plug them in. Studios geared for scoring have two levels of lighting, one for bands that's more moody and another that has ceiling-mounted floodlights for scoring and during setup. (There's nothing worse than trying to do a setup in a dimly lit studio—invariably, there are mistakes while plugging cables into the wall panel.)

For sessions in which players are seated, sit down in each chair and verify that it doesn't squeak or creak. Bucket-type plastic chairs are no good for most musicians, particularly string players, and you should never use chairs with arms. Folding metal chairs with flat seats and straight backs are best. In a small studio, get all the cases out of the room, because they make the space feel cramped.

For efficient communication no matter what is being recorded (except vocals), set up a room microphone in the studio to pick up whatever conversation is going on. The room mic may (or may not) be recorded, but many recordings have some of the room mic of the rhythm session added in for a bigger drum sound. If you foolishly try to hear what's happening through the drum kit's overhead mics, you can be guaranteed that at some point, when you have the gain way up to be able to hear the guitar player speaking at the other end of the room, the drummer will decide to test out his snare sound.

Always set up a couple of extra microphones that are plugged in and ready to go so that if an extra or a replacement is needed, it's there. Always know which and how many microphones are connected to the mixing desk. Write down what channel each is plugged into, and if they're going to be moved in the course of the session, put numbers on the mics or the stands (using masking tape) to keep track of which mic is being used.

Positioning and Leakage

Any time there is more than one acoustic sound in the same room, almost all of the microphones in the room, to varying degrees, will pick up some of that sound, regardless of whether that's desired. For instance, a microphone set up to capture percussion will also capture some sound from the electric rhythm guitar if it's in the same room and both musicians are playing at the same time. When a mic picks up sound from an instrument other than the one it's primarily recording, that's called *leakage*. It's desirable to eliminate leakage or limit it as much as possible.

When recording a live band, you'll need to balance the desire to avoid leakage with the necessity of maintaining a helpful and friendly vibe in the studio. Bands typically like to be set up so the players can maintain good eye contact with each other and can be easily seen from the control room. Putting them in separate rooms or erecting isolation walls between them might be great for minimizing leakage, but it's lousy for setting up the kind of atmosphere and camaraderie that creates the synergy for inspirational recordings. And if the inspiration's not there, who cares about leakage? Positioning the mic close to the sound source—for instance, right against the guitar amp's speaker—will reduce the leakage from other instruments, but then it won't sound the same as when the mic is pulled back from the amp. These are all tradeoffs that you must consider to arrive at the best possible sound.

For a three- or four-piece band, the guitar player usually can be placed to one side of the drummer, and the bass player can be positioned on the other side. The bass will likely be connected to a direct box, though there may be a bass amp, if for no other reason than to allow the bass player to rehearse while everything is getting connected and sounds are getting mixed into the headphones. You may choose to have a guitar amp; it can hopefully be set up in another room (keeping the cord as short as possible) or well baffled. Keep in mind that the guitarist should be playing a rhythm part and would later play the lead as an overdub, so one would hope that while "loud" may be an aspect of the rhythm part's sound, if it is so loud that there is a leakage problem for the other mics, try to have the guitarist turn down. The keyboard player can usually set up opposite the drummer (or in the control room), and the keyboards are also run into the board direct. In many cases, the only things that are acoustic in the studio are the drums and a scratch vocal.

A scratch vocal is sung when the rhythm tracks are recorded, so that everyone gets a feel for what the song is about while recording the rhythm tracks. The scratch vocal is then used as a guide throughout the production process until it is replaced by a final vocal, though sometimes the scratch vocal makes it all the way to the final mix. When you're recording a scratch vocal in the same room as the drums, if the vocalist is loud, he will also be captured in the drum overhead mics. (Larger studios often have gobos with windows that can be used to create a semi-isolation vocal booth inside the studio. See Figure 9.5.) To minimize the problem, hook up a scratch vocal mic where the rest of the band is so the singer can use it during rehearsal. Then, when they're ready to record, send the singer into the vocal booth (or the adjoining hall) where another mic is set up. If the singer goes to the booth too soon, he will not be able to work as closely with the band in the inevitable fine-tuning that is required of the basic arrangement, and he will become alienated from the process.

Photo courtesy of Carl Clifford.

Figure 9.5 Tall gobos to create in-studio iso booths.

Laying Cable

Once the mics are on booms (but are not necessarily positioned), lay out the headphone and mic cables. The cables should run from the mics to the mic input on the board (wall panel, loom, or snake) and lay flat and out of the way so no one trips on them. When laying cables, avoid going under anything so that a cable can be moved without hassle. Keep audio cable and power cables separated (or cross at right angles) to help prevent noise and buzzes, especially if there are any unbalanced audio cables being used. Allow a fair amount of slack in the cables so the mics can be easily positioned after everyone is set up. As the microphones are plugged in, be sure to note which input each mic or direct box is plugged into. If the studio has duplicate inputs (that is, several wall panels with the same inputs), make sure that two microphones are not plugged into the same input and that the headphone and mic cables are in fact plugged into the correct input number. It's not unusual for a microphone lead to accidentally end up in the wrong socket on the wall panel. This is particularly the case when there is a full setup, lots of microphones and headphones, and a couple of people doing the setup. Many sessions have ground to a halt because a microphone (or other input) was plugged into the wrong input or a headphone was not working. This is not a good thing when you have 30 musicians getting paid for their time while you or the assistant engineer is scurrying around trying to locate the problem.

Studio Sound Check

If there is time, go into the control room and quickly check to make sure the microphones are working and verify that they're all plugged into the inputs to which you've assigned them. Under no circumstances should anyone tap or blow into a microphone. Talking into them is fine, but in the initial time-consuming phases of finding out which mics are working and where they're plugged in, having someone talk into the mic doesn't work well, particularly if the mics are already roughly positioned. (Talking into a kick drum mic is awkward, and you never know when the drummer is going to start hitting the drums.) I prefer to have an assistant gently scratch the windscreen of each mic in order. This approach relieves that person from having to say, "Check one, two," a million times. It is critically important to make sure you know which microphone is which when many microphones are in close proximity—for instance, the several that are on a set of drums, a horn section, or a string section. It's a real shock to set the level on the snare drum, turn it off, do the same with the floor tom, turn it off, and then discover, when all the mics are turned back on, that you've set levels for the wrong mics—the floor tom is incredibly loud in the snare mic, and the snare drum is blasting through the floor tom mic.

Attempting to get level and EQ settings on drums, guitars, and other non-electronic instruments with a stand-in musician is usually a waste of time because the stand-in is unlikely to play exactly like the person who will eventually record. The attempt to use a stand-in most frequently happens when the drummer wants to come into the control room to listen while the engineer works on getting drum sounds. One of the other members of the band will confidently claim he can play the drums so the drummer can listen in the control room. The truth is, when the drummer plays the drums, the sound will need readjusting because he will undoubtedly hit them differently than the stand-in did. But it probably sounds close, so before changing anything, do a test recording, have the drummer come back into the control room, and make suggestions based on that. The other thing is, every song will likely need changes to the sound, and as soon as the band is playing their first track, the drum sounds will probably need fine-tuning.

Of utmost importance is that you go into the studio frequently to check what the instrument sounds like before it enters the mics. Invariably, the musician will be making adjustments to the drums, keyboard, guitar amp, and so on, concurrent to the adjustments you're making, so keep checking. The first step is always to get it to sound good before turning on a microphone.

If the musicians have already arrived, don't bother to conduct a separate sound check; it just slows down the process. Have them start to rehearse the first song to set rough levels through the desk and a mix for the headphones. When they stop playing (as they will) to discuss things, then you can have the drummer hit the toms, hi-hat, and kick and fine-tune the kit. However, have the musicians scratch the windscreens before you begin to set levels for each mic (see Figure 9.6).

Headphones (Cans)

Headphones are also commonly called *cans* because in the early days, before plastic earpieces, that's pretty much what they looked like. Everyone must have the same model of headphones;

Photo courtesy of Tup Wanders.

Figure 9.6 As you're positioning mics on the drums, always ask the drummer to play his kit to make sure his sticks don't come anywhere near the mics.

otherwise, everyone will be hearing a different mix. The cans need to be capable of sounding good at screamin' loud levels. AKG and Fostex headphones have dominated the studio business for years (see Figure 9.7). They are expensive but worth it. They are also repairable when something breaks. At the high sound levels coming out of the cans, the kick drum will usually imitate a firecracker, and the rest of the drum set may be described as sounding like cardboard boxes being hit. The lowest range of the bass will also be lost. Never let anyone judge the sound quality that's being recorded based on what they hear in the cans. Always have the musicians come in and hear a speaker playback on which to base their suggestions. That being said, the cans need to sound as good as they possibly can. If the headphones sound awful, everyone will play differently, and you'll be facing a lot of unhappy *musos*.

Make sure you have enough cord going from the headphones to the wall. If the cord is too short, sometime during the session, someone will trip over it, and it will be ripped out of the wall or the headphones will be torn off someone's head. Studios that do many string-horn sessions will have single-headphone headsets, which are preferred by violin, viola, cello, and trombone players because of how they hold their instruments. All headphones (including those at the console) should be powered from a single (or stereo) amp through a central distribution system. Some studios let each player mix his own phones, but what invariably happens is that everyone tries to

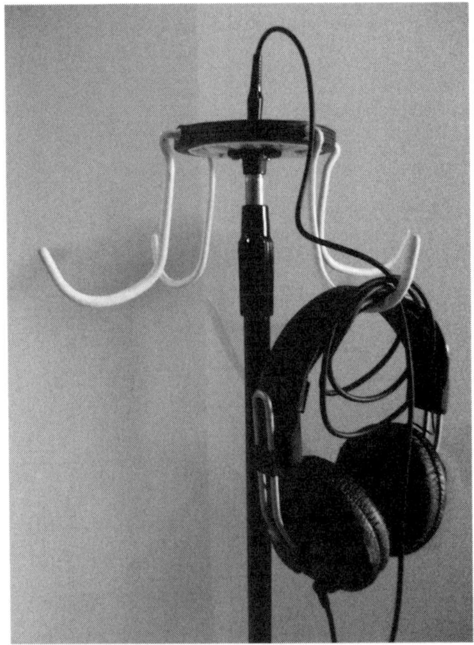

Figure 9.7 A headphone holder and Fostex T40s.

"produce" their headphone mix, and it slows down the whole session.. That being said, if the session is just a few rhythm players, giving them control of their headphone mix will solve the age-old differences between the mixes the drummer, the bass player, and the vocalist prefer. For big sessions, it is less hassle to have just one system and one mix.

Send a signal through the headphone system, go into the studio, put each phone on to make sure both phones work, and wiggle the cord to make sure its connection is solid and continuous (it doesn't crackle). Finally, verify that the talkback is working so communication can begin as soon as the musicians arrive.

The phones for the drummer needs to be particularly tight fitting because through the course of a song, a drummer can move around a lot, and if his headphones start to slip, he may not be able to readjust them. It's not too extreme to suggest that the drummer tape the phones to his head. It's important that pop-music ensemble overdub players (string sections, horn sections, background vocalists, and so on) hear the track and themselves when they record. The style of music and the nature of a pop arrangement require that the musicians play with extreme precision a score they have just seen. They don't want to hear the lead vocals or other lead lines, but plenty of rhythm and the basic chords. Most of the time, strings, brass, and background singers will want to hear a little bit of reverb on what they are doing. When they hear themselves dry, it doesn't sound as natural, so they don't play or sing as well. It's best to make the headphone mix mono because most background, horn, or string players work with one headphone off so they can hear what they're doing. Often, they will only want to hear what they've previously played (or sung) and very little of what they're currently playing (or singing). On the other hand, when lead vocals are being recorded, the singer will want the phones to sound like a finished stereo mix. Often, when I would do vocals, if it was just the artist and me, I would also listen on headphones while recording so that I could make sure what the artist heard sounded as good as it could.

In a classical or scoring session, there may be less need for everyone to have a set of phones, but it's still important for the rhythm players, percussionists, conductor, first violin, and possibly the section leaders and soloists. In large setups, it's better to put them out and not have them used than to waste time hooking them up while dozens of musicians are sitting around. However, be sure to unplug the phones that aren't used so they don't generate leakage into the room.

It is common in scoring or symphony sessions for the conductor to have a separate mix for his phones that will include the orchestra mix (if the session is for scoring the sound cues on film) plus a talkback from the conductor's assistant in the control room. This person will be following the score and checking what's coming through the speakers. His job is to follow the score, keep track of all the takes, and be the conductor's ears in the control room to ensure that the performance and the recording quality are perfect.

One other thing about headphones: If you get a quick mix in the phones, then go about setting final record levels, be sure to keep checking back with the phones. If you don't, this is what will happen: The musicians are listening to themselves, and when they get louder because you're readjusting the record levels, they will sing more softly, back away from the microphone, or turn down. Again, you turn up the levels, and the cycle continues until the musicians take off the phones somewhere near a microphone, and the entire system goes into ear-shattering feedback. I always explain to the musicians that in the beginning the phones will be changing as I set levels and get a mix, and they should play as they want to and if anything suddenly is too loud, just wave.

Don't ever do the headphone mix on the main speakers; always use the same headphones as everyone else is wearing, and from the same amplifier to which they're connected. And don't use the talkback until you have on a set of phones to make sure your voice doesn't blow a hole right through their ears. Start by turning down the talkback and then, while listening on the headphones, do a test while turning up the talkback level to an acceptable level.

Click Tracks and Scratch Tracks

Even if a drum machine is not a part of the production, most rhythm tracks are played to a metronome or a drum machine that provides a reference tempo. Drum machine sounds seem to be less painful to the ears compared to a click. When the click is running through the headphones, make sure it isn't leaking into the drum overhead mics. Otherwise, in a quiet part of the music or in the fall-away at the end of the song, the click will be heard. Once it's recorded that way, there won't be any way to get rid of it in the mix without muting the overhead mic tracks.

Once the drums have been recorded, the click track can be muted, but if there is a drumless intro or a freeform section and the click is necessary to record a piano, acoustic guitar, or vocal, there can be a click leakage problem. The click from the headphones can be inadvertently recorded through the guitarist's or vocalist's mic. The obvious solution is to turn down the click, but most players—and drummers, in particular—need the click very loud. Closed, tight-fitting headphones help, but if it's extremely loud, nothing will contain it entirely. It may be necessary to manually lower the click level during the quiet parts of the recording, such as the intro, and then turn it back up when the drummer comes in. If the ending of the song isn't a fade out, turn off the click at the final beat.

For everyone's sake, the click should be stopped while the band is working things out. Turn it on right before they begin to record and off at the end of the take. The click or drum machine should be recorded on a separate track for future reference. While listening to the band record, don't listen to the click, because there will be a tendency to base the quality of the track on how closely everyone maintains tempo. If the track has the right feel, a little tempo drift won't matter and may well contribute to the "feel" of the track.

A somewhat similar problem will present itself if any guide tracks (such as a trial solo or scratch vocal) leak through the headphones into quiet overdubs, such as acoustic guitars, small percussion (finger bells, and so on), or violins. The situation is made worse if the scratch vocal is somewhat out of tune and sung in the wrong places with the wrong words by someone other than the final vocalist. (It happens.) The best idea during overdubs is to keep the headphones at a fairly low level; otherwise, this little bit of guide track will contribute a certain amount of ghosting (tracks that have been deleted can still be heard in the background of tracks that are used) in the final mix. Also, during overdubs, be sure to unplug everything else that might generate noise, such as unused headphones, guitar amplifiers on standby, clocks, and so on.

Make sure the speakers in the control room aren't so loud that they can be heard in the studio (a common problem in home-built studios). This form of leakage in the tracks will affect the clarity of the recordings, and in some cases force the use of a track that was to be erased—or, at worst, re-recording the tracks that have the leakage. An example is where a rough lead guitar part has leaked from the speakers into a later overdub (say an acoustic rhythm) track, and now that a new lead guitar has been recorded, hints of the old one can still be heard in the acoustic. An identical problem happens if there are changes to any guitar part or vocal that was recorded in the same room with the drums (for instance, a guitar solo). That's why it's best to put the scratch vocalist or any guitar amps in a separate room from the drums, or the leakage in the drum overhead mics will lock you into the tracks that were recorded with the drums.

This chapter has been about setting up and operating a session in your home or in a studio. But in no way does it cover everything that can happen. It contains what I think is useful in getting a session under way. Invariably, unexpected situations occur. Many of the suggestions have come from my own experience, because occasionally things will go wrong, and what's in this chapter are those that have stuck in my mind. Over the course of sessions, different things will stick in your mind, and hopefully you can avoid some of the problems that I've experienced. Being as prepared as possible beforehand makes dealing with problems that much easier to solve.

In the next chapter, we'll look at the person who is reputed to hang out with musicians—the drummer—and getting drum sounds. I have a fondness for drummers because I was one. Recording drums is one of the hardest things to do because everyone has a different idea of what a great drum sound is. And, of course, this varies with the music, the band, the drum kit, the drummer, the style of music, and so on.

But first, to finish this chapter, I have included a step-by-step outline for setting up and breaking down a session and running various types of sessions. Most things will apply, but a few things may not, depending on your situation.

Setup and teardown:

1. Sketch instrument placement using a studio floor plan.
2. Select microphones and gather any other equipment (stands, cables, sandbags, headphones, direct boxes, power cords).
3. Position acoustic separators (gobos).
4. Position stands appropriate to instruments.
5. Place microphones on stands and set them to one side for musician arrival. Use sandbags as required.
6. Run leads from microphones to the studio connection box.
7. Place chairs, music stands, lights, power outlets, and so on.
8. Connect the headphone system.
9. Move into the control room and either load the files for the overdub session (all sessions are overdub sessions after the first session for a given recording) or, if it is a first session, ensure that there is sufficient storage on whatever medium is used for the planned session. (If there's not sufficient storage, you can run backups on files that can be deleted to free up storage.)
10. Verify that the files loaded are correct and the right version (the latest version, presumably), and that the required software plug-ins are operating correctly.
11. If a sequencer is controlling real-time sound modules or processors, make sure those devices are correctly loaded and taking commands.
12. Set the console to the appropriate mode for the required application (recording, overdubbing, or mixdown).
13. If it is an overdub session, create a quick rough mix in the control room.
14. Verify that microphones, headphones, and talkback system are operating properly.
15. Verify that any required forms, markers, pencils, adhesive tape, and so on are available.

16. At the end or during the session, make rough mixes to hard drive for transfer to CD at the end of the session.
17. Back up all session files and finalize all paperwork.
18. Zero the mixing desk, which means returning all controls to their zero settings.
19. Return all items to their normal storage area in the specified condition.
20. Return backup tapes or disks to storage.
21. Remove and dispose of accumulated trash in the studio and the control room.
22. Assist with the setup of the next session.

A standard approach for recording a basic rhythm session:

1. Set the mixing desk input selector so that channel faders are controlling mic inputs and are routed to the recorder and monitor controls all follow the output of the multitrack recorder.
2. Assign the input channels to the appropriate inputs of the recorder and track.
3. Set the recorder to ready/record on all or selected tracks and select input or auto/input mode.
4. Verify that talkback is operating in the headphones and that a room mic is functioning.
5. Each musician in turn will play his instrument. (I suggest you start with the drums and one sound after another—kick, snare, hi-hat, tom-toms, overheads, bass, guitar, vocals.) Regularly check how the instruments sound in the studio.
6. In a timely fashion, while maintaining good communication with musicians, set record levels, add EQ, adjust microphone and instrument placement, make required track assignments, add any signal processing that will be recorded (compressors and so on), and develop the monitor mix.
7. Have musicians play in ensemble and make final adjustments as required.
8. Improve the headphone mix once levels to the recorder are properly adjusted (keeping in mind the level the musicians require, taking into account the essential sound they need and the amount of sound that already exists in the studio).
9. Add reverb and other effects to monitor and/or headphone mixes. (Monitor reverb should continue on playback.)
10. Fill out a track sheet and keep take sheets using a pencil.
11. Record a take, then play it back for assessment and review by all.

12. Make adjustments based on participants' likes and dislikes about the recording.
13. Do another take until everyone is happy.
14. Complete a rough mix to CD for later evaluation by musicians and anyone else.

A standard approach for an overdubbing session:

1. Assign the mixing desk input channels to recorder playback (also called tape or remix).
2. Those mixer channels beyond the available playback outputs (such as Channel 17 for a 16-track studio or Channel 25 for a 24-track studio) are used for input signals, while the monitoring of overdubbing inputs and outputs of the recorder is through playback Channels 1–16 or 1–24.
3. Set the recorder to ready/record on selected tracks and select auto/input mode so that the track being recorded on will play back up until the moment you go into record, at which time it will go into input so you hear what you're recording.
4. Assign the channel input to open track(s).
5. Verify that talkback is operating to headphones and that the room mic is functioning, and begin communication.
6. If overdubs are happening in the control room, verify the signal path.
7. Have overdub musicians play their instruments.
8. In a timely fashion, while maintaining good communication with the musicians, mix the monitor and headphones and make required track assignments, record level and EQ (or other signal processing that is to be recorded), set final microphone and instrument placement, and monitor adjustments.
9. Add reverb and other effects in monitors and/or headphones; reverb should continue in playback.
10. Update the track sheet with notes of preferred takes.
11. Record and play back. Punch in/punch out as required. (Punch in/out refers to going in and out of record on an existing track. DAW systems are less critical to the need to erase what is already there when recording on an existing track, as there are essentially unlimited tracks.)
12. Make adjustments based on participant likes and dislikes about the recording.
13. Continually update track sheets and fine-tune monitor mix.
14. During vocal overdubs, monitor through headphones or check often to make sure they inspire the singer.

10 Miking Drums

Getting a great drum sound is one of the hardest things to do for a number of reasons. A set of drums is large, loud, and acoustically complex. The environment in which you record them presents a wide range of variables that will play a big part in the quality of sound and the recording. Some things that affect the sound include what you have on hand (equipment and acoustics), and some things the band brings with them (equipment and attitude). Of course, everyone will have expectations, and in the end success will be about meeting them.

This will happen to you: The band rolls in, and the drummer sets up and says he wants to get a sound like *blah de blah*. He sits down and starts whacking his drums, and they sound dreadful. The heads are old and badly tensioned, the fittings all rattle, half the metal strands on the snare are broken, they're badly tuned, the kick pedals squeak, the hi-hat creaks, and the drum seat groans louder than a drummer at the end of a long solo. The second shoe drops when you ask, "What do you think of the sound you've got now?" The answer comes back, "I think it's close" Of course, it's nothing like the sound of the drums and drummer that you've been asked to get.

At the heart of getting a drum sound is what *they*—the drummer, producer, or band—think a good drum sound is. We've all heard what we think are terrible-sounding drums, and yet you can be sure that when they were played, recorded, and mixed, an engineer and a drummer (and probably a producer and the rest of the band) invested a lot of time and effort to get them to sound that way. So a good drum sound is really in the ear of the beholder. Yes, there is a consensus of what's good in the context of some iconic bands, some drummers, some recordings, some producers, some engineers, and so on. But on a given day, in a given session, everyone will have a different view on the passionate, creative decision about how the drums are going to sound. A good starting point is for the drummer to bring in a couple of recordings he likes.

The first hour of the session will be professionally critical for you as an engineer. The drummer and the band will have expectations when they walk into the studio, and they will decide whether you can pull it off in that first hour. Invariably, that time will be spent getting drum sounds. What happens in that time will validate the client's decision to use you, and his belief that you can get the sound he is looking for. If things go well, you've earned the respect to negotiate the myriad decisions and compromises that happen throughout the session.

What you have to work with determines what your options are and how many alternatives you have to choose from. Here's a short list of things to consider:

- **How big are the drums?** They can occupy a lot of space or not much at all. Is it a basic set with two cymbals, hi-hat, kick drum, snare, floor tom, and small tom? Or five cymbals, hi-hat, two kick drums, four small toms, two floor toms, snare, temple bells, tambourine, wood block, gong, wind chimes, tympani toms, cowbell, hair-skin drum, roto toms, gamelan, and so on?
- **How does the drummer play?** Is he contained and economical? In other words, are his moves close to his body, consistent and practiced, or is he flailing all over the place? Do the drum heads have dents everywhere, or is it obvious that the hits almost always occur in the same place? This determines how close you can mike the drums.
- **How big is your space, and how much of it will you need for the rest of the band?** Hopefully, the guitar player will show up with one amp, and not a wall of Marshalls.
- **How good do the drums sound before you do anything?** A set that sounds good in the studio is key to a good-sounding drums recording. Hint: Be sure you own the most common drum keys, because you will undoubtedly have to tune many sets of drums. A surprising number of drummers don't have a clue as to what a recording set of drums should sound like. (More on this later in this chapter, in the "Getting Sounds" section.)
- **What rattles, vibrations, and squeaks does the kit have, and how hard is it to eliminate them?** Drums have hundreds of screws, bolts, wing nuts, hinges, and clamps. In the course of moving, setting up, tearing down, and playing the drums, all the fittings will loosen. This is seldom obvious during live dates, but it is painfully so when you're in the studio.
- **How many microphone inputs do you have? How many simultaneous record channels do you have? How many mics and stands do you have? How many quilts and gobos do you have?** Let's face it, what you can do will depend on what facility and equipment you have.

If this all sounds scary, remember that as long as you sort of know where you're going, you'll be fine, and the more drum sessions you do, the more it will become second nature.

Throughout this chapter and the balance of the book, I will be specific about microphones and placement. That being said, the suggestions I've made are based on years of sessions, and they are my generalities and starting points. But getting great sounds is a bit like mastering the English language. There are many rules, but there are also exceptions. Treat my suggestions as a starting point, and be flexible.

Where to Put the Drums

If at all possible, don't put the drums in a small booth, because too many phase problems can result, and usually the drums will end up sounding small. Also, make sure the floor under the drums is solid. I usually set up the drums in the middle or to one side of the main studio space, and if isolation is needed, I will have the guitar player set up his amp in the drum booth or in the hall connecting the studio and control room.

I prefer a hardwood floor with a small rug underneath the kick drum, hi-hat, and throne. This keeps these three pieces of the kit from sliding on the floor. The rest of the floor remains exposed wood. A wood floor creates early reflections and adds to the "liveness" of the drums. If the floor is carpeted, try laying a few small sheets of 1/4-inch plywood or masonite board on the floor around the kit. The sheets need to lie flat on the carpet so they don't vibrate, and you should try to keep all the mic-stand bases on the solid floor so they don't shake. If you've built a solid riser for the drums, attach a cleat at the front so the kick drum can be anchored to it and thus won't move forward.

Setting Up the Mics

There are thousands of combinations of microphone setups for miking drum kits and percussion sounds, but by and large, most people do it one of the following ways.

In the first instance, it will depend on how many mics you have, how many mixer inputs you have, or how many simultaneous record channels you have—and, of course, what else you plan to record at the same time. Tape recorders have tracks, and the number of tracks you can record at a time is set by the design. Most of the better computer-based multitrack computer programs have pretty much unlimited tracks, but only so many tracks can be recorded at the same time, depending on the interface hardware you have.

If it's a basic kit (kick, snare, two small toms, floor tom, hi-hat, and stereo overheads), you need eight tracks of simultaneous record if everything is on a separate track. It you have a 16-or-more rig, you probably can do that. But if you only have 8-track simultaneous record, you'll have to pre-mix.

If you need to work within a simultaneous 8-track record configuration, combine and pan the tom-toms with the drum overhead microphones into a stereo left/right overhead combination. For a five-piece set, the highest rack tom goes to one track, the middle rack tom shares both of the tracks that make up the stereo pair, and the floor tom goes to the other track. The two overhead microphones are assigned left and right. The overhead microphone nearest the high rack tom goes to that track, while the overhead microphone above the floor tom goes to the track shared by the floor tom. How much of the overheads you add to the mix will determine how "open" or "tight" the drums will sound. Those two tracks, along with a separate kick, snare, and hi-hat track, will make up the overall drum sound and take up five record inputs, leaving you three tracks/inputs for a bass, scratch guitar, and vocal.

Mono Recording

For mono recording of drums (such as for some TV and PA applications), the simplest approach is one mic over the kit, augmented with a kick-drum mic and a mic on the snare. A small-diaphragm condenser or some other equally compliant mic should be used for the overhead for rock dates, but I might use a larger-diaphragm condenser for jazz or classical sessions. The choice of microphones for the drums will vary with taste. A medium-diameter dynamic on the snare is often a preferred choice, and for the kick drum, more than likely a larger-diaphragm dynamic. If the hi-hat part is important, and you want a close, percussive attack, an additional bright-sounding mic on the hi-hat could be used (see Figure 10.1).

Figure 10.1 Three- to four-mic setup.

Specifically, where the hi-hat and floor tom are in relation to the kick drum will depend on whether the drummer is right- or left-handed. If you're looking at the drums from in front of the kick drum, a right-handed drummer will have the hi-hat to the right of the kick, and the floor tom to the left. For a lefty, it will be reversed. In all of the descriptions that follow, I am assuming it's a right-handed drummer.

For the kick drum, I use a short 6-inch stand or a medium stand with a boom to position the mic about 3 to 6 inches inside the front of the kick drum, through the hole that many kick drums have in the front head. (More on this in the "Getting Sounds" section later in this chapter.) The mic should be off center from the beater. If you're using a short stand, put a sandbag on the base to ensure that it doesn't move with the kick-drum beat. My favorite kick-drum mic is a Sennheiser 421 or AKG D 12 (see Figure 10.2). I might choose an Electro-Voice RE20 if I want a deeper sound or a Shure SM57 for a higher, punchier sound. I also like the Fostex M521 and the AKG D 112 (see Figure 10.3). The Neumann U 47 FET (see Figure 10.4) and the Neumann TLM 170 (see Figure 10.5) are also highly regarded kick-drum mics.

For the snare, I use a medium-high stand with a boom sitting in front of the set, to the hi-hat side of the kick drum. The stand should be set even with the snare so that the boom goes under the cymbal and just between the small (or *rack*) tom and the hi-hat. Make sure that the boom doesn't touch the drums when they're being played. At the end of the boom, the mic angles

Figure 10.2 AKG D 12 Classic dynamic for kick and guitar amp.

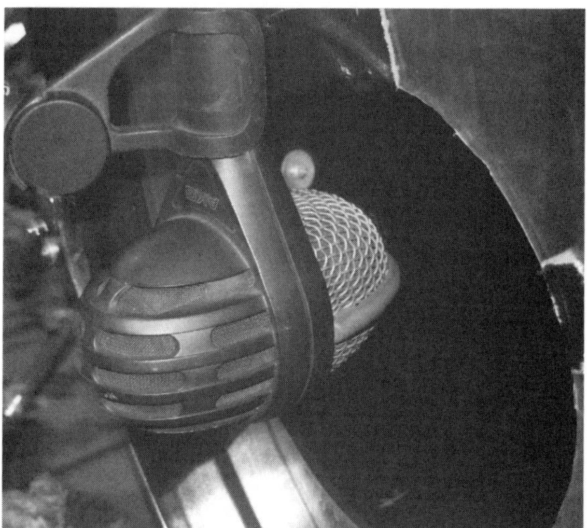

Figure 10.3 Kick drum with AKG D 112.

downward at about 45 degrees so that it is pointing toward the center of the drum about an inch above the head and beyond the rim 2 to 3 inches (see Figure 10.6). The mic holder should be about an inch above the rim so that when the snare moves around, it doesn't hit the mic and boom.

Figure 10.4 Neumann U 47 FET.

Photo courtesy of Georg Neumann GmbH.

Figure 10.5 Neumann TLM 170 R.

Figure 10.6 Shure SM57 positioned on snare.

A bit of trial and error is now called for, because you'll find subtle differences in the sound as you vary the angle of the mic and where it is pointing to on the snare head. Whatever you do, be very sure the mic is not going to get hit by a stick. The drummer could be fine when hitting the snare, but depending on cymbal placement, when he hits the cymbal just above the snare mic or the tom-tom just beside it, his sticks could graze the mic. The snare-drum mic and its stand should be checked regularly to be sure they maintain the position, because they will move with all the sound vibration. It's a very good idea to sandbag the bass of the stand because the boom is extended quite a way, and you don't want the mic falling against the head. For a snare mic, I often use a Shure SM57 or a Sennhesier 421. The AKG C 451 is also a common snare mic.

For a mono setup, the overhead stand's base works well at the front of the floor tom. Unless you have large studio-mic stands, you'll need to extend the stand to its full height and the boom as far as it will project over the drums. The stand must be sandbagged for stability. I start with the mic positioned 2 to 2½ feet above the highest cymbal and a foot or so in front of where the drummer's head is most of the time. The mic I select for the overhead is pretty generic, and it's often a pragmatic decision based on what mics the studio has. I like the Neumann KM 84 and KM 184, or AKG 451, with a cardioid pickup pattern for overheads. For a more jazz or classical sound, I might go with a Neumann U 87 and an AKG 414 (cardioid pattern), or any number of other large-diaphragm condensers. I prefer to turn on the roll-off switch to reduce the very low end entering the overhead. The hi-hat mic stand goes to the outside of the hi-hat. I like to position the mic pretty close to the top hi-hat cymbal, about 2 inches or so from the edge. The mic is angled slightly away from the drummer and where he will be striking the top cymbal. I have always used a Neumann KM 84 on the hi-hat, and any other microphone was used only when the studio did not have a KM 84 (see Figure 10.7). Don't ever set the mic near the opening between the two cymbals. The opening and closing will cause the microphone to sound like someone is popping P's into the mic.

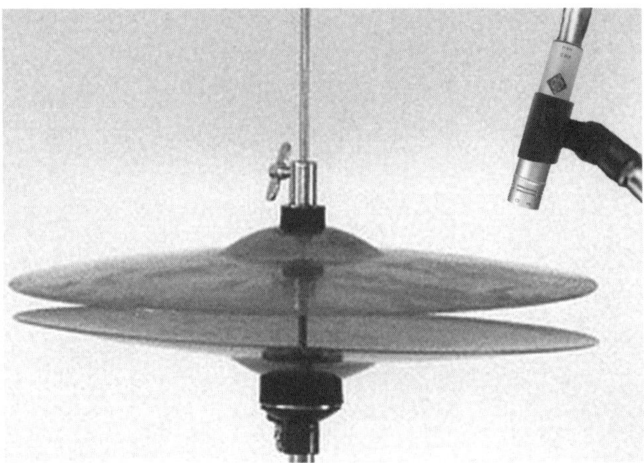

Figure 10.7 Neumann KM 84 on a hi-hat.

Be mindful that drums are extremely loud and percussive by their very nature. If you are using condenser mics, you may find you need to use the internal mic pad to prevent overloading the internal microphone's preamp. In the case of the 451, this is a separate attachment that goes between the capsule and the body of the microphone. Figure 10.8 shows a full three-mic setup.

Stereo Recording

A good stereo drum sound can be achieved with one mic on the kick, one on the snare, an additional microphone on the hi-hat, and a pair of identical mics for overheads. All five mics will be assigned to two record tracks. Pan the first two mics to the center (or equally between two tracks), and pan the overheads left and right for the desired amount of stereo image. Pan the hi-hat to the side shared by the overhead above the hi-hat (see Figure 10.9).

Specifically, all the mic details in the mono setup would be the same except for the additional overhead. The overhead used in the mono setup would move to above the floor-tom side of the kit, and a second identical mic and stand would cover the hi-hat side of the kit. If I have the space, I usually move both the overhead stands in front of the kit, to the left and right of the kick drum. The stand for the second overhead would be the same as the one used in the mono setup. The height for the two mics would be roughly the same as in the mono setup, but how far apart they are will be determined by the stereo technique you choose to use (AB, XY, and so on). As

Figure 10.8 Three-mic drum setup. Snare: Sennhesier MD 421. Kick: Shure SM58. Overhead: AKG 451 with a cardioid-pattern capsule.

Figure 10.9 Five-mic stereo placement.

previously mentioned, I prefer an AB approach for drums and for rock in general. The overhead pair will face downward, and they are separated by a couple of feet or more depending on the size of the drum kit. At times, I might move them forward, above the rear rim of the kick drum, and then tip them slightly back toward the drummer and out toward the tom and hi-hat, respectively. In a stereo AB approach, it would be rare for me to use anything other than a pair of small-diaphragm condensers, with my favorite being a cardioid pair of AKG 451s.

The position of the overheads will need further fine-tuning when you check how the stereo pair sounds when heard in mono. A tip that seems to work is to use a piece of string to measure the distance from the center of the snare to the overhead mics. If you make sure that they are all the same distance from the snare, then the biggest potential phase problem is averted because the snare will sound solid on the overheads. You might also try a third mic behind and over the drummer, also measuring out the same distance from the snare. The snare sounds solid; it's then just a matter of finding the best place for the other parts of the kit.

Mixing everything to stereo is usually done only when there are very few recorder inputs available or if the drums are a small part of a huge orchestra. But if you're mixing straight to video, no matter what you're recording—rock, pop, country, or whatever—it all goes down to stereo.

Glyn Johns and Recorderman

A couple of worthwhile stereo drum mic setups that use four microphones are the Glyn Johns and the Recorderman methods.

Glyn Johns is one of the best rock sound engineers who has ever recorded. His approach will only work well if you have a good drummer and a good-sounding room to record in. It uses four microphones—two overheads (usually large-diaphragm cardioid condensers) and a kick and snare mic (mics as noted earlier). See Figure 10.10.

1. The left overhead mic is about 4 to 6 inches above the floor tom, aimed toward the hi-hat across the center of the snare.
2. The right overhead mic is about 2 to 3 feet above the drum kit, facing downward between the rear of the kick drum and the snare.

Most of the sound will come from the overhead pair with the snare mic (3) and the kick (4) added into the center for impact and snap.

The second approach was suggested by the Recorderman in the popular forum www.recording.org. You'll need a few feet of string. Place the left overhead mic directly over and 2 to 3 feet above the center of the snare, being mindful of the amount of space the drummer needs when he goes to the cymbals and toms. Assuming you're working with a right-handed drummer, place the second mic just beyond the drummer's right shoulder. You'll fine-tune the position of this microphone with the assistance of the string.

Stretch a string from where the beater hits the kick drum to the first mic. Maintain that and stretch the rest of the string from the mic to the center of the snare. While maintaining the string tension and the point where the mic touched the string, swing the string toward the second mic. Reposition the second mic so it touches where the first mic touched the string. In other words, the distances from the mics to the kick and snare are the same.

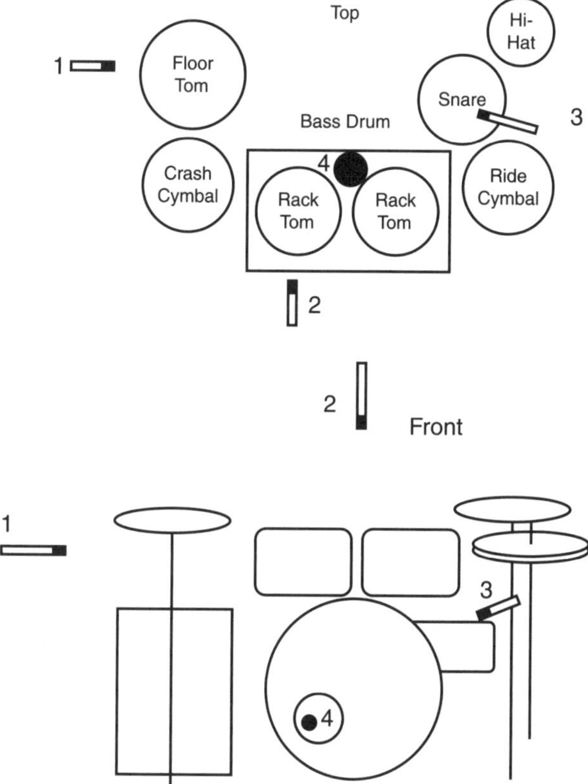

Figure 10.10 Glyn Johns four-mic drum setup.

Pan these two mics left and right and listen with headphones. While the drummer hits the kick, adjust the "beyond shoulder" mic's angle until the kick is in the center of the mix. As in the Glyn Johns approach, the overheads provide most of the sound, and the snare and kick are added as a matter of taste to get more snap and as individual components for the purposes of processing (such as reverb on the snare).

Multitrack Recording

Most people who are recording drums to a multitrack use one microphone on every tom-tom, one on the kick, one on the snare, one on the hi-hat, and a pair of overheads. If the drummer has an array of tom drums, bidirectional mics positioned between each pair of toms will do the job. See Figure 10.11.

For the hi-hat, mic choice and placement are much the same as before.

For the snare, use the same placement as before for the top microphone. There are those who also like a microphone under the snare to get more of the metallic rattle of the snares. I've never liked that sound, and I have never used a mic under the snare, but there are some who do.

Figure 10.11 Multitrack mic placement.

A Shure SM57 would work well under the snare, or for a very bright sound, a condenser. A short stand with a boom might be able to go just under the stand that's supporting the top snare mic, or a 1-foot stand just under the snare. This bottom mic should be 3 inches or so from the bottom of the snare. When the top and bottom microphones are combined, it might sound best to reverse the polarity of the bottom mic (see Figure 10.12).

For overheads, as in the stereo approach, most recordings will use a pair of the same microphones.

If the studio sounds good, and the only sound in the studio is the drums (in other words, everything but the drums is going direct, and any guitar amps are set up in an isolation booth), I usually have another pair of mics set up across the room to get the sound of the drums in the space of the room. It adds a lot to the "bigness."

Toms of any size are miked much like the snare. If the set has just one or two small rack toms and one or two floor toms, use one stand and mic for each drum. Set the stands to the outside of the kit. Set the booms to bring the mics into the drum at a fairly steep angle so that the boom is not overextended or sticking out into the rest of the studio so they are not accidentally knocked over by anyone passing by the drums. The trick is to bring the booms under the cymbals and away from the drummer. Allow plenty of space below the cymbal, because a vigorous crash can make the cymbals sway and swing substantially.

I usually start with the mic at a slight angle to the tom surface. (This is hard to say in degrees because it depends on the angle of the drums themselves.) The mic is about 1 inch from the rim and a couple inches off the surface. I like large-diaphragm dynamics on the floor toms (EV RE-20) and medium-size dynamics on the small toms (Sennheiser 421 or Shure SM57). In studios that have a lot of AKG 451s, I'll use them on the toms. I also like a cardioid Beyer M160 and the

Figure 10.12 Snare miked above (Shure SM57) and below (AKG 414).

RØDE M3 (see Figure 10.13) on toms, and if there is more than two small toms, I will use the bidirectional M130 for a pair of drums.

A few last comments on drum miking. In recent years there has appeared a new generation of mics designed especially for drums—in particular, those made by Electro-Voice (see Figure 10.14) and Sennhesier (see Figures 10.15 and 10.16). The microphones will meet the taste of many engineers and at the same time eliminate the forest of mic stands that surround most drum setups. That being said, choose them because they get the sound you're looking for, not because they are convenient.

Again, this is not my thing, but some engineers will also position microphones under the toms. Shure SM57s probably would work fine for this, but I've never liked that sound. The only time I recall miking a set of toms below the heads was for a Billy Cobham album. He had North Drums (very popular in the '70s). There were four or five across the top, much like regular toms, but the shell diameter expanded as they went down toward the floor and then curved out toward where an audience would be. We used a few mics several feet in front of them. The horn effect of

Photo courtesy of RØDE Microphones.

Figure 10.13 RØDE M3 cardioid condenser on rack tom.

the shells amplified the head vibrations, and of course Billy knew how to play them like no one else could. They were like tuned cannons.

Latin Percussion

Over the years I've worked on many Latin sessions where the rhythm section was much more than just a drummer and drums. Many Latin dates will include congas and timbali and may also include marimbas and a hand percussion. The trick here is to walk around the instrument while it's being played to figure out where the best sound is coming out. It may sound best above the sound or just as likely near the floor.

Don't ever record congas or other Latin percussion on carpet. It will sound terrible. If you have a studio with carpet, put down some sheets of plywood or masonite to liven up the early reflection of the percussion. If you have a large glass window, don't position Latin percussion instruments too close to it, because the glass can create undesirable reflections.

The percussionist will arrive with cases and cases of stuff; you should work out where he can store it while still being able to access it. Many times it will be junk that has turned into found

Figure 10.14 Electro-Voice PL35 dynamic supercardioid polar pattern. Integrated swivel and drum rim clamp.

and prized percussion objects that he takes great joy in "playing." Percussionists like to work fast when they are overdubbing and will quickly change from one thing to another as they work through what they want to do. So don't get hung up on changing everything with every sound, but go with the flow.

Handheld percussion of almost an infinite variety can be recorded with a single (see Figure 10.17) or a stereo pair of microphones. (I like the Neumann KM 84, AKG 451, RØDE NT55, and Sennhesier e614.) Position the mics 2 to 3 feet away from loud percussion (cabasa, guiro, tambourine, cowbells, and all sorts of other things that shake and rattle), and 1 to 2 feet for quieter percussion (wind chimes, finger bells, talking drums, and rainsticks). MS miking can also work well on small percussion. You can do some reasonably close miking and get a very present sound on the cardioid mic, and then the side mic eliminates the "shaker in your ear" sound. You also might find vocal windscreens are needed, because some percussion can cause the mic (in particular, condenser mics) to sound like someone is popping into it.

If percussion is being recorded with a full band (such as a Santana session with conga, bongo, timbales, and ethnic drums), most drum-type percussion can be miked pretty much like a floor or rack tom and/or overheads. But when overdubbed, they will be more open if the mics are

Figure 10.15 Sennhesier e905 on snare and e904 on tom cardioid dynamic microphones designed for drums.

pulled back from the instrument. The decision to use both close and far miking mixed together is a judgment call, but something like congas will almost always be created by mixing mics near the heads to pick up the hand slaps and articulations, and mics a couple of feet away that bring out the fullness of the drums.

The close mics would be much like those used on toms, and the more distant mics would usually be a Neumann 87, AKG 414, or similar.

Getting Sounds

Getting sounds for drums is both technical and aesthetic. It's a matter of mic choice and placement, correct preamp and mixing-desk gain structure (level settings), drum placement, adjusting the acoustics, the use of signal processing (EQ, gates, compression, and so on), making sure the drums are recorded at the right level, deciding whether to gate, and perfecting drum tuning and EQ. And of course, all of that has to be appropriate for the production and the likes and dislikes of everyone in the studio at the time. Opinions will come from everywhere, and you just never know whose will prevail. As long as you're working on your own projects and the only one you

Figure 10.16 Full drum-mic setup using Sennhesier mics.

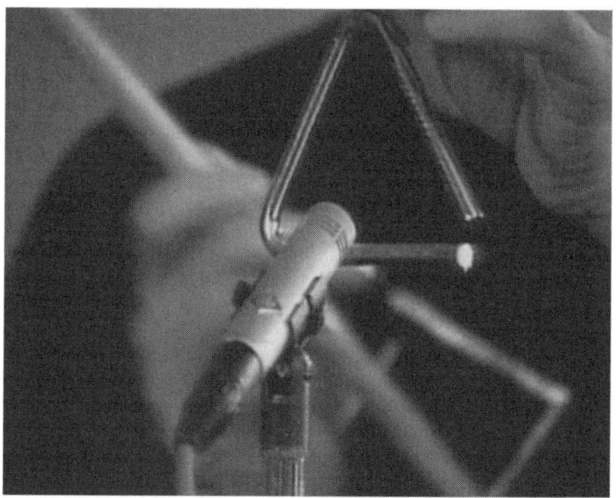

Figure 10.17 Neumann KM 84 recording a triangle.

have to satisfy is yourself, you can be pretty firm about how you want things, but when you're working with the artistic judgments of others, be flexible and accepting that there are a lot of differing opinions about what's good and what's not.

Every kit sounds different when played by different drummers in different rooms at different times at different temperatures and humidity. And every song can need a different sound. The idea that every cut on an album should have the same drum sound is ludicrous. Just what the world needs—another album on which every cut sounds the same (yuck). There should be a consistent texture, but not a "sameness," unless every song has the same beat, the same chord progression, the same lyric form, and the same instruments.

Once the drummer is set up, move all the stands and microphones into position. It is likely that the drummer will be making adjustments as well and could be in his own world. So make sure to let him know when you're getting in front of the kick drum or anything else he could hit. The ears he could destroy are the only ones you have, and he is relying on them. At this point, find out whether the drummer needs a music stand for more than holding the headphones; moving one in will be a real hassle if it's needed after all the mic stands have been positioned.

Ask whether the drummer thinks he might hit any of the mics or stands. Find out what the drummer will be playing and what type of song he'll be doing. A lot of time can be wasted getting sounds with the drummer hitting the snare with a stick, when it is later discovered that brushes are used throughout the song. Similarly, you can spend a lot of time getting sounds on a huge set (15 pieces with chromatic temple block and Tibetan wind chimes), only to discover that all the drummer will be using are the snare, kick, and hi-hat.

It's also important to make sure that there are no squeaks in the pedals (use silicon spray or WD-40) or hardware and fitting rattles. Use rubber cement or rubber washers to keep the fittings that can't be removed or tightened from shaking. Drum and mounting hardware won't rattle until you hit them, and when you do, the sound of the hit masks the rattle, so eliminating this audible junk is not as easy as you might think. The best recording tom-tom drums are held in position by a freestanding frame. The common design that has a post coming out of the center of the kick drum tends to cause the kick and tom to have inter-resonance problems (one drum vibrating the other). A great drummer can get a great drum sound on almost any set of reasonably made drums, provided he knows how to tune them. Though drums don't have specific pitch, they do have tone. Most drummers with a five-piece kit will tune their drums roughly to thirds. An even tension should be applied to all the lugs, and many drummers will tap the head with the stick near each lug to determine the desired even tension. Once evenly tuned, slight tension changes in one or more of the lugs will cause the toms to change pitch over time (that sound where when the drum is struck, it then goes down in pitch). Drum-key torque wrenches are used by some drummers (see Figure 10.18), but ultimately it comes down to tap, tap, turn; tap, tap, turn. Often, but not always, a set of drums that has been on the road is higher pitched than a recording drum kit. If the heads have previously been too tight, they may not be capable of sounding good when they are tuned down. After you tap, tap all the way around, give them a few good whacks to settle them in across the shell lip. Then tap, tap some more.

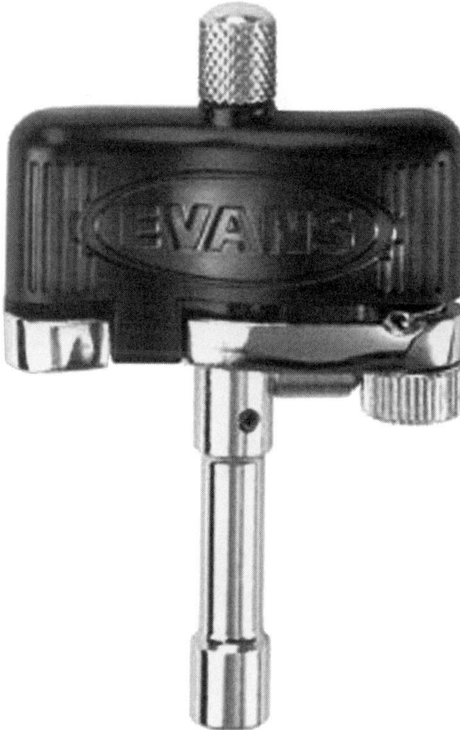

Figure 10.18 The Evans DATK Torque Key has a handle that can be preset to a desired tension in order to help achieve even head tuning.

I was a drummer and was always comfortable sitting down and tuning the drums if the drummer was happy for me to do so. If you do much drum recording, learning how to tune drums will be a worthwhile skill.

I frequently remove the bottom heads from all the toms because if they are left on, they usually contribute unpleasant overtones and sympathetic ringing. If you explain that this is what is needed to get a good sound, the drummer will almost always cooperate. A few drummers who know how to tune their instruments and who are looking for a bit more of a compressed jazz sound will leave the bottom heads on. When properly tuned, the pressure inside the double-headed drum will provide a certain amount of atmospheric damping on the vibrating heads. For rock dates, pulling off the heads is the best bet.

You should also remove the front of the kick-drum head. A lot of drummers will have a front kick-drum head with a big hole to one side of center, which is fine because what's left of the front head keeps the rim hardware from rattling. Most studio drummers will put either a pillow or a blanket inside the kick drum to dampen the shell's vibration (see Figure 10.19). The best idea is to line the inside of the drum shell all the way around with a 4-inch piece of closed-cell foam rubber that is as deep as the shell. This will eliminate the rumble and vibration in the drum shell.

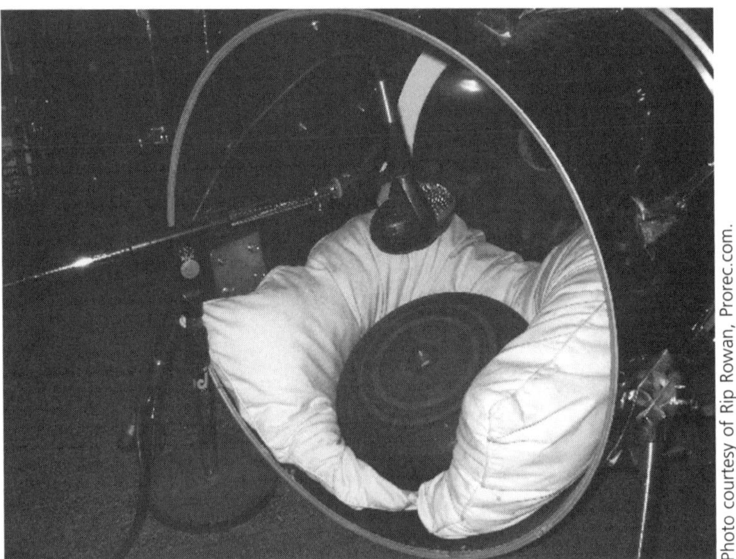
Photo courtesy of Rip Rowan, Prorec.com.

Figure 10.19 Kick drum with pillow inside and weighted down with a mic-stand base. AKG D 112.

To get a big, open sound, I suggest removing all the internal mufflers on all the drums including the snare. Internal mufflers are useful for live work; however, they put pressure unevenly on one side of the head, giving the drum's decay some nasty overtones. Just loosening them won't cut it because they usually rattle. In place of the dampers, use small pieces of gaffer's tape and little pieces of cotton or gauze to create even damping. Stick these patches in a couple of places along the rear of snare and tom rims. Experiment with how much of a pad you need and where it should be stuck.

Probably one of the best snare drum sounds comes from taking an old snare drum head and cutting off the ceramic hoop (see Figure 10.20). Then cut a 5- to 8-inch hole inside the circle so that you end up with a ring that is just big enough to sit on the snare drum. Don't tape it down; just let it sit on top of the head. It will stay put. This gets rid of any ring, and it works great. I always kept one of these in the studio, and I used it often. The thickness of the bottom snare head and the size and tightness of the snares are a matter of taste.

The type of heads, the material they're made from, and how old they are will also matter. Newer heads are better, but brand-new heads are not. They quickly stretch during their first few hours and are constantly changing during a session. When replacing the heads, be sure the shell rim is smooth.

Figure 10.20 A ring made from an old snare drum head makes a great damper.

Before heading into the control room, ask the drummer to play the entire set, and make your final mic placement settings.

To get a good drum sound, it's important for the drummer to remember that he is recording and not playing live. A drummer playing a gig will usually hit the drums hard and the cymbals even harder. For a vast majority of recordings, a session drummer will hit the drums hard and the cymbals much lighter so that the cymbals don't overwhelm the drums and the tonality and smoothness of the cymbals is enhanced.

Finally, make sure the drummer's headphones fit well and that there is enough cord for them. Tell the drummer he'll be hearing you in the cans, but he won't hear his drums until you've got levels. Remind him that while you're getting levels, he needs to strikes the drums as hard as he'll be striking them in the recording and that his hits must be consistent. Some drummers quickly tire of hitting the same drum during the sound check, and they hit them progressively more lightly. Others get angry and start hitting them harder!

Unconventional Snare-Drum Sounds There are an unlimited number of interesting modifications and variations to snare-drum sounds. Occasionally, Ringo Starr used to bang his snare through a towel (preferably a thick one stolen from an expensive hotel). There have been periods when everyone was taping leather wallets to the snare (often containing mail-order prayer cloths), then came the use of industrial-strength tampons. Over the years, there have been dozens of "everyone's doing it" things to do. (I prefer to tape to the snare the key case that comes with a Mercedes Gullwing.)

Years ago, I recorded an album with Jonathan Richman (of Modern Lovers fame). On several cuts, his drummer used a 1957 DeSoto hubcap as a snare drum and a small Salvation Army marching drum for the kick. The floor tom was a meter-round basket-bottomed hair drum of stretched genuine imitation zebra skin, and the drum legs were made from cow hooves. The entire album was recorded in a reverb chamber. (Those were the days!) The same album also had the definitive version of "Neanderthal Man," which featured one of the engineers (me) rhythmically dropping the closed end of a very large mailing tube to create a particularly appropriate "ugh" drum sound. (For trivia's sake, I also played the typewriter carriage return and bell in the original "Government Center.")

Adjusting Drum Levels

Once in the control room, put on the headphones and make sure you can hear yourself in the talkback and that the drummer can hear you as well. It is essential that you let the drummer know what's going on. Also, being in someone's ear is different than standing a few feet away from him, so be mindful of how loudly he is hearing you.

Be sure you're ready before asking the drummer to start hitting the drums, and tell him to stop when you have technical problems or when you're making changes or plugging things in. Most important, tell him when you don't need him to continue to hit something.

Start by checking to make sure all the microphones are plugged in where you expect to find them on the mixer. Ask the drummer to hit the kick drum first, and as soon as you know that mic is working, ask him to scratch one at a time as you raise and lower each of the other microphones until you've verified everything is in order.

I usually start with the kick drum, then snare, hi-hat, and toms, and then I ask the drummer to play the whole kit to get a sound and levels for the overheads. Be mindful of preamp gain or the need for pads when adjusting levels so that the internal mic amps, the mixing desk preamps, the mixing desk output amplifiers, and the recorder inputs don't overload and distort. This is called *adjusting the gain structure* of the signal flow.

Gain Structure Microphones are designed to handle a wide range of dynamics, from the quietest of sounds to the loudest. But in order to be useful, a quiet sound requires considerable amplification of the signal between the capsule and the recorder. The same microphone's capsule is able to handle very loud sounds, but if the same gain is applied to loud sound, the various amplifiers along the signal path will overload and distort. So, various adjustments need to be made depending on the loudness of the sound entering the microphone's capsule. This process is called adjusting the gain structure (see Figure 10.21).

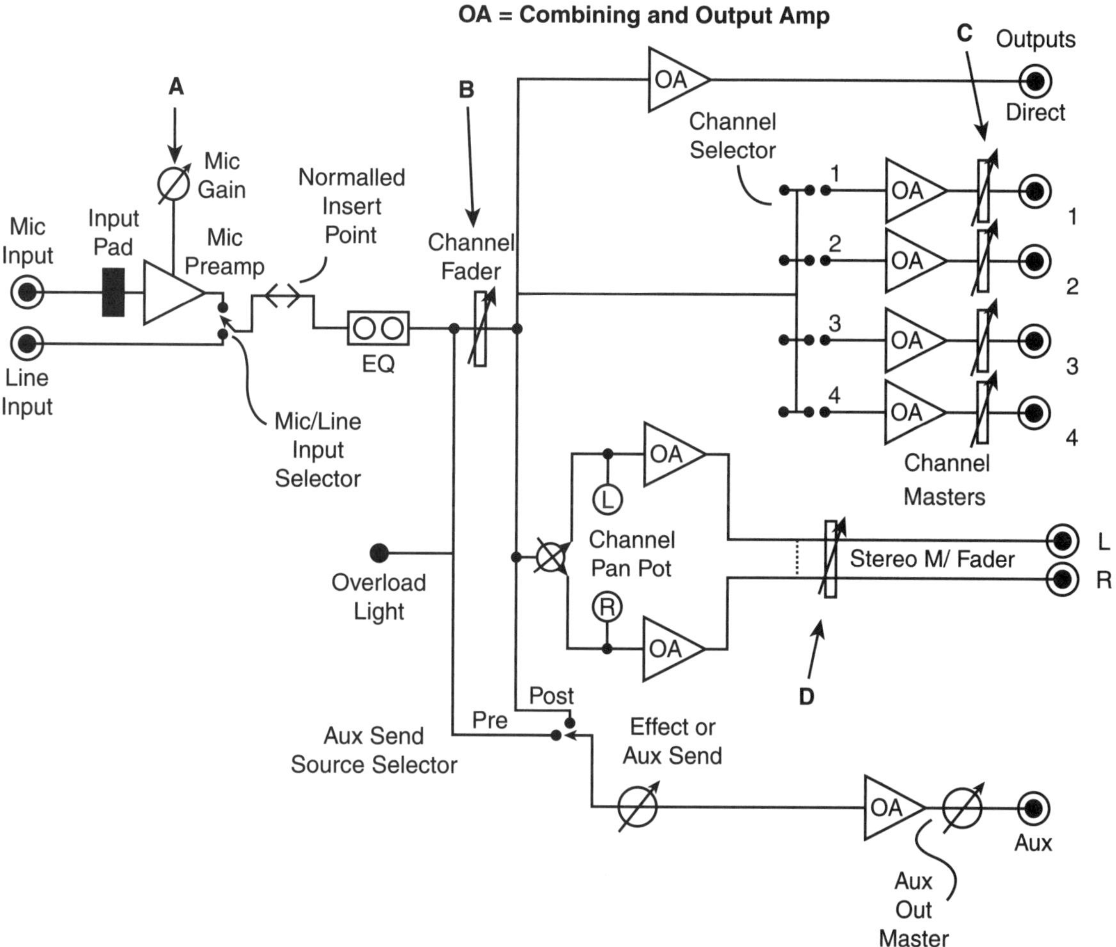

Figure 10.21 Mixing desk schematic showing signal path and point where gain can be adjusted.

Dynamic and ribbon microphones seldom have internal pads, but as described in Chapter 7, they are common in condenser microphones to prevent the internal preamps from overloading. Some mixing desks (no Neve has a pad) will also have a channel input pad before the desk's microphone preamplifier, which will have an input level (or trim) control (Point A in Figure 10.21). The channel input pad is activated if the input signal is so great that the preamp level control can't be turned down enough. The pad increases the range of attenuation by usually 20 to 30 dB. There is often an input overload indicator at this point in the circuit to indicate whether the signal level is overloading the preamp. In many preamp designs, the overload light is after the EQ amplifier so that the effect of any boost of EQ can also be taken into account. The signal then goes to the channel fader (Point B in Figure 10.21) and another amplifier. The channel fader is used to control the level of the signal in the mix. If several channels are being submixed, the signal will go through a submix amplifier and fader (Point C in Figure 10.21). The submix fader may also be the stereo fader, or it may be a separate master fader (Point D in Figure 10.21).

On the channel, the submix, and master faders, there is a position that is determined by the electronic design of the mixing desk to be best for the mixer's signal-to-noise and headroom. On many of these faders this is indicted by a zero mark (which is to say below this point is –dB and above it is +dB level adjustment from its optimum operating level position), and it gives some indication of the settings that are to be followed to achieve the best gain structure. A safe place to start when setting levels is to raise all the channels and submix faders (if used) to the 0 position, and then trim the signal until it's correct using the input pad and preamp. If you use a lot of boost EQ, and the signal is peaking too high, turn down the preamp (see Appendix B, "An EQ Primer").

It's difficult to suggest record levels, because it will depend on the recording medium (tape, digital, analog, hard disk, and so on). In general, digital recorders have less headroom, while analog is more forgiving of peak levels. I'm a bit conservative with digital and less so with analog tape. Also, percussion has significant transients, and some meters do not respond as quickly as others. I take the view that you should assume a flashing peak-level indicator is telling you that if distortion isn't happening at that instant, you're in the danger zone. Once you set levels, keep checking peak levels, because when the band starts recording, levels may creep up. Levels will also change with each song. Ultimately, if you find the playback has some distortion, lower the levels. Needless to say, it's not good if the take that everyone loves has obvious and undesired distortion.

If you have to use a lot of excessive equalization, take a step back and return to the studio to see what the drums sound like in the studio. You might want to change the tuning, the mic or the mic placement. It could also be that the drummer's thoughts on how he wants his drums to sound are quite different than yours might be from the control room.

This book is about microphones, and signal processing can fill many more books, but I've included a short appendix (Appendix B) at the end of the book on how to use equalization that might be helpful.

For toms that are combined with overheads into a stereo pair, when the toms are struck, the level meter should read about –1 dB for the two that are assigned to the left and right. The center tom that shares both tracks is set to a lower level (about –4 dB). At this level, its total loudness (or energy) in the stereo mix will be as loud as each of the two separated toms. The output of the overhead microphones is blended in with the toms according to how much cymbal splash you prefer. In any case, the individual toms should be substantially louder than the overhead cymbal ambience.

Once you have levels, have the drummer play the whole kit, and turn everything on to see how all the mics work together. Do whatever fine-tuning is needed, and then turn up the drums in the headphones. It will need to be substantially louder than you expect for the drummer to hear the drums in the phones over the leakage from the drums around them. Record some of the drums, and then ask the drummer to come into the control room for a playback. Don't let him judge the sound through the headphones, which bear little resemblance to the way the kit sounds in the control room.

Gating Drums

When recording analog or if you need to combine the overheads and toms into a stereo mix, some engineers and producers use gates on snare, tom, or kick drums. Gates are most commonly used during mixing (as an external device or as a function of a digital workstation), but if mics are being mixed together while recording, they may be used at that time to eliminate the leakage coming into each of the individual mics from the rest of the kit.

What Is a Gate? Basically a gate is an automatic on/off control. When the input signal drops below a certain level, the gate will automatically turn down. For instance, a gate can eliminate low-level leakage between every snare-drum beat that's coming from the hi-hat or other nearby instruments (see Figure 10.22). As the snare rattles away into leakage, the decay goes below the threshold, the gate turns off the sound, and when the snare drum is struck again, it instantaneously turns on. The result is that the leakage is eliminated between every beat of the snare drum (see Figure 10.23).

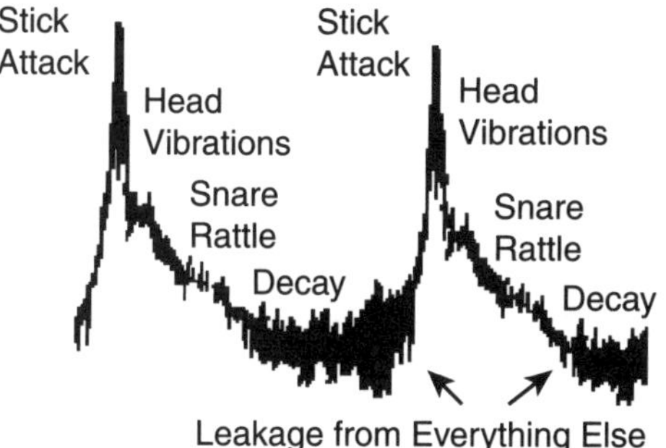

Figure 10.22 Snare envelope with leakage.

Gates are frequently used to "tighten up" the kick drum and snare sound and to eliminate from the tom mics the constant rumble that occurs in sympathy with the kick and snare. The best result can be achieved if the gate's controls are set for a fast attack time, a medium release time, and the range adjustment is set to very deep—and it's best if only one signal is being controlled by each gate. If a gate is used on a single track, it's safer to use it during mixdown than to worry about it during recording.

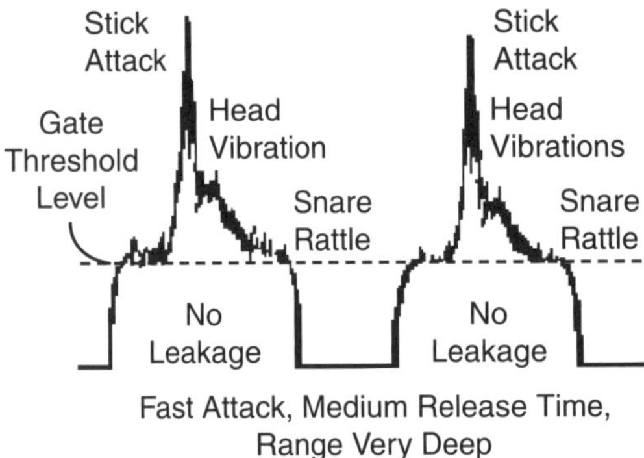

Figure 10.23 Envelope of snare with leakage gated.

Most gates have an external trigger input so that an equalizer can be inserted into the level sensor circuit. For instance, if the leakage in a snare drum mic is nearly as loud as the drum, the gate's level sensor will have difficulty discriminating between the snare and the leakage. Without changing the quality of the snare sound that's passing through the gate, the equalizer in the external trigger (see Figure 10.24) can be used to enhance the stick hitting the snare while diminishing the leakage frequencies. The sound through this equalizer won't be heard, since it is only used to enhance the gate's sensitivity to the snare drum (so it can be radical) in order to achieve a dynamic difference between the snare and the leakage.

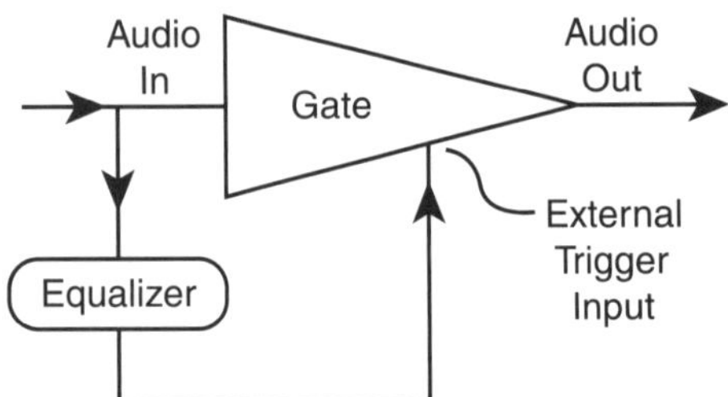

Figure 10.24 Diagram of gate with equalizer to fine-tune external trigger signal.

The most common need for a gate while recording is when the tom mics are mixed with the overhead drum mics (see Figure 10.25). To eliminate leakage on the toms, you'll need a gate for each of the tom microphones. If you try using gates on the combined signal after the toms are combined with the overheads, the gates will not be able to stop the leakage on each of the toms and will cause the cymbals to dynamically "pump."

When it is necessary to record with a gate, it is critical for the settings to be exactly right. If the gate threshold and release are set incorrectly, the resulting recording cannot be fixed later. The threshold of each gate has to be sensitive enough to turn on when each of the drums is individually struck, but not so sensitive that it turns on if any of the other drums are struck. The release

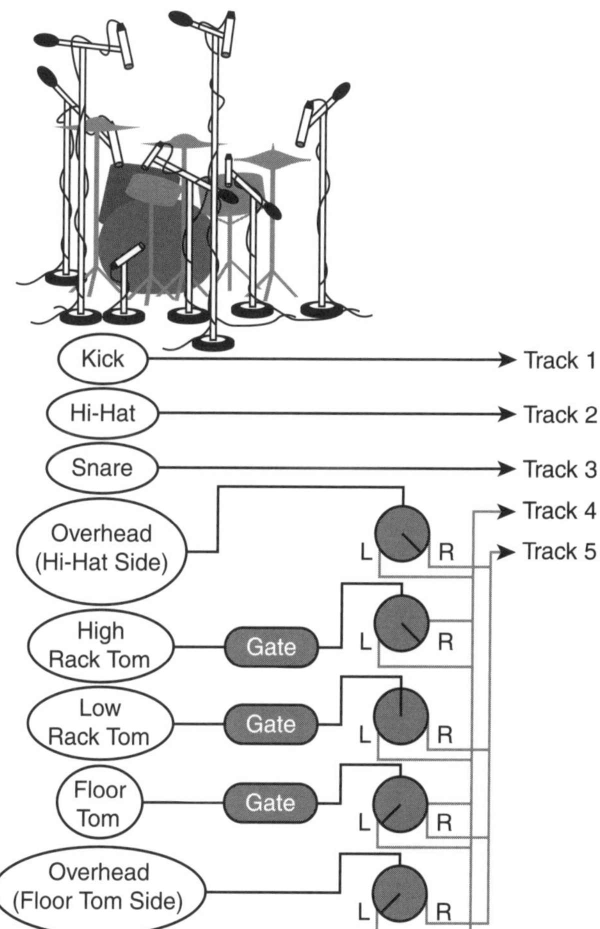

Figure 10.25 Gates on toms mixed to stereo.

time is set to the desired decay so that it turns off before over-ring, rumble, or snare or kick-drum leakage intrudes. Through the whole session, and particularly when the band moves from one song to another, recheck the gate adjustments so they don't open if the wrong drum is struck, because that will cause erratic leakage and a constant changing of the overall drum sound. At the same time, verify that they do open when the appropriate drum is struck; otherwise, that drum will be picked up by the overheads only. Getting all the threshold and release settings just right is a little tricky but not impossible, and it dramatically tightens the overall drum sound.

When only one or two tracks are used for drums, gates may also be needed while recording the kick and snare. For jazz or when brushes are used on the snare, gates may not be appropriate because the snare-to-leakage level is very low when brushes are used.

It's Not the Drums, It's the Drummer I once worked on a pair of back-to-back sessions. The first was a booking for a commercial ad agency. We had three hours to record and mix three 30-second spots. The second session was with a rock band of some note. They had booked six hours to get drum sounds for an album that was to start the following day.

For the agency date, Hal Blaine (legendary studio drummer) had been booked. The set Hal was to play was from Studio Instrument Rental, and it was not one of his regular sets. In fact, it was one of the worst kits I had ever seen SIR deliver. The band's roadies showed up about the same time with a large set of expensive custom drums. By the time Hal arrived, the rented set was all miked up. He was also surprised by the low quality of the set, but he hit around on the drums and said he could make do. He took a roll of duct tape and a drum key out of his briefcase and got to work. I moved into the control room and imagined we might end up using the rock band's kit, but when I raised the faders, the junk set with the lousy heads sounded pretty good. Ten minutes later we were recording, and the set sounded great.

We finished the commercial session on time, and the SIR set was moved into a corner, out of the way. The roadies for the rock band assembled their killer set, the "heavy" rock drummer arrived, and we began. Six hours later, I'd had it. The drummer insisted on getting his sound, but nothing he did made them sound great. Finally, I got him to let me have a go. He headed out to the lounge for a smoke, and while he was gone I moved out his custom set and moved in the set that Hal had tuned. I told the drummer to go into the control room and listen to what I had. Because of how the studio was laid out he couldn't see the set, just my head and the cymbals. I played time and went around the kit a few times. Through the talkback I heard, "Great." The next morning, we called Hal and asked if he would come in and show the drummer how to get a sound. Hal and I had to swear to the "heavy" drummer that no one would ever know.

These days, a lot of drum sounds come out of machines. Drum machines don't take hours to get sounds, and they keep better time than many drummers. Nor do they require a whole studio in which to set up or a lot of microphones. Further, drum machines don't groan throughout the recording session. Even the drummers have embraced the machines. Today, many drummers are making use of the technology, whacking away at black pads connected to sound modules. Modern digital recording often makes use of drum sound replacement, where ordinary acoustic drum sounds are replaced with exceptional-sounding drums. It's all about taste, isn't it?

If you're working with a drum machine, but you'd like to have a live-sounding snare, take the snare output of the drum machine and feed it to a small amplified speaker in another room. Set the small speaker face down on top of a real snare drum, and turn up the amplifier so that every time the drum machine snare occurs, the snare of the real drum will sympathetically rattle.

Position a mic on the real snare drum and mix it in with the sound of the snare coming out of the drum machine. The sound coming through the mic will sound surprisingly real, as though there were a drummer hitting the snare. This same technique works well on any poorly recorded snare-drum track. If the original snare sounds bad, gate it, send the gated signal to the miked snare in the studio, and mix the two together.

But rock-and-roll bands will continue to want the more physical "organic" sound. And I admit, I'm a retro guy—I love real drums and the synergies of a live rhythm section. I like a sound that's unique for that production and doesn't sound like thousands of other productions that use the same samples. I like the synergy when a real drummer plays with a real bass player and a band of musicians. The good news is that drum sales don't seem to be off these days, and there seems to be no shortage of great drummers.

Although I make fun and say that drummers are people who hang out with musicians, I love drums and played them before my career went in a more technical direction. I enjoy working with real drums and a great drummer. I've also found many drummers are interesting conversationalists and philosophers (some more unorthodox then others). Looking back over my career, I recall some of those conversations fondly and as vividly as the recordings of those sessions. I guess some of it is that drummers have more time to hang out. What they do is the cornerstone for all the overdubs that are to follow, but after an intense few days of rhythm sessions, their job is done. They might do some percussion and background vocals, but most of their time is hanging out, reading the paper (or the comics), and philosophizing.

The next chapter turns to the guitar in its many forms, and how to get the sound the guitarist imagines in his wildest dreams.

11 Miking the Guitar and a Bit on Bass

In Chapter 10 I covered recording drums, and without a doubt they are central to rock and roll, but if there is any one instrument that most epitomizes rock and roll and modern pop music, it's the guitar—in particular, the electric guitar. Even if the guitar player can't sing and his songs always need co-writing, if he can smoke a lick, he can be the star and have the band named after him. Guitarists and their guitars are sexy.

On stage the guitarist and his instrument are one. The audience hangs on every note of a performance, but it is fleeting and only in the moment. In a recording, the guitar parts can be played and recorded over and over and analyzed in every way. Such scrutiny builds an audience's expectation that when the guitarist takes center stage, the solo will reflect the solo they have come to know and love on the record. Little do they know that the solo was most likely constructed from dozens of takes. The final assembled solo is then learned by the guitarist to be played on stage. Do all guitarists construct a solo? Yes, to varying degrees—some to the extreme, one note at a time. Can the great guitarists stand on stage and just deliver? Of course they can, but when they record there are no boundaries to what they can do. They can experiment, massage, and modify throughout the recording process to achieve the best result for the production. (The term *best* is naturally very subjective.)

Guitars can sound sweet, gentle, and embracing; they can cry and weep; they can be aggressive, angry, dangerous, and in your face; and of course they can be everything in between. The right sound can be pretty much anything. The tricky bit is sensing what's best for a given production. The band may be a four–piece, but the recording may have a dozen guitars playing different parts with different types of sounds—acoustics, electrics, 6-strings, 12-strings, different amps, stereo, mono, harmony, rhythm, lead, bottleneck slides, power chords, harmonics, whammy bars, overdrives, Leslie cabinets, tremolos, and so on.

The sound for a given part or track is the result of almost an infinite combination of variables, starting with the way the guitarist plays. Then there are the characteristics of that instrument, because every guitar is different. After the guitar are all the effect "pedal" possibilities. The sound is also the amp design and its general condition (old tubes/new tubes, loose fittings, vibrating grill cloth, slightly torn speaker, cabinet vibrating, dodgy connections, and so on). Finally, there is the room you're recording in and the mics you select. The recorded sound of the guitar is the result of all these factors.

An important lesson I learned early in my career was to strive for the amp sound to be as close as possible to the final sound, then touch it up if needed with control-room processing. Adding guitar effects post-recording can work sometimes, but it is risky for a number of reasons. While there can be anxiety that a decision made today would later prove not to be right for the total production, the sound of the pedals and amp effects is integral to the guitar sound and is unique. Simply put, a $4,000 digital processor won't sound like a cheap processor, and if the latter has the sound, go with it.

The Wisdom of Eddie A common problem arises when a planned effect is not added until mixdown. Because the effect is not a part of the ongoing process of production, but a figment of someone's (active) imagination, through the course of subsequent overdubs, the sonic space for the effect becomes filled. Then, to add the effect in mixdown means that something will have to go, or the entire sound image will become cluttered. *Cluttered* is defined in the Eddie Eaires Official Sound Engineering Handbook as "too much shit happening at the same time."

You may not have heard of Eddie before, since his book is only available in Esperanto, but in the Balkans he's very big. His thought-provoking quotes often make it into the English tabloids, although their meaning is sometimes lost in the translation. Often misquoted is his famous statement, "Friends, Romans, countrymen, lend me your ears; mine are plugged with wax."

But when it comes down to it, "best" for the production or an individual part will be decided through a process of creative evolution and negotiation between everyone involved, and in particular the producer and guitarist. It may start with something they may have in mind, or it may just as likely be a passing thought that comes together as the sound emerges to where, at some point, they know it when they hear it.

I used to go crazy recording endless tracks of guitar solos, all too good to erase, but none good enough to use. But in the end, when the solo had been assembled, and it soared out of the second chorus for eight bars into a modulated last verse, or when it brought the song home in the chorus fadeout, I would know it had been worth it.

The bass, on the other hand, is most often very straightforword. This chapter covers some of those times when it is not, particularly when the bass player uses an amp or when a traditional "upright" acoustic bass (or double bass) is to be recorded.

So where do we start a chapter on recording the guitar when there are no wrongs and anything could be just right for a certain part?

If you are recording a basic rhythm guitar that is one of several guitar tracks, one microphone (mono) will probably do it. In general, the more featured the guitar part, the more likely that it should be recorded in stereo (see Figure 11.1). All the various stereo techniques discussed in this book can be used on an acoustic guitar and/or a guitar amp.

Figure 11.1 Stereo pair on a solo acoustic guitar.

Doubling a Rhythm Part A basic rhythm guitar part is often preferred for the rhythm session. Many times I like to fatten up that sound by having the guitar player double the part. After the rhythm track is completed and before moving on to the next song, I will send the guitar player back to the studio. By having the guitarist double the part right after recording the first track, the part will be fresh in his mind, and the sound and performance a near-perfect match. The doubled rhythm will be much fuller, with the original panned to one speaker and the overdub panned to the other.

Acoustic Guitar

A great recording of an acoustic guitar starts with a decent-sounding guitar that stays in tune, new strings, someone who can tune it, and of course, someone who can play. Keep in mind that the focus of the sound does not come from a specific area of an instrument, but its entire body contributes overtones, harmonics, and timbre. Sticking a mic into the sound hole of an acoustic guitar will pick up a lot of rumble, mud, and finger noise. Besides, think about it: Who do you know who listens to a guitar with his ear in the sound hole? The instrument needs to interact with a rich acoustic environment in order for sympathetic vibrations in the wood to generate overtones and sustain that contributes to the sound.

Many acoustic guitars have pickups, and when used can be treated more or less like an electric guitar, but let's start with how to record an acoustic with microphones. Unless you have the acoustic guitar in a separate room or the studio is large, it is difficult to get a good acoustic guitar sound when drums or other loud sounds are happening at the same time. I usually suggest that the acoustic might be recorded as an overdub, or if it does have a pickup, that the pickup output may do for a guide track.

It's best if the player is seated, but make sure the chair doesn't have arms and doesn't squeak. If you don't have a wood floor, this is one of those times to put down an 8-feet-by-8-feet sheet of plywood or chipboard on top of the carpet. Set the chair at the edge of the wood with the guitarist facing the rest of the floor.

I like a bright, compliant microphone with a fair amount of output to bring out the liveliness, brilliance, and overtones of the guitar. My choices are often the Sennheiser MKH 8040 (cardioid), AKG 451 (cardioid capsule), Audio-Technica 4051, or Neumann KM 84. If I want a bit more bottom, the AKG 414 or Oktava MK-103 is a good choice.

Mic placement will vary with conditions. If the acoustic is part of a rhythm section (for instance, in a country music session), I suggest a single mic on a boom pointing at the sound hole about 4 to 6 inches from the instrument (see Figure 11.2). You'll have to watch how the guitarist plays and moves to the music to know just how close you can get the mic without it being hit. This close won't necessarily give you the best acoustic sound, but the track will have a minimum of leakage.

Photo courtesy of Sennheiser.

Figure 11.2 Close-miked acoustic guitar with Sennheiser MKH 8040 cardioid condenser.

Close miking will also be necessary if you're recording a song demo in which the singer is also playing a guitar. In such cases, place the mic (AKG 451 and so on) at the same distance as mentioned a moment ago, but above the guitar's sound hole and pointed slightly downward and away from the singer. The vocal mic is also on a boom and positioned below the mouth, pointing slightly upward (AKG 451 with a cardioid capsule and a windscreen). The angling of the mics will result in less leakage.

You might find that a coincident (XY) positioning (or Blumlein, using for instance a Royer SF-12) at a right angle to the floor (see Figure 11.3) will minimize the phase problems that may arise when mixing the guitar and vocals.

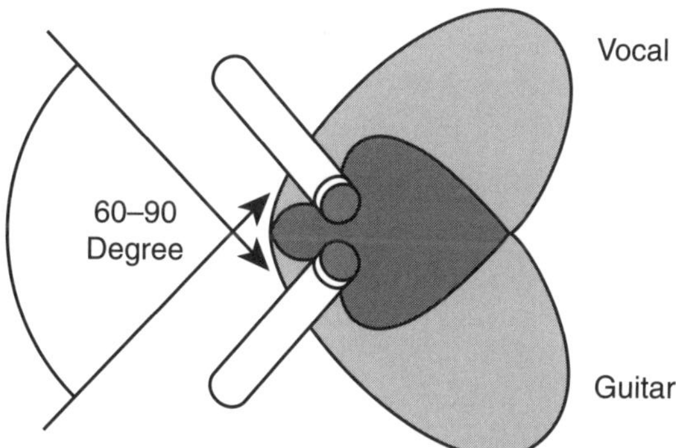

Figure 11.3 XY coincident pair used for guitar vocal combo.

My preference for an acoustic guitar is to record it as an overdub so I can get a more open sound that picks up all the sound and reflections of the instrument in the space. Point the mics toward the center of the guitar 2 to 3 feet from the instrument. Stereo mics are placed at the extremes of a 30- to 45-degree arc in front of the guitar. If you use one mic, start on axis to the front of the guitar, but experiment along that arc. I set the mics about 6 to 10 inches off the floor so that some short, early reflections that enrich the sound are also picked up.

This placement approach is a pretty good starting point for 6- and 12-string acoustic guitars and any other similar instrument, such as dobros, mandolins, bouzoukis, ukuleles, banjos, and so on. There is always some fine-tuning, so move the mic(s) around using a bit of trial and error until it sounds best for the production. Some people will use a less symmetrical approach and mix together one mic nearer to the guitar and one farther away to introduce a certain amount of room sound. When more than one mic is used, always check for phase problems by panning the mics to a single speaker. (Refer to Chapter 8 for remedies.)

A few other things to watch out for: Keep an ear out for heavy breathers, guitarists who like to hum along to the music, toe-tapping, and buttons/jewelry rattling against the body of the guitar, all of which are easily picked up by the mics, particularly when the part is quiet and there is compression on the mics. (See Appendix A, "Compressors and Limiters: A Brief Overview.") As previously mentioned, make sure that headphone leakage is kept to a minimum, particularly for click tracks and guide tracks that are not intended to be included in the final mix, as it will leak into the acoustic mics.

Some finger noise might have to be tolerated to get the right sound, but it can be a problem. Steel strings, depending on how they are wound, will be the worst. Flat wound strings contribute the least finger noise, but they may not necessarily provide the desired sound. You will get fewer finger, pick, and fret squeaks the greater the distance is between the guitar and the mics. If there is a lot of finger noise, try to get the guitar player to lift his fingers instead of sliding them from fret to fret, though this can be a hard habit for a guitarist to break. On more than one occasion, I have erased the finger noise between notes or chords when the guitarist moved from one fret position to another. In a DAW, erasing finger noise is pretty straightforward, but the best is a guitarist that doesn't do it. Many acoustic guitars have pickups, and some engineers use them for recording. The result will have a distinctive electric acoustic sound, and that's fine if that's what you want, but be aware that recording using a pickup will sound different than miking the acoustic in the usual way. In some cases, the sound is a mix of the pickup and the miked sound.

Electric Guitars

Every possible combination of amp and guitar will create any number of unique guitar sounds. Many volumes have been written about guitar and amp tone, and every guitar player magazine describes "the sound" of that issue's hot player. While closely related to getting a great acoustic guitar sound, it is beyond the scope of this book to go into every possibility relating to the sound of electric guitars. New strings, quiet pickups, a properly adjusted guitar, a hum-free amp, new tubes that have been matched (if it's a tube amp), the types of speakers in the cabinet, and so on contribute to the overall sound of a great electric guitar recording. Epiphone introduced one of the first lines of guitars intended to be used with electronic amplification. This was the Epiphone Electar amplifier, made in 1938–39. They were used by such jazz greats as Charlie Christian (see Figure 11.4).

Photo courtesy of Mike Schultz.

Figure 11.4 Epiphone Electar amplifier.

There are two things worth noting: First, a big guitar amp sound can often be created with a small amp that provides better control and tone. Second, all pedal effects should be run with power supplies, not batteries, and only those pedals that are used should be in the guitar's signal path. Suffice it to say that a good-sounding amp and guitar are the starting points for a great recording.

Knowing How to Play the Game A famous guitar player once arrived at the studio with his hand-built custom amp. He hooked it up to a 4-inch speaker installed in a 5.5-inch cube roughly made from particle board. He pushed the amp and speaker beneath the recording console and plugged in an old microphone—the companion to an early Revere tape deck (popular in high school AV departments in the '60s) that he had modified by splicing on a standard three-pin XLR connector. It was a pretty unusual approach, but because the famous guitar player had a commanding track record, the engineer was willing to give it a try. The guitarist began to play along with the track, getting into his sound. After the first pass, the engineer diplomatically said, "Gee, that mic has an awful lot of distortion." The guitar player gave a satisfied smile and replied, "Yeah, I've been looking for that sound for years." Knowing how to play the game, the engineer unhesitatingly volunteered, "Yeah, it's great! We're ready to record."

Here are a few approaches to recording an electric guitar.

Although a guitar amp is almost always used for electric guitar sounds, occasionally the guitar will also be recorded through a direct box. And there are times that a direct box output will be recorded as a separate track from the amp sound. Again, it will depend on the part and what the guitarist is hoping to achieve.

If the basic rhythm session is mostly about getting a great drum sound, both the bass and the guitar may record direct so the only sound in the studio is the drums. The guitar track is then just a guide track and will be replaced by an overdub.

Another possibility is that during remix, the recorded direct sound will be fed through a "reamp" to a guitar amp and miked (see Figure 11.5). All professional recording equipment operates at a balanced +4 line level. In order to interface these signals to guitar amps or stomp boxes, the line-level signal needs to be reduced significantly without adding phase shift, distortion, or noise and without any loss of frequency response. A reamp is designed for that one purpose. The reamp uses a circuit that allows its transformer to mimic the output impedance of a guitar pickup so that the guitar amp input circuit behaves as though it were connected to a guitar.

Some guitarists may also use an effects box that simulates an amp. While it's not quite as tactile or as organic as a blasting amp, and you can't get amp/pickup feedback as is sometimes desired, it is much easier to deal with in a confined space or where no studio really exists.

Figure 11.5 The reamp optimizes the signal between professional audio equipment and a guitar amp.

To use a direct output from a guitar, it is essential that the headphone mix sounds great.

Electric Lady The idea of reamping a DI guitar track has been around for a long time. In 1970, I was fortunate to be hired as an assistant engineer at Electric Lady. When Studio A was completed a few months earlier, Jimi seldom left the studio. But when Studio B was completed, the staff was expanding to accommodate outside clients. I was part of that expansion. At that time, high-output tape formulas had just been introduced, and the Ampex MM1000 recorders at Electric Lady had difficulty erasing this new tape. So, to avoid ghosting from previous takes, Jimi's tapes were never rewound and recorded over. The recorder went into record at the beginning of the session and ran almost continuously until the end of the session. There were often many takes of the same song—sometimes the songs were incomplete bits and pieces, and sometimes it was nothing more than Jimi and the band talking as they worked. Every 20 minutes or so, a new tape went on the machine. There were closets full of 2-inch tapes. When Jimi died, the label wanted rough mixes of all the tapes.

It took months to go through all the tapes. Eventually, various tracks were selected for remix. Often Jimi's amp sound wasn't as good as it could've been (or there was no amp), but in almost all cases, the guitar was also recorded direct. During remix, Jimi's amps were set up in the studio and connected to the DI guitar track and the amps were miked. Electric Lady had a ceiling that was made up of curved surfaces of slightly different sizes, so when the lights were dim, it looked like clouds with bits of light poking through. There were times when it was extremely eerie, with everything totally quiet except for Jimi's voice talking through the speakers, and then his amp blasting in the studio where he had been just a few months before. His presence was definitely there.

When an amp is used in a rhythm section session, it is likely that gobos will surround the guitar amp (see Figure 11.6). If it's not overly loud, the front may be open so the guitarist can see the amp controls. Where the amp is very loud and/or there is concern about the guitar getting into

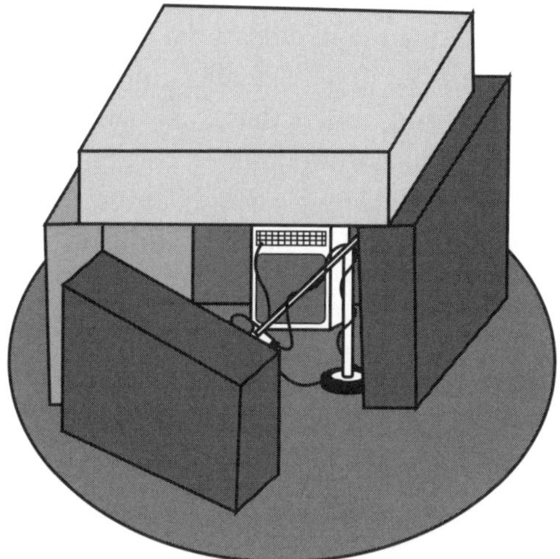

Figure 11.6 When recording several instruments in the same room, it may be useful to make a fully enclosed enclosure of foam rubber gobos. The front gobo will be closed once all settings and microphone adjustments are completed.

the drum overhead mics, gobos can completely surrounded the amp, with a gobo laid across the top to completely close in the amp. The obvious problem is that any amp adjustment is a nightmare. If the guitar amp has a separate speaker and amp head, set up the amp outside the gobos and run a short cord to the speaker. If the amp is cranking, it may be acceptable to suggest that it be turned down and that a louder version could be recorded as an overdub.

In a rhythm session, if there are a lot of other instruments playing in the room, the guitar mic will go right up against the speaker grill (see Figure 11.7). The mic should be positioned to one side of the

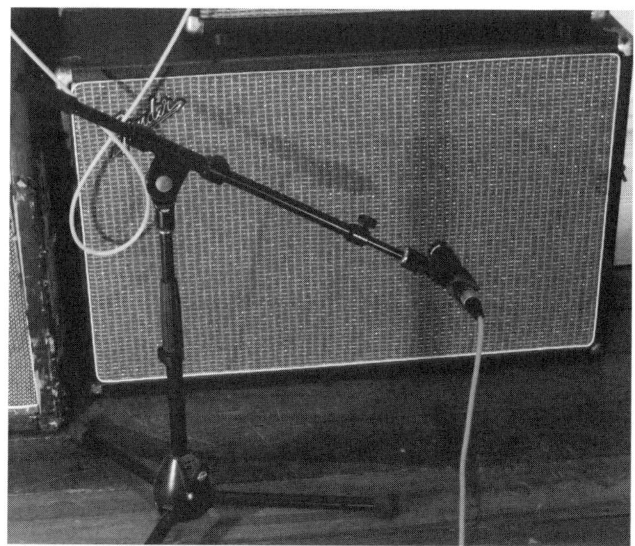

Figure 11.7 Close-miked electric guitar with a Shure SM57.

cone and at a slight angle away from the center. If it is positioned in the middle of the cone, there will be unexpected phase problems and a lack of richness and presence. If it's a smaller amp (Fender Deluxe, Princeton, or Champ), set it on a chair to reduce the low-end rumble that comes when the amp is sitting on the floor. The Shure SM57 (or 58) remains one of the most popular recording mics for electric guitar. To get a good chunky rhythm sound, you might also try a Sennheiser MD421 (see Figure 11.8) or an Electro-Voice RE20 (see Figure 11.9); both can handle the sound levels.

Photo courtesy of Sennheiser.

Figure 11.8 Sennheiser MD421. A classic cardioid dynamic microphone for guitar, bass, kick, and other drums.

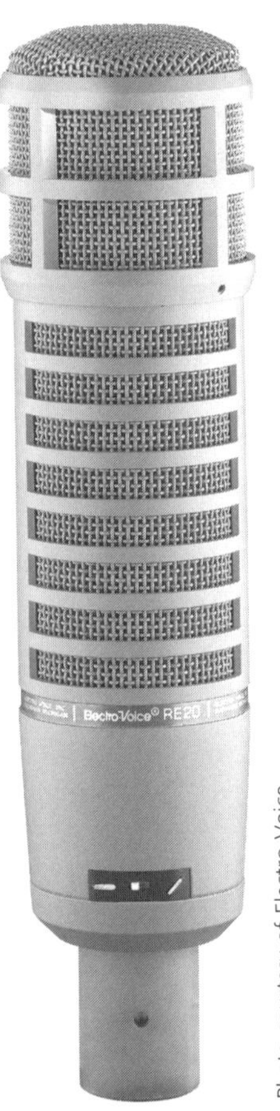

Photo courtesy of Electro-Voice.

Figure 11.9 Electro-Voice RE20. A classic cardioid dynamic microphone for guitar, bass, kick, and other drums.

For an overdubbed electric guitar, I prefer to place the amp on a 6- to 8-inch rubber block, so the amp is decoupled from the floor, and the mic(s) can be in direct line with the speakers. I use a reflective surface on the floor in front of the amp and under the microphone(s). If the production seems to call for a chunky sound, mike the guitar amp like a rhythm session, but otherwise, a good starting point is with the mics 2 to 4 feet away from the amp and 6 to 8 inches off the floor.

You may also decide to use some gobos to change the acoustic characteristics of the space around the amp. This is particularly important if the amp cabinet is open-backed, as is the case with several classic Fender designs. The sound coming out of the back is to blend with what's coming out of the front. If it's too close to a wall or is blocked off by gobos, the amp won't sound quite right. Such designs need a certain amount of space between the back and a reflective surface for the rear sound to bounce back to the front.

All these designs are different, so you'll need to experiment. With an open-backed cabinet, you might also try a mic behind the speaker that's mixed with the front mics, but be careful of phase cancellation. In many cases the rear mic will need to have its polarity reversed.

In some cases guitar/amp feedback will be an essential part of the sound; in other cases it won't. If the guitarist intends to stick the guitar right up against the front of the speaker to get feedback, make sure the mics are neither in the way, nor blocked by his body when he is in front of the amp.

Similar to miking an acoustic guitar, use as a guide the 30-degree arc in front of the amp and place the stereo pair at the two ends of the arc, pointing toward the speaker (see Figure 11.10). For a closer and deeper sound, move the mic(s) toward the amp. For a more distant, open, and "natural" sound, pull the mic(s) back.

As for what mics I like for electric guitar overdubs, I like my old standby the AKG 414, the Neumann U-87, or more recently the Oktava MK-219, or the RØDE NT1-A. (If the mic has adjustable patterns, I would most often use cardioid.) For something a little different, try a Royer 121. The figure-8 pickup pattern captures some of the room as well as the guitar amp.

Playing from the Control Room

Often a guitar player will want to play from the control room in order to hear exactly what is being recorded. So, a cable will be needed to connect the guitar to the amp in the studio. If there is no interference, a wireless system may work just fine, but if a cable is used, here are a few suggestions.

To eliminate the loss of signal and high frequencies from a long, high-impedance lead, the guitar should be connected to a direct box in the control room with a low-impedance line from it to another direct box (or a reamp) in the studio, which is connected to the guitar amp (see Figure 11.10). The direct box in the control room balances the guitar signal and drops the impedance, and at the other end, another direct box (or reamp) raises the impedance and unbalances the signal right before it goes into the amplifier. There is a certain amount of

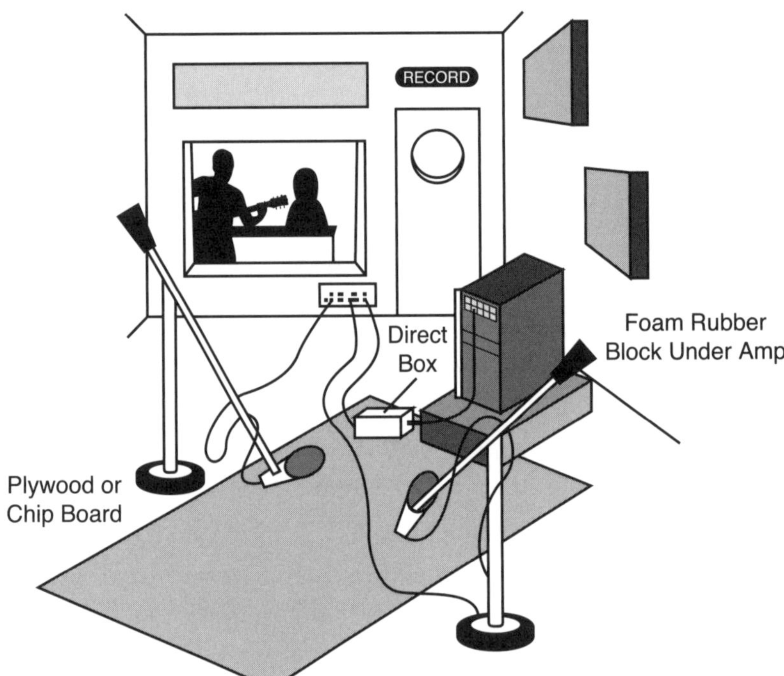

Figure 11.10 Stereo mic placement for solo guitar amp. Guitarist is playing from the control room.

loss through the two transformers, but it's nothing compared to the signal loss through a long high-impedance line. The direct boxes have both male and female 3-pin XLR plugs so that the low-impedance sides of the transformers of two direct boxes can be easily connected with a standard microphone cord. Many studios have a permanent "playing from the control room" setup with a cable and connections just for this purpose.

I quite like working with the guitarist in the control room when there are many overdubs. It improves communication and speeds up the production process. But it's very important to determine how much the guitar is prone to pick up the sound of the monitor speakers or even talking in the control room. This will depend on the settings and the design of the guitar, so it's a good idea to solo the track's playback in a quiet section of the track to make sure the leakage is acceptable. Hollow-body electrics will be the most susceptible. In many cases, the best way to avoid the problem is by monitoring through headphones while recording.

While pickup hum is always a problem (as covered in Chapter 6), it will occur more frequently when the guitar player is in the control room because of the electromagnetic radiation from all the equipment, display screens, hard drives, and power supplies. The level of hum will change depending on where the guitar player is standing and the direction he is facing, so have the guitarist move around the room to locate the area where the hum is least noticeable. Sometimes the hum can be minimized by connecting a wire between a well-grounded point in the control room and the tail piece of the guitar. Also ask the guitarist to turn down the guitar when it's not being played, or the compression will greatly exaggerate any ongoing background hum.

Big Sound from Small Packages

Many guitarists find they can get "the sound" by running direct through some sort of guitar effect, amp modeler, such as the SansAmp PSA-1, or tube-amplified device that substitutes for a guitar amp, then using a small self-powered speaker and miking it. A 4-inch self-powered speaker, such as the Fostex 6301, is pretty good for this application. In a recording environment, a practice amp, such as a Fender Princeton or a Peavey Windsor, will often sound "bigger" than a large amp, and it's often much easier to get controllable feedback with a little amp.

Give This a Try To add more complexity to the sound, when you're doubling a guitar part, move the microphones a little bit before recording the second track.

Depending on the recording medium (tape or some DAWs), you will be able to varispeed the recording. This means you can vary the pitch by changing the tempo (or speed of the tape). For instance, slightly slowing down a tape's playback also lowers the pitch and the tempo. If you can varispeed, try tuning the track down slightly and retune the guitar to the track. (It's a good idea to have a tuning note at the top of the track.) When the track is returned to normal tuning, the new track will sound brighter, and fast parts will sound crisper.

Slides into solos and licks can make the guitar part sound more exciting and can provide a sense of anticipation to the beginning of a solo. Several times I've recorded a track of finger slides. Adjust the guitar amp to feature the string slides, and then mike as usual. This track is then blended into the mix.

Getting great-sounding harmonics can be difficult; they are often best managed as an overdub on their own.

A Bit on the Bass...

Like guitars, there are electric basses (4- and 5-string) and acoustic basses. (The latter is often called a *double bass*.)

It's not unusual for the bass player to only record "direct" through a DI box. I've done many sessions where the bass player showed up without an amp. Many others will want a combination of DI and amp.

To get a bass sound, I'll start with a note on using a DI with the electric bass. I'll then move on to miking a bass amp and then an acoustic bass.

Compression is commonly used while recording a DI electric bass. The envelope (see Figure 11.11) of the electric bass has a pluck that is significantly louder than the sustain. In order to bring the pluck's level closer to the sustain's level, a compressor is widely used during recording (see Figure 11.12). A bass amp sound will have less attack than a direct sound because the mass of the speaker is unable to respond to the transient of the pluck, thus the amped sound needs little (if any) compression. A compressed DI bass will form a solid, up-front beat for the rest of the band. A compression ratio of 4:1 with a threshold setting that affects just the peaks will tighten the sound without affecting the dynamics too much. (See Appendix A for a brief overview of compressors and limiters.)

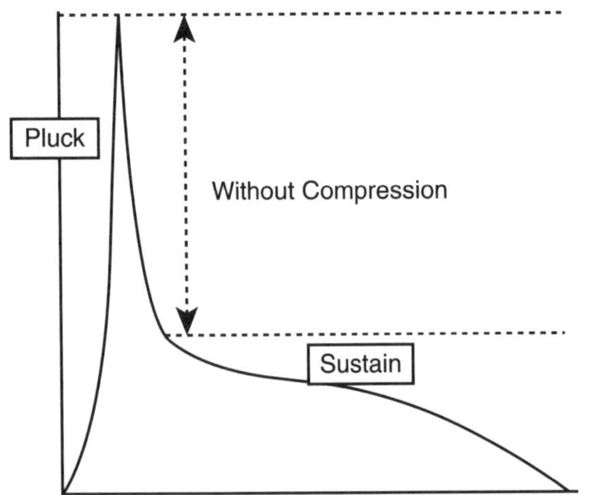

Figure 11.11 Bass envelope without compression.

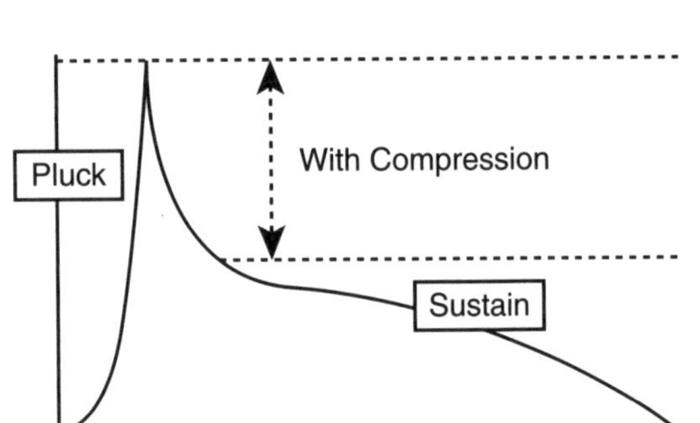

Figure 11.12 Bass envelope with compression.

Bass cabinets and speakers can wear out and contribute distortion. Low-frequency waves are powerful enough that, over time, they can loosen the various laminations in a cabinet—for instance, the glue between sheets of plywood, or where corners are sealed, or where inner sound board is bonded to the exterior covering. The speakers themselves can generate an opposing magnet field as the cone moves back and forth and can demagnetize the speaker, causing it to sound less sharp than when it was new.

When a bass player uses an amp, hope that it won't be outrageously loud, because bass is nearly impossibly to isolate from its surroundings. I've also found that very loud bass speakers lose distinctness as they reach their point of breaking up, though I'm willing to concede that it's a matter of taste.

To mike an electric bass amp, you'll probably want to go with a mono setup. Although I have miked a bass with a stereo pair, it is seldom satisfactory because the long bass waves tend to create nasty phase problems between the two mics. When the stereo pair is panned left and right, the sound of the bass seems to move around the center and doesn't give a solid sound most people want from the bass. When the track is heard in mono, the bass may lose some bottom and sounds like it's going through a phase-shifter effect.

The bass will usually be connected to the DI as well as the amp. The two signals may go to two tracks or be mixed. When using a mic and direct box, always check for phase and polarity problems. It is common to find that the direct signal will be out of phase with the mic signal due to phase shift in the bass amp's electronics. You may get a better sound by reversing the polarity of the direct signal (refer to Chapter 4) or, if you're using a DAW, you can align the waveforms by introducing a short delay into one of the two signals.

If the amp is small, the bass player may prefer the amp to sit on the floor because this enhances the low end. If it's larger, you might suggest setting it on a block of rubber to decouple it from the floor, particularly if the floor is not solid. Like the electric guitar, you should place gobos around the amp. Although the gobos won't contain the long bass waves, they will reduce the leakage coming from the drums and guitar into the bass mics. Set the mic about 12 to 18 inches from the amp off center to the center of the cone. If the cabinet has more than one speaker, choose one—don't place the mic between the two (or four), because it is likely you'll have weird phase problems.

Also, some bass cabinets have an active driver and a passive cone. In other words, they both look like speakers from the outside, but only one of them is actually connected to the amp. The other cone is driven by the sound pressure changes inside the cabinet. Bass players using such boxes usually know what's going on and can tell you which cone is active, and that will be the one to focus the mic on. My mic choices are all large-diaphragm mics, such as the dynamic AKG D 12, Sennheiser MD421, the EV RE20, the ribbon Coles 4038, or a Telefunken RM-5C. There are many large-diaphragm condensers that could be used, such as the AKG C 12 in bidirectional.

An acoustic bass has a sound very different than the electric bass. It generates a traditional jazz, pre-electric popular music, or classical bass sound. These days it is rare for an acoustic bass to be used for recording anything other than jazz and classical. Some have been modified to have a built-in contact pickup that is commonly used when playing a gig. When recording, the pickup might be used, but it is much more likely that the bassist is looking for an acoustic sound. If the instrument is played in a room where there is a lot of other sound from the drums, piano, guitar, and so on, you might try using a small-diaphragm, physically short condenser (such as a Neumann KM 84, RØDE NT55, or Mercenary KM-69), wrapping it in some foam, and wedging it into one of the two F holes. If the part doesn't require very low bass, you might also try a lapel mic attached (use Blu Tack) to the underside of the fingerboard, right where it ends over the bass's body.

Some bass players use an AMT S25B for live gigs, and it also does well for recording (see Figure 11.13). The S25B is a specially designed condenser cardioid for acoustic bass. The

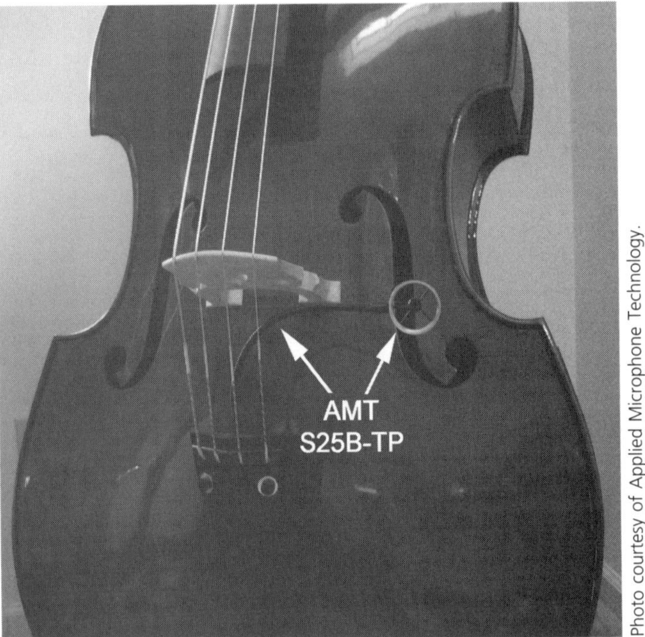

Figure 11.13 AMT S25B-TP condenser mic and suspension.

Figure 11.14 Blue Bottle large-diaphragm tube condenser with (B2) bidirectional capsule.

Photo courtesy of Sennheiser.

Figure 11.15 Sennheiser MKH 20 omni condenser.

mic is suspended in a four-point isolation ring at the end of a gooseneck that connects to the tailpiece, thus eliminating sympathetic vibrations and handling noise. The mic's position stays constant no matter how much the bass player moves around.

My preference would be to have the mic 8 to 12 inches or so away from the instrument, roughly 2 to 4 inches above where the player is doing most of the fingering or bowing, and with a slight downward angle on the mic. On bass I like a large- or medium-diaphragm condenser, such as a Telefunken Ela M 251, a Blue Bottle microphone with a B2 (bidirectional) capsule (see Figure 11.14), a Neumann U 47 FET, an Audio-Technica 4050, or a RØDE NT1-A. A Sennheiser MKH 20 is also interesting. The MKH 20 is a midsize condenser capsule in an omni housing (see Figure 11.15). While the omni is more prone to pick up leakage, I think it also provides a richer low end then a cardioid.

The guitar is at the heart of rock and roll. The bass is central to most pop music production, and great sound is essential. This chapter has provided a foundation and a starting point for getting any number of unique guitar and bass sounds.

In the next chapter, we'll look at the acoustic piano and the many ways to capture one of the most difficult and complex instruments to record.

12 Miking Piano

A precursor of the piano, the harpsichord, was a favorite instrument of England's Henry V and Queen Catherine in the early 1400s. A harpsichord is much like a piano, as it has a sound harp and strings that are played by a keyboard. The difference is the harpsichord plucks the strings rather than hitting them, as the piano does. By the early 1700s, an instrument called a *pianoforte* appeared. It was louder than the harpsichord, and its keyboard had a mechanism that struck the stings. From this instrument, all pianos have evolved.

For more than six hundred years, the piano and the instruments that predated the piano have been at the heart of popular music. Keep in mind that what we call *classical music* was, in its time, pop music. Brahms, Puccini, Bach, and Mozart were pop stars of their day.

For centuries, the piano has held a place of pride in the parlors of numerous family homes. Even the working class had a prized upright in their home, and more than one person would be able to play it. Singing around the piano was the evening's musical entertainment prior to the gramophone. Even after the record arrived, many families had a piano, and children learned to play it.

Fast-forwarding through the 20th century, every type of music has been performed and recorded on the piano. When samplers appeared, many expected that they would replace real pianos, but their demise was grossly exaggerated because, given the opportunity, most keyboard players still prize those times when they can make music on a great-sounding piano. Yes, electronic keyboards can generate a passable piano sound, but only an acoustic piano can fill an acoustic space in a certain way. Musicians will choose concert halls and recording studios based on the reputation of the piano that is there. A 9-foot grand piano is probably not going to be included in the instruments available at a small studio, but many studios do have a 5-foot baby grand or a good-sounding upright. A good-sounding piano, well recorded, adds much more to a production than just the sound that comes out of an electronic keyboard. The sound and tactile feel of a piano can inspire a performance.

Pianos are complex instruments. They are large and have myriad moving parts that can groan, squeak, and clunk. Components of a piano's total sound come out from everywhere, and they will sympathetically vibrate to any sound in the space it shares. A piano's construction, how it is set up and tuned, and the room that it is in will all contribute to how it sounds.

The Piano Tuner and Finding a Piano When you decide to have a piano and make it a feature of your studio, the phone number of a piano tuner will become one of your top-10 speed dials. It's a good idea to look around to find the tuner for you before you get the piano, because the tuner can help you choose the right piano and may actually know when a good one becomes available. The tuner you're looking for is someone who can do more than basic tuning. He needs to know how to keep the mechanism quiet, properly regulated, and feeling good to play. The tuner will occasionally also need to change the characteristics of the hammers. There is a considerable difference in the hardness of the hammers, depending on the style of music. (Rock/pop music will generally use pianos with harder hammers, and classical and jazz pianos will often have pianos with softer hammers). It's an added bonus if the tuner will tune for you in trade for studio time.

It is rare for anyone in the studio business to buy a new piano. They often come in trade for studio time, or someone calls the studio offering a piano for a good price. I know of a few studios that placed a small ad in a recycler shopping guide saying they were looking for a great-sounding piano that didn't need to look too good. Many of these pianos have not been maintained, so they will not sound very good when you first see them. Perhaps the piano is available because the person who played it has died or is no longer interested or able to play it. Hence, you need to have the piano tuner before you acquire a piano to make sure that it's a diamond in the rough. It's also worth mentioning that many times the owner who is parting with a great piano considers the instrument a loved part of the family and will be looking to find it a new home that will appreciate it. This may be more important than the money.

If the piano is a feature of the studio, it should be tuned regularly. When a prospective client tours the studio and sits down at the piano, it should impress him. And, of course, if a client wants to use the piano on a whim, it should sound as good as possible. If the studio is prone to having radical changes in humidity and temperature, it's recommended that a piano humidifier/temperature controller should be installed. A particularly good system is made by Dampp-Chaser (www.pianolifesaver.com).

Recording Piano

The best approach for recording a piano will depend on the sound and design of the piano and the style of music. In pop music and overdubbing, the part will also determine the recording approach. Unless there are track or input limitations, I always record the piano in stereo because its size provides one of the best and most natural sound panoramas. The listener is able to imagine the pianist's hands as the sound of each note travels between the speakers.

Pianos can be divided into uprights and grands. As most musicians know, a grand has its sounding board and strings parallel to the floor, and an upright has a soundboard and string vertical to the floor.

In general, an upright will be miked from the front, and a grand from above the sounding board. If a deeper low-frequency range is desired, the back (or bottom) of the sounding board will be miked. For most piano recordings, a very compliant, bright microphone—usually a condenser—is the preferred choice. (I'll mention my mic choices as I discuss the different setups later in this chapter.) If the mic is placed reasonably close to the instrument, a capsule pad may be necessary to keep the internal preamp from overloading. Identical microphones are often used to make up a stereo pair, but depending on how the instrument is miked, two different but compatible mics may sound best. For instance, if you're close miking (as is often done when recording rock), a couple of small-diaphragm condensers will work well, but when you're farther from the strings (for a more classical, pop, or jazz sound), a larger-diaphragm condenser mic will be a better choice on the low end, with a small capsule for the higher piano strings.

Piano in a Rhythm Session

In general, in a louder session that intends to have a piano as part of the production, it may be best to suggest using a *scratch* electronic keyboard while cutting the basic rhythm tracks and save the acoustic piano for an overdub. However, if the acoustic piano is an important part of the track, and playing it rather than an electronic keyboard creates a better feel, then it should be used. It's really a matter of how much leakage, from whatever is in the studio, will enter the piano mics and what is acceptable.

To record a piano as part of a rhythm session, open the piano lid just enough to get the mic booms inside the piano. Usually the short lid support gives just enough opening. For a percussive rock sound, position the mics as high as you can above the hammers (about 3 to 4 inches, without touching the lid) and a couple of inches to the rear of them. Separate the mics by about 2 feet and angle them slightly inward, depending on the note range where the musician is playing (see Figure 12.1).

My mic choice is a pair of AKG 451, Neumann KM 84, RØDE NT55, or Oktava MK-012 cardioid capsules. For a richer low end or more sustain, position one mic near the high hammers and move the low-end mic to over the fourth or fifth hole in the piano harp (see Figure 12.2). For this positioning, the mic selection could be the same as the previous placement, or I might use a large-diaphragm condenser for the piano's sound hole. My mic choice for a large diaphragm would usually be a Telefunken Ela M 251, AKG 414 or C 12, or Oktava MK-220.

The piano should be wrapped in quilts (or a piano bag, as mentioned in Chapter 7) and surrounded with gobos to help prevent leakage from the other instruments into the piano microphones. Having the piano near an absorptive wall will provide a bit more isolation, but allow enough space to move microphones without the assistance of a contortionist.

Even with a lot of effort put into isolating the piano, there will be a certain amount of snare leakage and externally generated low-end rumble from the kick (and possibly a bass amp). How much will depend on how loud everything else is in the studio. The entire piano will resonate with the loud rock sounds that are happening in the room. Unfortunately, tight-miking a piano

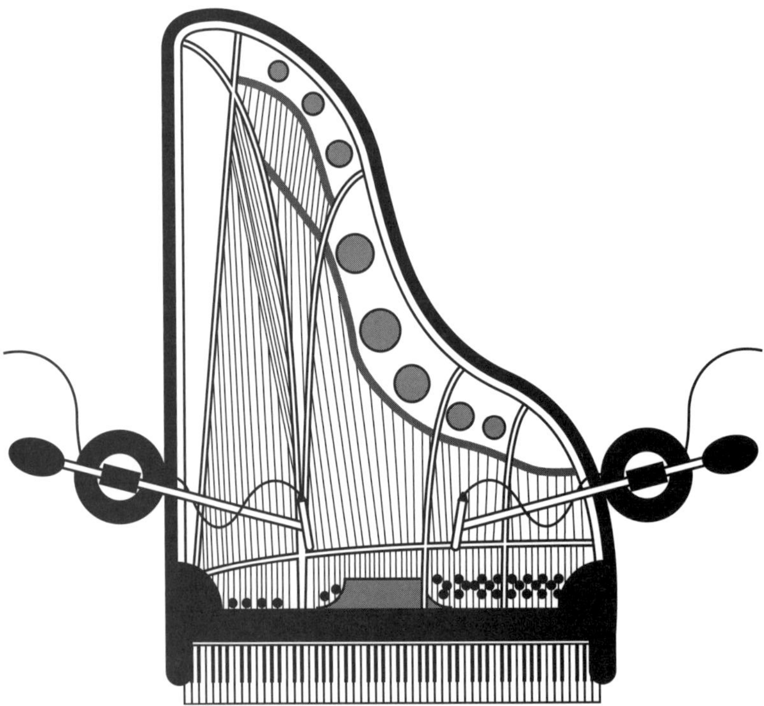

Figure 12.1 A stereo pair of small-diaphragm condensers positioned above the hammers of a grand piano. (The lid has been removed.)

surrounded with padding and gobos has its disadvantages. The sound inside the restricted space of the piano cabinet can sometimes vibrate so much that, depending on the part, the sound can lack clarity, and the piano will end up having to be re-recorded anyway. Another problem is that the pianist won't be able to hear very well what he or she is playing. If the sound in the room is not that loud, fold back the quilt where the pianist is sitting.

Then there are times, such as when recording a modern jazz trio, when I'll set up the band as if they were playing a live performance and use a minimum of leakage control. The open sound in the room will often inspire the best performances, particularly when improvisation is central to the composition. Since these sorts of recordings seldom require re-recording individual parts, whatever leakage there is adds to the organic quality. However, it is important to make sure while recording that the control room mix sounds pretty close to what will be a final mix and everyone is happy with it. If there are many changes during remix, all the leakage will also be affected, and everything will sound highly processed.

When the piano is recorded by itself, you won't need to surround it with gobos and quilts. I prefer to move it away from the walls and, in the case of a grand piano, open the top to its maximum height or remove it all together.

Figure 12.2 Stereo technique for piano I learned from Wally Heider. (The lid has been removed.)

Removing the Piano Lid For overdubbing a piano, I have on occasion removed the lid of a grand piano or the removable front and top of an upright. I think it gives a cleaner sound that doesn't bounce around inside the piano. The lid on most grand pianos is secured by hinges that are held together with removable pins. Pull the pins, and two people can gently lift off the lid. In the case of the upright, the front and top come off any time someone tunes one. There are usually a couple of knobs on the inside holding on the front, and the top will usually just lift off. Whether you would do such a thing in a featured classical or jazz session would be a matter of the performer's taste in the sound.

Grand Piano

For a grand piano overdub, if the lid remains on, open it up to its full extent. For a percussive rock sound, the placement is very similar to when the lid is closed (see Figure 12.3), but the open lid provides more space for the mics to move a little higher above the hammers and strings.

For a less percussive, more open and spacious sound, position the mics 8 to 10 inches above and 12 to 14 inches to the rear of the hammers, separated by about 12 to 18 inches and angled slightly toward the hammers (see Figure 12.4).

Photo courtesy of Sennheiser.

Figure 12.3 A stereo pair of Sennheiser MKH 40 cardioid condenser mics positioned above the hammers.

My mic choice for grand piano overdubs is a pair of AKG 451, Sennheiser MKH 40, RØDE NT55, or Oktava MK-012 cardioid capsules. For a richer low end or more sustain, position one mic near the high hammers and move the second one to above the last few holes in the piano harp. In the latter positioning, the mic selection could be the same as the previous placement, or I might use a large-diaphragm condenser for the low end of the piano (see Figure 12.5). My mic choice would usually be a Neumann U 87 or M 150, a RØDE Classic II, a Telefunken Ela M 251, a Sennheiser MKH 800, an AKG 414 or C 12, or an Oktava MK-220.

Sometimes a mic is placed underneath the piano, but I've never cared for that sound, and this placement tends to pick up a lot of pedal noise.

For classical piano music, open the lid to its full extent and move the mics back from the sound board and into the room.

Referring back to Chapter 8, I prefer a type of AB approach using two omni (as opposed to cardioid) directional microphones—one at the end of the piano, about five degrees to the right of center, and one about parallel and approximately a foot behind the keyboard and facing the piano's opening (see Figure 12.6). Both mics should be about 3 to 4 feet from the instrument, about 4 to 5 feet off the ground, and slightly tipped downward toward the piano harp. If the

Photo courtesy of Sennheiser.

Figure 12.4 A pair of Sennheiser MKH 800 variable pattern condenser mics in cardioid.

sound has too much of the room, I would go to bidirectional or cardioid patterns facing the piano. The microphones of choice would be a pair of AKG C 12, Telefunken Ela M 251, AKG 414 or C 12, Oktava MK-220, RØDE Classic II or NT 1000, or Groove Tubes MD1b mics.

While the approach I've outlined is my preference, I have recorded pianos using all the other stereo approaches described in Chapter 8. Refer to Chapter 8 to see these various techniques compared.

Upright Acoustic Piano

As described in the "Removing the Piano Lid" sidebar, the front of an upright piano is pretty easy to remove, and my preferred rock-and-roll approach to recording an upright is to remove the front (see Figure 12.7). The pair of mics is positioned 6 to 8 inches away from the strings and about a foot above the keyboard, with the mics tipped downward toward the hammers. My choice in mics would be a pair of AKG 451 or 414, Oktava MK-012, Neumann KM 84 or KM 184, or Studio Projects C4 mics.

To get a more open upright piano sound, continue to have the front of the piano open. Position the mics 4 to 5 feet from the piano, behind the pianist. Separate them by approximately the width of the piano, and place them 4 to 5 feet high and slightly angled inward toward the pianist.

Figure 12.5 Sennheiser MKH 40 (cardioid) condenser at a near right angle to the keyboard, aimed toward the high end of the piano, and a Sennheiser MKH 800 (cardioid) at the end of the piano, pointing toward the low end of the piano.

Figure 12.6 Classical miking approach.

Figure 12.7 Stereo miking for upright. Front panels above and below the keyboard have been removed.

If for some reason it's not possible to remove the top and front of the upright piano (or if you're doing a rhythm session with other sounds in the room), there are a couple of miking approaches that can work. The top of an upright is most often hinged. When the lid is opened, you usually have an opening of 6 to 8 inches. Position a couple of mic stands with booms at both ends of the piano. Raise them to their full height (5 feet or so) and extend the two booms down into the piano opening. The cramped space will make positioning a bit difficult and will limit the choice of mics to ones that are short (such as a Neumann KM 84 or KM 184, a Mercenary Audio MFG KM-69, or a Berliner CM-33). Position the mics so they are pointed toward the strings and separated from each other by about a third to half of the width of the keyboard. This will give a good stereo sound, but it may be a bit boomy, requiring some low-frequency roll-off.

If the space between the piano harp and the front of the upright's cabinet is too narrow, position the booms just above the opening and separate as before. Point them down toward the hammers. This will create a reasonable stereo image with a degree of hammer percussion. Boominess will continue to be a problem. Damping the sound board may help by attaching heavy quilts to the rear of the piano.

This chapter has covered the many ways you can record an acoustic piano. These approaches will hold you in good stead nearly all the time. But there will be times when experimentation is in the air. Such experiments with the piano are referred to in experimental music circles as *prepared piano*. How much experimentation you might do will depend on your willingness to alter the piano. Miking the piano, then running the signal into a guitar amp with tremolo or a Leslie cabinet can be pretty interesting and does not alter the piano.

There are many ways to make a unique piano sound. Two that I recall use tacks and paperclips. Thumbtacks in the hammers create the sound of honky tonk, and paperclips dangling off every string and vibrating with every note of a slow piece of music create a very menacing sound. So, in closing, don't be afraid to experiment when the opportunity permits.

In the next chapter we'll take a look at vocals and solo—the icing on the cake.

13 Miking Solo Acoustic Instruments and Vocals

In previous chapters we covered the main instruments that make up popular music production—drums, bass, guitar, and piano. This chapter explores how to record vocals and the many types of solo acoustic instruments that come into the studio. You probably know what a trumpet, violin, or bagpipe is. But when you hear them up close and in the flesh, it's different than when you hear them on a recording or on a stage 50 feet away. For instruments that you often work with, such as the acoustic guitar, you'll build up experience so you'll know what you're going to do, but the first time you hear an Aeolian wind harp, a beer bottle organ, a daxophone, or a bamboo saxophone, you'll have to figure out where the best sound comes out. And while there is no mystery about where the sound for vocals comes out, every vocal session can be different. Every singer is unique, and the best way to capture their vocal may be the way you usually record vocals—but it can also turn out to be something completely different. It will be the right microphone (whatever that might be), set in the right space, and coupled with the best mood and setting for the singer to deliver a performance that is magical and beyond just the sound.

Taking a Solo

Most of the time, a solo instrument should be set up in a "live" area of the studio. In a dead studio, plywood on the floor may be needed. One of the stereo microphone techniques (usually AB) should be used so that the solo steps out in front of the speakers. Needless to say, to record in stereo at least two tracks are needed, but depending on what you're attempting to achieve, you may decide to use more tracks and additional mics, particularly if you're planning a surround mix.

In general, solo acoustic instruments should be miked at a distance, in order to pick up the overall sound that comes from the entire instrument. This gives the sound space. How much distance depends on the instrument and the space in which it's played. So, does that mean 6 inches or 4 feet? It's very hard to say what the best distance is for any particular instrument, and there will always be exceptions.

For a particularly unique sound, a combination of close and distant miking may also be appropriate. For instance, for a "breathy" flute sound, as was associated with Jethro Tull, you'll need a close mic right near the flute player's lips, and one or two more distant mics for the overall flute texture.

Many times the larger an instrument, the more likely the sound will emanate from all around it. The first step will always be to have the musician play the instrument and then move around it, listening for the place in the room where it sounds best. Be sure to add height to your movement, because the best-sounding place will often be near a reflective floor. Essentially, use your ears as a starting point and position the mics where the instrument sounds best.

Specifically, in general (yes, I know that's a conflict of terms, but it's hard to avoid being too general while not being too specific), if the instrument is something small and not very loud, I would probably start with a pair of microphones a foot or so from the instrument, separated by 9 to 12 inches (see Figure 13.1). To reduce comb filtering, none of the distances should be equal. While the 3-to-1 rule provides the least chance for comb filtering, you may not be satisfied with the greater distance from the instrument or the wider stereo separation.

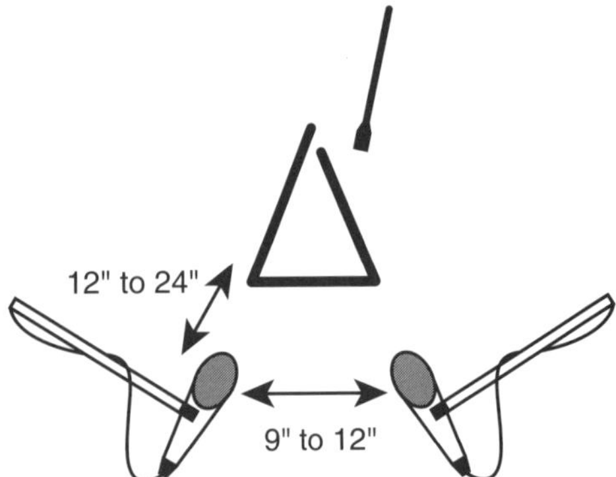

Figure 13.1 Miking small handheld instruments.

A larger, louder instrument might have its mic placement 3 to 5 feet from the instrument and separated from one another by 5 or 6 feet. There are times when closer (1 to 2 feet) will sound better for the production, and other times when farther away (6 to 8 feet) is better. A 2- to 3-foot range will usually have a harder-edged pop sound, with more of the sound coming straight from the bell of the horn, the stick's contact with the drum, the attack of the strings, and so on. As the mics move away from the instrument, the sound will mellow, and the attack will blend into the sound of the surrounding reverberation.

The stereo image may also work well if one of the two mics is closer to the instrument, and the other is farther away (for instance, one mic is 18 inches from the instrument, and the other is 30 inches);

see Figure 13.2. Finally, always be mindful that when you have two mics in close proximity to each other, there will be comb filtering (see Chapter 4), so always check how the mics sound when they are combined to mono.

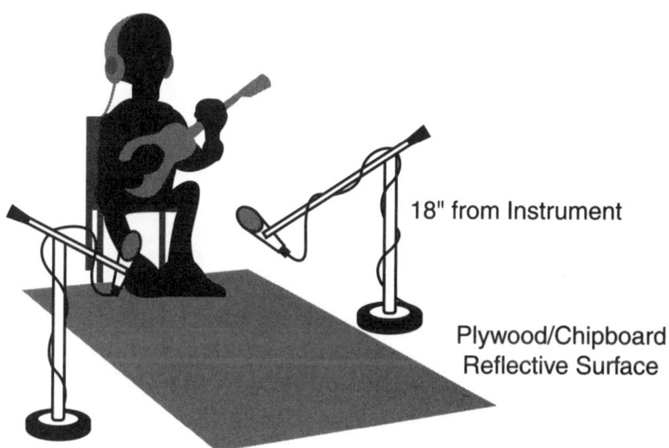

Figure 13.2 An interesting stereo image may also come when one of the mics is positioned closer to the instrument and the other farther away.

Depending on the instrument, you can have problems if the musician moves the instrument around while he plays. This can cause any phasing or comb filtering to draw attention to itself as the distances between the sound source and the mics change with the movement. Also, the instrument will lose its center as it moves between the pair of mics. (Or perhaps that's what you want.) A shifting center is most obvious with small instruments (such as handheld percussion, flute, recorder, and so on), where the mics are closer together and nearer to the sound source. If this is happening, mark the floor with an X and give the musician a target to play toward by positioning a third mic 2 to 3 feet in front of the performer and between the microphones. Position it at a comfortable height for where the performer holds the instrument, and don't bother to plug it in (unless you just want to be wild and crazy).

Microphone selection will vary depending on the instrument, but the suggestions in previous chapters will apply. I've also added a few extra ones. For instruments that have a higher musical range, I would usually choose a brighter small-diaphragm condenser mic, such as an AKG 451 (see Figure 13.3), Neumann KM 84 or KM 184, Studio Projects C4, Berliner CM-33, or Oktava MK-012 (see Figure 13.4). I think the Samson CL2 is also a very good value (see Figure 13.5).

For a richer low end, I like larger-diaphragm condensers, such as the Neumann U 87, AKG 414 or 214, Oktava MK-220 (see Figure 13.6), AKG C 12, Telefunken Ela M 251, RØDE Classic II or NT1000, or a Groove Tubes MD1b (see Figure 13.7). If the mic had selectable patterns I would most often go with a cardioid pattern, but the choice of patterns will be decided based

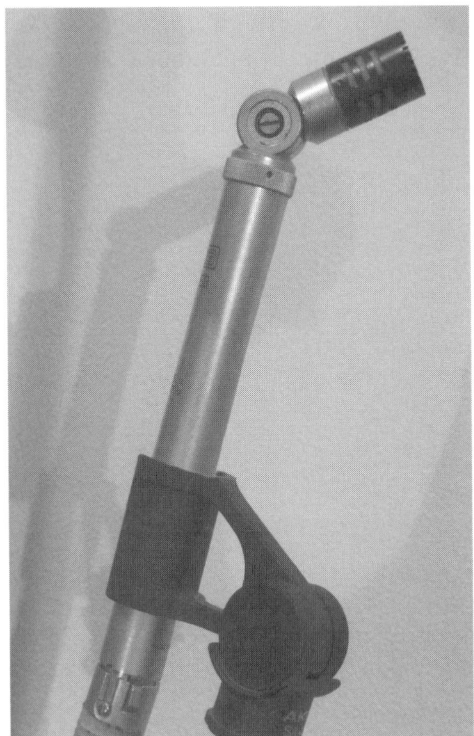

Figure 13.3 AKG 451 CK 1 cardioid capsule with swivel.

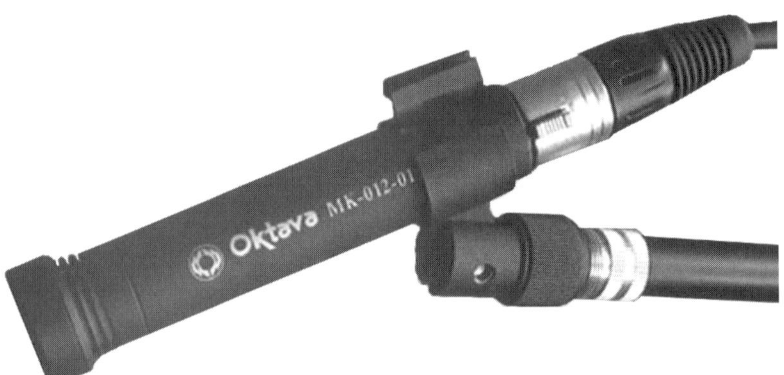

Figure 13.4 Oktava MK-012 with cardioid capsule.

on how much of the room I want to include in the sound—I'd use a cardioid for less room and an omni for more room. It's also worth a reminder that when many cardioid mics are close to the sound source, there is a proximity effect that enhances the low end. This can be desirable or not, depending on the sound.

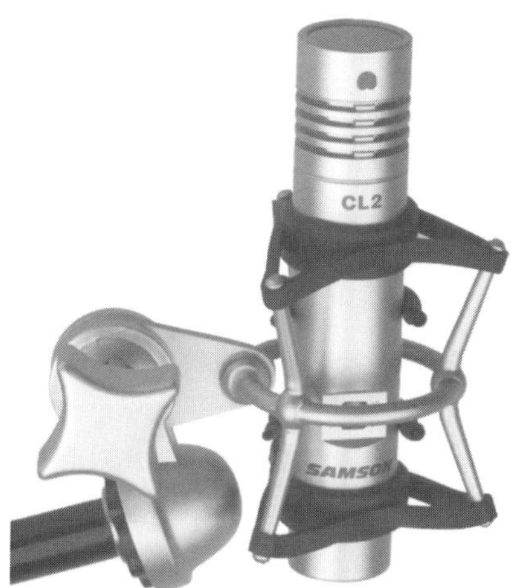

Figure 13.5 Samson CL2 cardioid.

Figure 13.6 Oktava MK-220.

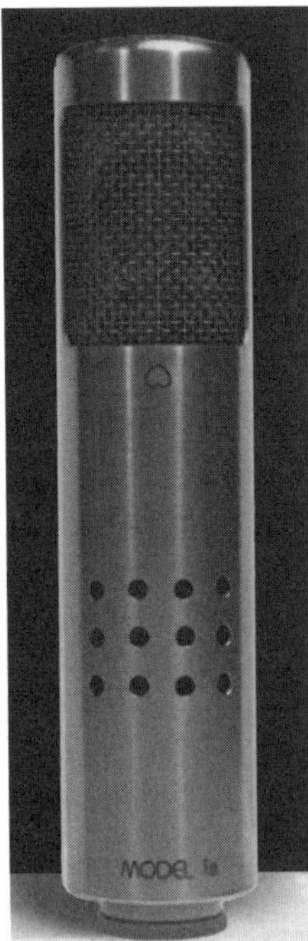

Figure 13.7 Groove Tubes MD1b vacuum tube condenser microphone.

Variations on Recording Solos

- If the solo is a precise part, doubling (recording two identical solos) may create a fuller sound. In the mix, over-balance the two stereo recordings of the doubled solo. In other words, one of the solos will have its stereo pair with the right side slightly louder than the left, and the double will have its left slightly louder than the right. This technique creates a solo that is larger than life. This technique isn't appropriate for everything, as doubling some parts causes them to lose their personality, but when it works, it can be very effective.
- *Sometimes*, the sound of a traditional acoustic solo instrument, such as a flute, violin, or harmonica, can be enhanced by miking it; connecting the mic to a guitar amp (or a Leslie cabinet), usually through a transformer direct box or reamp setup; and miking the amp (see Figure 13.8). In this case, the acoustic violin is miked in stereo, and the amp has a pair of mics a few feet from the amp as well as a mic up against the grill cloth. The amp would most likely be placed in another room.

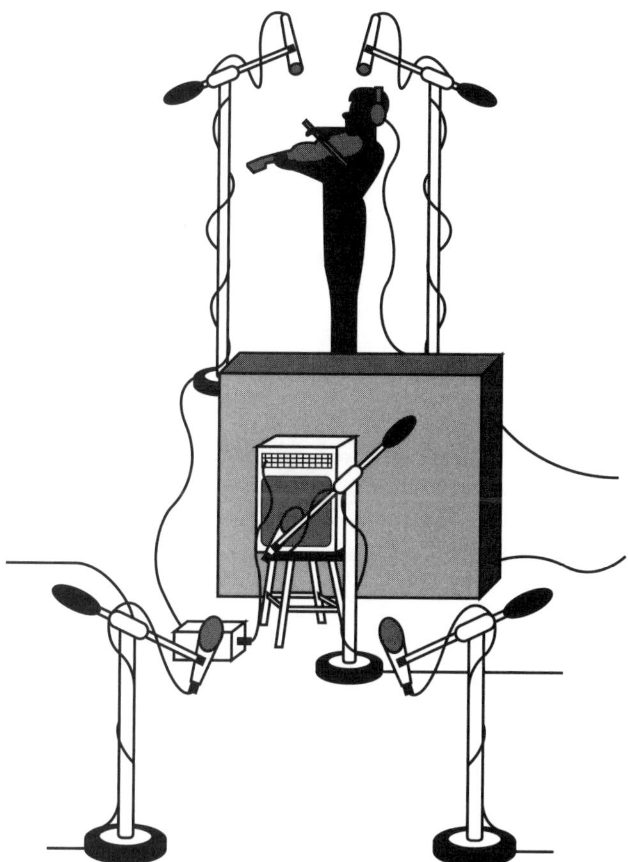

Figure 13.8 Amplifying an acoustic instrument.

Background Vocals (BG Vocs)

The background vocalists (often called *BG Vox* on track names) find inspiration and blend better if they hear a track that is nearly complete. At the very least, there must be a scratch lead vocal. Many times the BG Vox are recorded by the lead singer with the help of one or two other singers, with the exception of those times when the BG Vox are the opposite gender to the lead singer. And many times, the background parts are doubled or tripled to increase the "size" of the chorus parts. When recording two background vocalists, position one on each side of a single bidirectional mike (such as a Neumann U 87 in a bidirectional pattern or a Groove Tubes VELO 8); see Figure 13.9. For more than two voices, an omni pattern is best.

Using separate mics and mixing the voices together doesn't create the right blend. By hearing themselves (it's common for background vocalists to take off one headphone), they will achieve a more natural balance. Experienced BG vocalists will step back from the mic when they are loud and move closer when they are soft, with an average distance of about a foot. If variation in

Figure 13.9 BG Vox on a figure-8.

the height of the singers is a problem, the shorter singers should stand on a box, a crate, or anything else that gets them all at the same height. The entire group should stand on a rug to eliminate foot-shuffling sounds. Toe tappers should remove their shoes, and all noisy jewelry should be removed (see Figure 13.10).

Of course, there are times when more voices are called for (or they just appear because the producer has invited all his friends because he/she wants a big chorus). With more than four to five voices, it may be necessary to use two omni mics with the group in two clusters around the two mics. Set the mics enough apart for all the singers to be comfortable, but still close enough that the singers can make easy eye contact so they can make strong vocal entrances and accurate cutoffs. If you have a full chorus, it's best to mike them with a couple of microphones in stereo, with the singers in a slight horseshoe.

The more singers you have, the greater the possibility of headphone cords and junction boxes being tripped on, or someone walking into the microphone boom counterweight. Use the largest stand/boom you have, and make sure it's sandbagged (as described in Chapters 7 and 9). Ideally, the stand should be large enough to have the boom and its counterweight above head height. Be sure that there are two or three music stands for lyrics, and pencils with erasers to make notes. Make sure the stands are padded to reduce reflection (see Chapter 7). Also, position the singers within reach of the piano keyboard. If there is no acoustic, set up an electronic keyboard and a small amp (be sure it's a quiet one) so they can work on parts and get pitch.

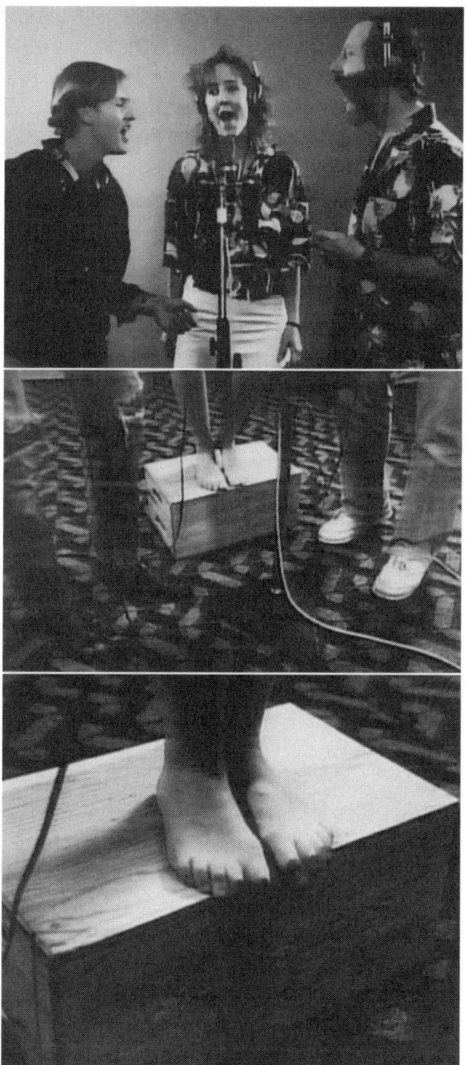

Figure 13.10 BG Vox on an omni condenser.

Doubling Chorus Parts When doubling chorus parts, record the BG Vox a section at a time. This makes the doubling tighter. In other words, once the first chorus part has been recorded, stay on that chorus and double it. Many times the double will be stronger than the original because the singers have the first track to lock onto. Then go back and re-record the first track so it is as strong as the double. Once everyone is happy with that chorus, move on to the next chorus. Those who have DAWs might cut and paste that chorus into all the choruses, though I personally would prefer to have each chorus unique. Once the choruses are all finished, record the BG Vox for the verses.

Lead Vocals

The best microphone for vocals is the one that makes the singer feel as if he or she is wearing "golden slippers." It's so important to remember that the technical quality of a microphone is seldom the subject of discussion outside of people who make recordings. What matters is how well a mic can capture a vocal performance that moves millions of people to want to hear the recording over and over and to buy it. For a given singer, that mic may be a pawn-shop special with a mangled windscreen that's slightly plugged with lipstick, but if the singer has faith in it, even though its sound may not technically be as good as the sound of another mic, it could become the catalyst for a moving, emotional, powerful, compelling recording. No matter what model of mic it is, if it does that, then it's the right mic. And while everyone does have their own opinion, there is most definitely an ad hoc consensus that certain mics are good for vocals.

Some mics are so consistently used on vocals that their reputation precedes the singer's experience with them, so there is confidence that a great vocal is in the making. A few mics are almost mythical for their ability to capture the elusive qualities in a singer's voice that can only be described as soul, emotion, and magic. These mics just have it, and many of them are expensive. It's fair to say that if you can only afford one good mic, it should be a vocal mic.

Photo courtesy of RØDE Microphones.

Figure 13.11 The RØDE Classic II is a tube-amplified large-diaphragm microphone that has gained a solid reputation over a short period of time. It has nine polar patterns.

For the majority of productions, the mic chosen for vocals will be a large-diaphragm condenser. They are almost always in the same family of mics that are also used for most acoustic instruments. As for my taste, I tend to like a bright vocal mic that picks up some of the room. I like a little upper midrange boost, but if it rolls off at the very top end, that suits me for most singers. Mics I like include the Neumann U 87, U 67, M 49, U 47; AKG C 12, 414, and 214; Oktava MK-220; Telefunken Ela M 251; RØDE Classic II (see Figure 13.11) and NT1000, and Groove Tubes MD1b. Generally ribbon and dynamic mics will not be the first choice for a vocal mic because they tend to have less high-frequency clarity, but there are a handful of notable dynamics and ribbons that can hold their own in the great vocal mic family.

Choosing a Vocal Microphone (on a Budget) While many of the microphones on my list are used for vocals by major recording artists and most are expensive, a few are widely used and, although expensive, they are ubiquitous in any premium studio. Probably the two most common would be the AKG 414 (see Figure 13.12) and the Neumann U 87 (see Figure 13.13); most studios will have a pair or more.

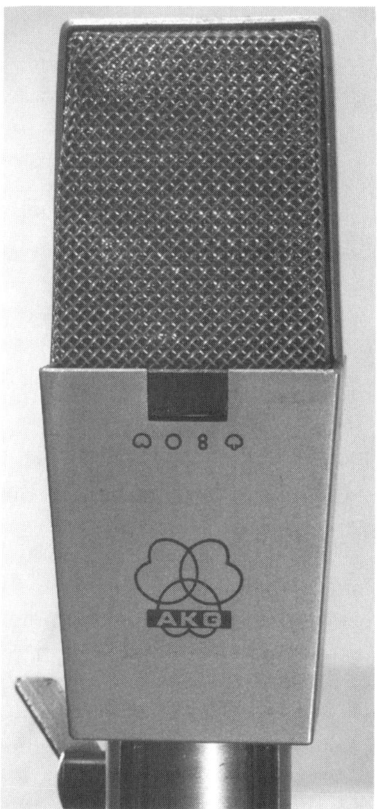

Figure 13.12 An AKG 414 condenser. One of the most universally used high-end studio microphones. Four-pattern transistor-amplified. Can be used on almost anything, including vocals.

Photo courtesy of Georg Neumann GmbH.

Figure 13.13 A Neumann U 87 condenser. One of the most universally used high-end studio microphones. Three-pattern transistor-amplified large-diaphragm.

But don't assume that the more you spend on a mic, the better it will be. There are many expensive microphones that are not all that good on vocals, and they'll go unnamed because I don't feel like dealing with angry letters from manufacturers. A more expensive mic will generally have better specifications—flatter response, low noise, good transient response, and so on—but these objective measurements mean little compared to the subjective opinion that a certain mic is great for vocals.

There are also a lot of less expensive microphones that are marketed as "just as good as such-and-such legendary microphone." They often look like expensive high-end microphones, but when you actually compare them, the budget mic is a pale imitation.

Some mics will sound better on male singers, others will sound better on females, and some will work well on both. Most people who have home/project studios often buy their first vocal mic based on how it sounds on their own singing voice, and that's probably as good a place to start as any.

Although the mics I've noted as favorites are mostly more than $1,000, there are some pretty good vocal mics that sell for less than $1,000, and even below $500. There are a couple below $300, but don't expect them to sound like a mic that costs 10 or 20 times as much. Still, they may be great on your voice. I've used a few of them and taken suggestions on others. All of them are current, and extensive reviews and surveys are available on the web.

Ultimately, when purchasing a mic specifically for recording vocals, try to test drive the mic before you buy it. The quality of a PA mic can be reasonably evaluated based on what is heard coming out of PA speakers at a music store, but you can't really tell how a mic is going to sound until you've played back a vocal performance recorded using it.

In the less-than-$1,000 range, it's hard to get past the Audio-Technica AT4033, but also try the Sennheiser MKE4032, the AKG C 3000 or SolidTube (see Figure 13.14), the BLUE B7 or B6 capsules on an AKG 451 amplifier (about $750 to $1,000 for each capsule/amp combo), or a Blueberry. The RØDE line has a few large-diaphragm condensers worth

Figure 13.14 The AKG SolidTube condenser microphone combines the sound of classic vacuum-tube technology with the benefits of advanced solid-state circuitry. Fixed cardioid.

Photo courtesy of RØDE Microphones.

Figure 13.15 RØDE NT1000 condenser cardioid. Transistor-amplified large-diaphragm. Very versatile.

looking at (NT1-A, NT2-A, K2, NTK, NT1000 [see Figure 13.15], NT2000), ranging in price from less than $1,000 down to $300. At a little bit more than $1,000, the Neumann TLM 103 (see Figure 13.16) or Shure KSM44 (see Figure 13.17) is excellent. At $500, the Audio-Technica AT4047 (see Figure 13.18) is very good.

A lot of people like the sound of a ribbon mic on vocals, and the AEA R84 is outstanding and costs less than $1,000. In the $350 price range, take a look at the Shure KSM27 condenser and the SM7 (a dynamic often touted as the Michael Jackson vocal mic on *Thriller*) (see Figure 13.19), the MXL V88 (see Figure 13.20), and my two favorites in the price range, the Heil Sound PR35 dynamic (see Figure 13.21) and the Audio-Technica AT2035 condenser (see Figure 13.22), which sells for around $200.

It also worth exploring the used-microphone market. Most people who have larger home/project studios already do this. It has been my experience that those who own good recording microphones take care of them, which also means that when they sell them, they're in good condition. But be sure the previous owner knows about mics and

Photo courtesy of Georg Neumann GmbH.

Figure 13.16 Neumann TLM 103 condenser. Fixed cardioid. Transistor-amplified large-diaphragm.

has not abused them. Microphones are delicate, and you won't know how good it sounds until you plug it in and use it.

If you have a pretty average mixing desk, you might also consider looking into a high-quality external mic preamp. They vary in price from less than $50 to more than $3,000. My preference is the Vintech X73, which is a near duplicate of the legendary Neve 1073 channel strip. Several hundred dollars less is the Chandler Limited Germanium Pre Amp/DI, and at under $300, the Focusrite TrakMaster Pro.

The Singer's Position/The Stand's Placement

How close should the vocalist be to the mic? Many cardioid microphones have substantial proximity effect and will boost the bass in someone's voice if they stand too close to the mic, so I would suggest that 4 to 8 inches is a good distance. On the other hand, some singers and

Figure 13.17 Shure KSM44 condenser. Three-pattern transistor-amplified large-diaphragm.

Figure 13.18 The Audio-Technica AT4047SV dual-diaphragm capsule design maintains precise cardioid pattern definition across the full frequency range of the microphone. Classic FET circuitry.

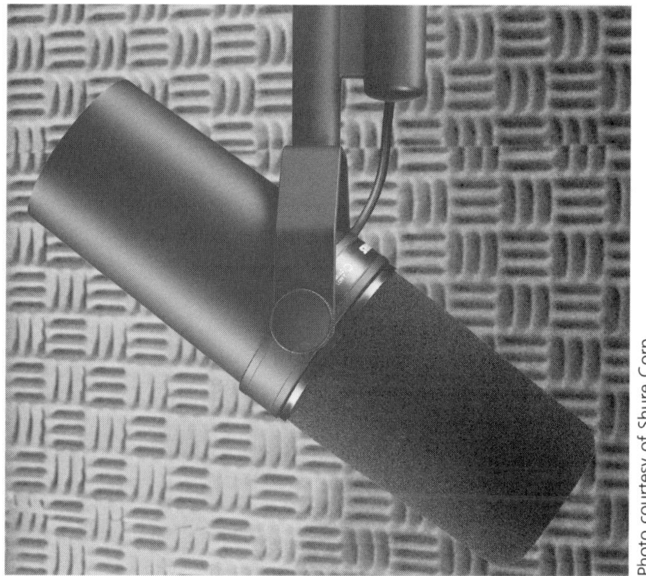

Photo courtesy of Shure Corp.

Figure 13.19 Shure SM7 dynamic cardioid.

Photo courtesy of MXL.

Figure 13.20 MXL V88 condenser cardioid. The preamp uses low-noise FETs.

producers want this quality, so the vocalist will work closer to the mic. The problem is then controlling sibilance and percussive noises (S, T, and P sounds, and so on).

Many times, a vocalist will crowd a mic because he is not hearing enough of himself in the phones, though sometimes the problem is caused out of habit, with many singers being very

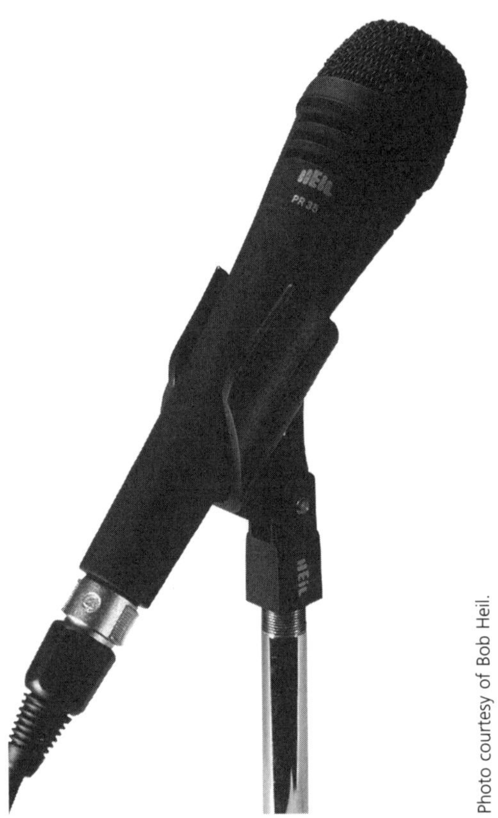

Photo courtesy of Bob Heil.

Figure 13.21 Heil PR35 dynamic cardioid. If you're a fan of the *Live at Abbey Road* TV series, this mic is frequently used on vocals.

accustomed to kissing the mic when they sing onstage. Some engineers will draw a white line or X on the floor to show the singer where to stand or will set a stool or chair between the mic and the singer. On a few occasions, I have set up two mics—one right in front of the singer who likes to eat the mic, and another a short distance from the first. I have on occasion recorded both, but most of the time the close mic was a placebo, with only the farther mic being used.

If the singer stands too far from the mic, the sound will lose brightness and edge in the consonant sounds and the transient quality. Getting the singer to stand where you want him is often a matter of getting the headphone levels right. If his voice is too loud, he will move back, and if he can't hear himself, he'll get closer.

If you have the space and can afford it, it is advisable to buy a large mic stand/boom. A large boom that can bring the boom and mic in over the heads of everyone is the best with BG Vox and provides a solid base for the mic when doing lead vocals. Examples include the Atlas SB-36 and the Ultimate Support MC-125, both less than $300. Unless you have a micKing stand ($450;

Photo courtesy of Audio-Technica.

Figure 13.22 Audio-Technica AT2035. Large-diaphragm cardioid condenser.

see Figure 13.23) or a Starbird ($1,000) with its very heavy base (a bit of overkill for the small studio), you'll still need to sandbag the base if the boom is fully extended.

Lead vocal mic placement varies from right in front of the singer to above and tipped slightly down toward the singer's mouth, but with the vocalist singing straight ahead. The latter is very effective if the windscreen you're using is unable to contain the percussive sounds of a particularly "poppy" singer.

Other Considerations

Sure, you need a great singer, great tracks, a great song, good gear, and so on. But even if you have all that, expectations of a magical session can go south because of the little things. Here is a list of things that matter beyond the singer, the track, the song, and the gear.

- Absolutely everything has to be set up before the singer arrives, and if possible the mix of the first song that's to be recorded should sound like a master in the headphones. Singers hate

Photo courtesy of Latch Lake Products.

Figure 13.23 micKing 2200 stand.

waiting. It breaks their momentum and mental preparation. When they come in they're ready, and if you're not, it can get nasty very quickly.

- The air conditioning and ventilation should be turned on long before the vocalist arrives. Know beforehand what temperature the singer likes. Humidity can also be a vocal killer. Too dry and too damp are both bad for singers. If the room air is not to a singer's liking, he may leave on the spot or he may lose his voice after a few takes.
- Smell does matter, and if the studio is prone to smell bad, get some fresh air in the room the night before. Don't use scented sprays; go with unscented air cleaners. Many studios have electrostatic air cleaners in the air-conditioning system that ionize the air and attract these particles to a filter.
- Have all the lyrics written out with the musical bar count and time reference noted for the beginning of every verse, chorus, bridge, instrumental, intro, and outro of the song. For DAW recording, set up markers in the project for verse, chorus, and so on. Also, all gaps in

the vocal where you can go in and out of record should be noted. I used to make up a chart for every song on the day the rhythm tracks were recorded (based on the scratch vocals).

Know exactly how long a bar is in real time. When working quickly, you should be able to consistently start the track within a bar of where the singer is to begin recording. You cue the singer with, "You'll hear a bar, and you're in." If you do this well, the singer will love you. You don't waste his time or his voice singing in the wrong place. It also prevents erasing the wrong chorus or some other part of the vocal. This sort of accuracy also improves the productivity of instrumental overdub sessions.

- The engineer and producer in the control room must have good eye contact with the singer(s) in the studio because there is always a high degree of nonverbal communication through body language, hand signals, and conducting. The better the connection between the singer and the producer and engineer, the more likely the session will go well.
- Nothing will drive a singer to distraction more than only hearing half of what they're being told through the talkback. Adjust the talkback to the studio headphones so it's easy for the singer to hear the engineer and the producer in the control room. If the producer has a habit of trying to talk to the singer without pushing the talkback switch (and many do), the engineer should get used to turning on the talkback for him. However, you have to be careful not to turn it on when the producer is saying something meant only for those in the control room. For instance, "This guy can't carry a tune in a bucket!"
- Many singers—in particular, experienced background singers—will often want to see the record light so they know when they're recording. On the other hand, there are some singers who tense up when the record light appears. Find out which the singer prefers and accommodate him. Or there are singers who want to know when recording begins but stop when a red light goes on, in which case change the color of the light to green (green means go, and red means stop).
- Always let the singer know when you're doing a playback. If he think he's singing and you don't go into record, he will get very annoyed.
- When recording vocals, the engineer should work quickly at setting levels, adding EQ and compression, and getting a monitor and headphone mix to the singer, because a surprising number of times, the first pass on the vocal will be the best. Unless the singer wants a full run-through, stop the first rundown as soon as you've got levels, let the singer know you're ready to go, and start recording (even the warm-ups). I usually keep the first complete take as a reference or starting point. Some producers just want to start recording without telling the singer, but the problem is the singer may stop in the middle or want to go back. People as different as Frank Sinatra and Chaka Khan have been one-takers.
- Don't ever erase a great take if you hear on playback some kind of distortion. It may be fixable. While such tracks may be less than perfect technically, they have that elusive soul. We're talking magic, so get levels quickly and start recording.

- Pay attention when the singer is listening on phones in the studio so if he has a comment or he wants to stop the playback, you can hear him.
- Take accurate notes on what mics were used, what EQ or other processor settings were used, what plug-ins and version numbers, which takes were played back, which take had the best choruses, who liked it, and so on. A singer may do a great take that's kept, but everyone decides to do a few more to get it better. Two hours (or two days) later, a request is made for the take with the good verses to be used with the take with the good choruses.
- If there's a technical problem, stop recording and have the singer relax while you sort it out. Make sure there are a stool or chair, a glass, and a pitcher of water near the singer (but not on the piano). You should also have available a non-sound-reflective music stand with paper, pencils, and an eraser. Mood matters, so the overhead lights should be turned off. Set up a floor lamp with a nice thrift-shop shade that provides enough light for the singer to read lyrics and notes. It creates a more intimate environment. On more than one occasion, I have organized some flowers in the studio.
- Be sure the singer is not standing under an air-conditioning duct or in its draft. (Also, such positioning will generate noise in the microphone.)
- If you change mics (or for that matter, anything else, such as headphones, reverb, the studio lighting, the tea boy, the color of the wallpaper, and so on) on a vocalist, you'd better have a good reason, because if the vocals are going well, you shouldn't tinker with anything.

Jagger's Mic So the album's almost finished. The vocalist loves the sound you've been getting. He has a good relationship with the mic being used, and it sounds great. Then, out of the blue, the mic decides to fail, and there's not a similar mic available. After a half hour of chasing down unknown noises, the problem has turned into a total session breakdown for the vocalist as well as the mic.

The first thing to do is to calm the vocalist and tell him you'll be right back—you're going to find another. Try to recall who owns a similar mic and if that person owes you a favor, and then call around. There may be a possibility of borrowing or renting a replacement. If that fails, look for your second-best vocal mic. Take it back to the studio where the artist is contemplatively sullen (at best) and is doodling on the piano a blues song about what's occurring. He now imagines that the special magical vocal quality has escaped him forever. His career breakout has been nipped in the bud by a broken mic. Those visions of a hit album are fading away; a speech after receiving an "Album of the Year" award is no longer needed. Into this blackness, walk in with the mic held preciously in your hand and say, "So and so [the biggest name he will believe] is a friend and he left this mic in my keeping. He bought it from a studio in England where the Stones did a lot of work, and Jagger [or whatever singer the vocalist idolizes] used it to do most of his vocals on their first six albums. This one's got the magic. As long as we're careful, it should be okay to use it, so let's see how it sounds."

If the singer buys it, great. In any case, if he believes the mic will sound as good as or better than the one that died, it will. If he doesn't buy the story, hopefully at least the tension has been broken, and you have until tomorrow to fix the suspect mic or to find another "golden slippers" mic before you begin the next day's session. Good luck in your quest.

Sometimes when you do vocals, something happens. For days and months (and maybe even longer), you're going along recording songs with different artists and making good albums. Then one day there is a moment when you push up the fader on a vocalist, and it brings goose bumps. No one says anything for fear of breaking the spell of whatever is happening, but those in the control room give each other knowing glances—but not too much, for fear of jinxing what's happening. Often the singer is in the moment and unaware of the effect he is having on the other side of the control-room glass.

For the next few minutes, hours, and days, you'll be the first to hear what millions will hear. When the session is over, you'll play it one more time, then again and again. The singer's song demands to be played one more time and is an addiction that stretches until the dawn.

That amazing, indescribable feeling that you're part of a hit record is like nothing I know, and it is why you do what you do. This hit will change people's lives, including yours. Here's hoping it's the first of more hits to come. And when the masters are shipped to the label and all of what everyone did is reduced to an album credit, you'll never lose the rush of hearing a record you made played on the radio. Even someday 30 years from now, as background music in a shopping mall, the sound of that song will return you to that moment when you pushed up the fader labeled Ld Vox.

In the next chapter, we'll look at a few approaches to recording "sections," such as string and horn sections.

14 Miking Classical Acoustic Sections

Let's be clear: A keyboardist playing something called *strings* or *horns* in a sampler (no matter how good he is) will never replace a professional string or horn section playing a great sweetening arrangement for a song. The challenge is getting a recording that has the sound quality of the best sample recordings. Of course, a scoring or concert orchestra presents an even greater challenge. These sessions are recorded by the most experienced engineers working with highly competent assistants. But everyone who engineers bands occasionally gets the opportunity to do a big acoustic session. If you do well, more may follow, and the more of them you do, the better you will become until you are one of those big session engineers.

Although you may not get the opportunity to record the London symphony, most places have a local orchestra, and many of them are very good. If you have an interest in working with orchestra, get to know the local conductor and build up a list of players who have ability and interest to play on non-classical dates. On several occasions I've recorded a classical ensemble's repertoire in return for their playing something I was working on.

Space and Setup

Sessions with groups of musicians (or sections) that are classically trained and/or are reading charts can be at best nerve-wracking and at worst a disaster if you have not planned ahead for what will happen on the day. Professional orchestra musicians are getting paid to play, and they will be required to record a master take within minutes of entering the studio. In most cases this will be the first time they hear/read what they are playing, yet an experienced studio musician will be ready to go as soon as he sits down and tunes up. Which is to say that, unlike a rock-and-roll band that is figuring out what they're going to do while you (the engineer) fine-tune the sound and correct any problems, session players will always be waiting for you if there are any sound issues or technical problems.

If you mess up, wherever those studio *musos* go for their next session, people will hear about how bad it went in your session. You'll also have a dissatisfied producer who is paying for the players and a conductor/arranger who knows how a sweetening session should go. If things go really badly, you won't get a second chance; the project will go to another studio for session overdubs. There's just too much money involved.

But it's not that hard to get it right; you just have to know what's going to happen, and you must be prepared for what the producer, the musicians, and the conductor/arranger expect. Did I say it was all about planning? It's about planning.

Space

Horns and strings are the most common section sessions. The size of the sections will vary with the music and the budget, but in general a string session will have a handful of first and second violins, a viola or two, a cello or two, and occasionally a bowed double bass. A horn section is more varied but will have trumpets, trombones, and most of the time saxophonists who may also play clarinet or flute. Most horn section players will bring along other similar instruments depending on what the arranger has asked for. For instance, the trumpet player may also have a cornet or a flugelhorn, a trombone player may also have a bass trombone, and sax players may bring alto, tenor, soprano, and baritone saxophones, as well as various flutes.

Usually the best way to produce tight horns and strings for pop recordings is to use a smaller section and have the ensemble double the parts (in other words, play and record the same chart two or three times on different tracks). A smaller section is more manageable and likely to play tighter with their previously recorded selves than if there were many more individual musicians. If you have limited tracks, rather than recording each section in stereo, mix the various instruments to mono tracks, then in mixdown take these two or three mono tracks and pan them left, center, and right.

Classical instruments sound best when they are played and recorded in a live and open space. Attempting to record too many instruments in a small space is a recipe for disaster. No one has any room to move, all the instruments leak into all the microphones, and the sound has no space to expand (and neither do the players who get uptight about the tight confines). Another problem when too many players are crammed into a too-small studio is inadequate air conditioning. Both high temperatures and high humidity will affect player attitudes and dramatically affect the sound of their instruments. High humidity usually makes acoustic instruments sound lifeless. As far as possible, the air temperature should remain stable during the session, or else the tuning of everything—in particular the wood instruments—will shift constantly.

Finally, it's important to realistically evaluate what your equipment and space are capable of. You can have an excellent studio for recording and mixing bands but that cannot handle section sessions. If you have a good thing going with a band or producer, it's far better to suggest you will take them to a larger studio, where you have established a relationship and where possibly you can do the engineering, than to hurt the relationship by trying to record something at your studio that's beyond its capabilities.

The latest approach for an advanced small studio that needs to record an orchestra is to use a digital link, such as Source-Connect, and a high-performance Pro Tools setup that connects the small studio control room located in one part of the world to a large studio on the other side of the planet. This allows direct-to-the-timeline recording with real-time, broadcast-quality audio using T1, cable, or DSL Internet connections. Such a studio is featured in the following sidebar.

Trackdown Scoring Stage If you've never been on a large, state-of-the-art scoring stage, these pictures of various sessions at Trackdown will help you get a feel for what major sessions look like.

Trackdown's Scoring stage is located on the Fox Studio lot in Sydney, Australia. It was designed and built in 2003 in the tradition of studios such as AIR Lyndhurst, Abbey Road, and the Newman Scoring stage on the Fox lot in Hollywood. Trackdown can accommodate a 100-plus-piece orchestra. The main hall has 4,800 square feet of floor and a 30-foot ceiling, with the space generating approximately a 1.8-second reverb time (which can be reduced as required). It has Tasmanian Oak floating timber floors, suspended acoustically reflective timber panels, rear pyramidal diffusing panels, suspended infinite ceiling diffusers, two attached isolation rooms, and clear sightlines from and into all rooms (see Figures 14.1 and 14.2).

Trackdown is equipped with several Pro Tools systems; its main system is a Pro Tools|HD Accel 2 system connected to a Yamaha DM2000 digital console. The control room is 5.1 surround monitoring–enabled, is capable of playing back up to 128 tracks, and operates up to a sample rate of 192 kHz. Pro Tools inputs via 56 channels of microphone preamplifiers (48 of which are custom built). Needless to say, the outboard and peripheral equipment is extensive. Video, MIDI, and CAT-5 lines connect between all rooms. Source-Connect allows real-time connection to similar facilities anywhere in the world.

To accommodate a scoring session (see Figure 14.3), the main hall has 48 mic lines into the control room. "On air" lights are triggered from an automatic in-record switch. There are eight mono or four stereo independent headphone sends and 70 single-sided and 30 double-sided headphones. The studio has 100 fully adjustable cushioned musicians' chairs, 100 music stands, eight orchestral risers (adjustable up to 3 feet), a greenroom, and large case storage area off the main hall.

Finally, the Trackdown microphone locker includes:

- Seven overhead mic stands, 45 medium mic stands, 5 small mic stands
- Three DPA 4006s
- One Neumann TLM 170
- Two Neumann KM 184s (matched pair)
- One Neumann U 87
- One Neumann U 89

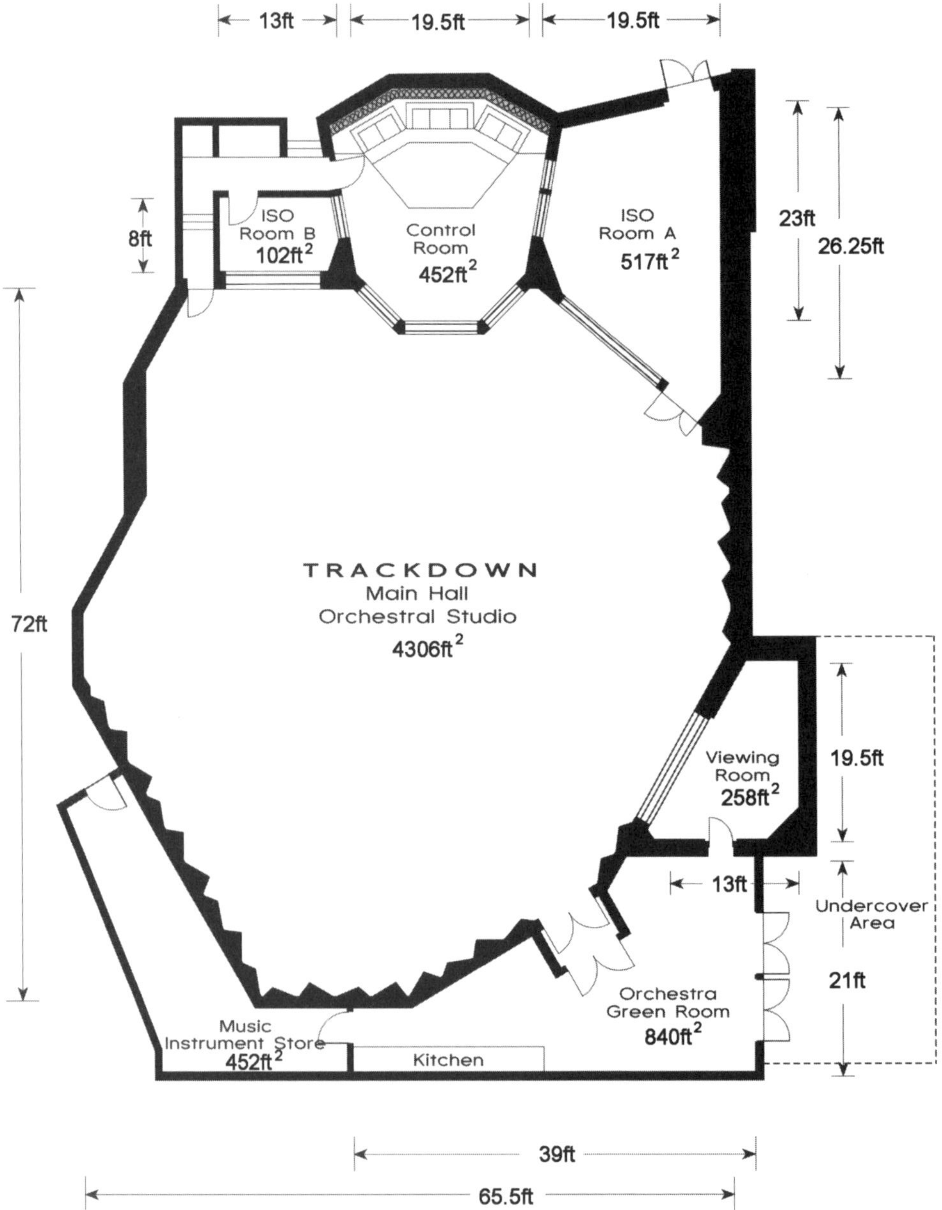

Figure 14.1 Floorplan, Trackdown Scoring stage.

Photo courtesy of Trackdown.

Figure 14.2 The main hall at Trackdown Scoring with a Yamaha C7 grand piano.

- One Neumann KMR 81
- Two Microtech Gefell M930s (matched pair)
- One Microtech Gefell MKG1Y (stereo)
- Two AKG C 414 Bs (matched pair)
- Two AKG 451 Es (matched pair)
- Sixteen RØDE NT5 (eight matched pairs)
- Six RØDE NT1000s
- Five RØDE NT2s
- One RØDE NT4 (stereo)
- Two RØDE NTG-2s
- One Audio-Technica AT4033
- One Sony ECM22
- One RØDE NT6
- Five Schoeps CMC 6-Us (bodies)

Photo courtesy of Sue Taylor.

Figure 14.3 Scoring orchestra. Note the horn and rhythm sections are in an arc to the rear of the setup, behind large half-transparent gobos. Behind the conductor is a large boom atop which is a Decca Tree with Schoeps MK 2H capsules on CMC 6-U bodies (see Chapter 8).

- Five Schoeps MK 2Hs (capsules)
- One AKG D 190
- Three DPA 4006s
- One Audio-Technica ATM21
- One Beyerdynamic M 88
- Three Beyerdynamic M 201s
- One Beyerdynamic M 55
- Two Sennheiser MD 211s
- One Sennheiser MD 421
- Three Sennheiser MD 441s

- Three Shure SM57s
- One Shure 545
- Two RØDE Classic IIs

Setup

Larger studios that are designed for orchestra recording usually have hardwood floors. If your studio has carpet, I would suggest putting on the floor sheets of plywood to increase early reflection, as previously described in Chapter 10.

The musicians in the studio need to be visible from the control room, but they should be placed back from the control room window to avoid slap echo off the glass. In many cases the best approach is to position the players so that the control room is off to one side of everyone. This allows both the musicians and the conductor to look into the control room by glancing to the right (or left), and everyone in the control room can see everyone in the studio.

Arrange the musicians in clusters of two or three, with the four or five clusters forming a horseshoe around the conductor. The bigger the ensemble and the closer it comes to a full orchestra and a classical music recording, the closer the setup should resemble a live concert setting. This style of setup is familiar to the musicians and the conductor and will make it easier for them to play as a unit (see Figure 14.4).

Film and TV scoring sessions will tend to set up differently according to the score and the instrumental mix. In many cases, scoring sessions will have a lot of strings that will occupy the area all around the conductor, and the horns and percussion will arc around the outside of the strings (as in Figure 14.4).

Large sessions are seldom produced by people who don't know what they're doing. Producers know how much it costs to produce a certain amount of music and how many hours it should take. To satisfy such clients, it is imperative that the entire setup be installed and completely checked out before anyone arrives. Don't book anything else in the studio once you've started setting up a big session. All it takes is one cable or patch being kicked, pulled out, or moved to really stuff you up.

For the biggest of sessions, the setup may need to be done the day before. Virtually everything must be verified for reliability and lack of noise. If there is video playback, time-code synchronization, lots of headphones, intricate talkback, a video feed, and so on, make a checklist a few days before and verify that everything is there and working. For a big date, if something has been left to chance, it will probably fail. Changing a mic is nearly impossible with 50 musicians seated and waiting. Have a couple of wireless mics on standby just in case a mic fails. It's arguably not as good as a wired mic, but it's better than having no mic at all on a critical instrument. When

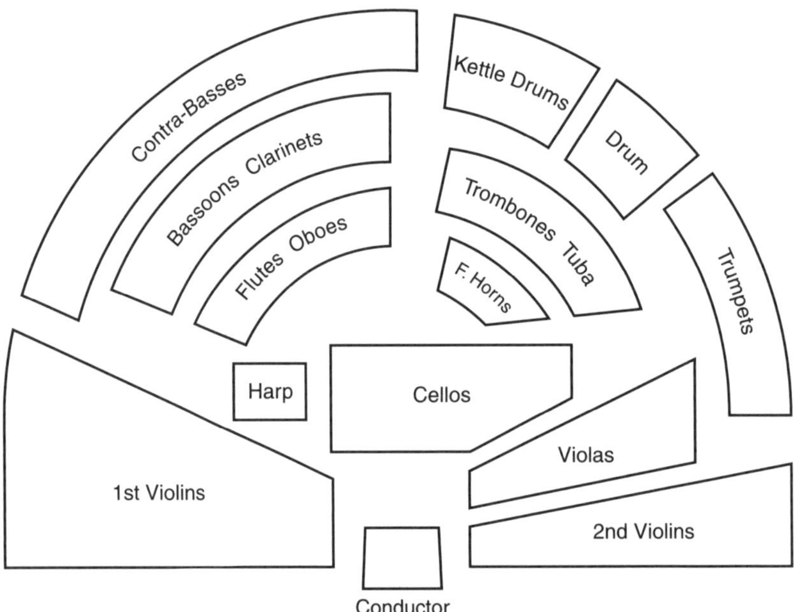

Figure 14.4 One of a few "standard" setups for a full concert orchestra as they might be in a large studio.

catastrophic failure happens, as it sometimes will, you can only hope that it happens to you after many previously successful sessions. And if it does, the studio will likely be obligated to underwrite all the costs for a replacement session. What's catastrophic? Maybe the recorder completely fails, a video sync fails, the air conditioning fails, power in the building goes down, and so on.

A common problem for studios that only occasionally have large sessions is finding enough mics, music stands, chairs, and lights. If you don't have enough, rent them and build the rental costs into the studio charge. In the end, the cost of rental is insignificant compared to the overtime bill for the musicians.

The need for adequate lighting cannot be overstated. Most rock studio lighting is too subdued for studio musicians who are reading charts. Put up clip-on floodlights pointing at the ceiling if you have any doubt about how well someone might be able to see the notes on the page, and make very sure they're not going to suddenly come crashing down. It's a nightmare trying to set up temporary lighting after the musicians have arrived.

In classical or scoring sessions, there may be less need for everyone to have a set of phones, but they will still be needed by the rhythm players and possibly by any or all of the percussionists, the conductor, the first violin, the section leaders, and soloists. Violin, trombone, and viola players will usually prefer single-speaker headphones, and many other classical acoustic musicians may also request the single-phone models.

Crowding into the control room during playback can be eliminated if there is a decent set of speakers in the studio. No one expects the studio monitors to provide a critical reference on tone or balance, but having a reasonable playback system will keep the musicians involved, will allow them to hear where they may be going astray if a retake is required, and will help keep the control room less crowded. The producer and some of the key players may come into the control room, but most of the others will be content to stay in the studio. During playback, go into the studio to hear what it sounds like and ensure that the speakers are not too loud (or soft). The trip to the studio will also give you a feel for what the musicians think and whether they need anything, such as more click, cue levels, the temperature turned up or down, and so on.

Ensemble sessions should have access to a piano even though it's not being used in the session. And, the piano should be tuned on the morning of the session. If there are prerecorded tracks that are being added to, check with the tuner that the piano is in tune with the tracks that are to be recorded on. This is particularly important if the tracks were recorded somewhere else, where the piano tuning may be ever so slightly different.

What Could Go Wrong? In any orchestral recording session, there is the potential for things to go wrong. You can't foresee every possible problem, but here are a few to be on the lookout for:

- Chairs that squeak, are not straight-backed, are too low and lounge-y, or have arms. Players' chairs should be quiet, straight-backed, and armless.
- Insufficient and unprofessional music stands. If you need to, rent them from a school music department. Also, be sure you have plenty of sharp pencils.
- The rhythm track does not have a tuning note at the top. What's worse is it's not tuned to A440, which means the musicians will be wasting time trying to get in tune with the track before they can record. Unless there is some reason not to do it, always be sure the rhythm tracks are tuned to the universal standard.
- Cables, headphone cords, power boxes, and power supplies being kicked and disconnected. So many people, so many wires—keep the two apart.
- No riser for the conductor. Find or make a riser that's sturdy and quiet and that the conductor won't fall off of. The best studio conductor platform will have a rail across the back.
- Fluorescent lighting that hums. If you need more light than usual in order to accommodate an orchestral session, be sure that your lighting doesn't induce hum into the process.

- Loud air conditioning. AC that's tolerably noisy for rock will be far too noisy for scoring sessions, and you may need to turn it off while recording. Needless to say, you need to make sure you turn it on during playbacks, or the temperature will quickly go through the roof and the humidity to 100 percent. Not only will the musicians get hot under the collar, but the instrument tuning will keep going out.

- Toilet problems of any kind. Make sure there are plenty of supplies and the bathroom is clean. Rock-and-rollers tend to tolerate grime more than session and classical musicians.

- A copy machine that isn't working. You will occasionally need to copy charts and sheet music for players, and you'll need to be able to accommodate large sheets. If you can't do it, know of a copy place nearby that's open and quick.

- Lack of space for cases. If your studio is too small for a large number of musicians *and* their cases, try to make arrangements ahead of time for stashing the cases in an alternate locale. Previously mentioned Trackdown has a large storage area for cases, but as shown in Figure 14.5, the amount of stuff on the floor of a major session is a minefield to negotiate, particularly when you're trying to fix a bad connection of some sort.

- No place to get lunch. If the musicians have a lunch break and no place is around, get a lunch wagon to come by at an agreed time. Or if it is delivered, it must be on time, have sufficient and generous variety, and then be cleaned up before the next break. If players have to get in their cars, they will never get back in time.

- A deluge coming. A studio roof blocks the occasional distant airplane, but rain in the extreme comes through loud and clear. It can be the direct contact on the roof or the water rushing through the drainpipes. Rock bands and even vocals may not be a problem, but when there are lots of microphones, the sound of rain will be picked up even if it's not obvious in the studio. There is nothing to be done on the day, but if you have a problem, fix it before you do big acoustic sessions. Put up something to keep the rain from directly falling on the roof and drain the water away from the walls of the studio.

- The roof leaking. If you have a leak, fix it as soon as you know about it. Leaks are more than drips falling on mics and instruments. They also get into the acoustic materials in the walls and ceilings, and suddenly your studio smells, and eventually the weight of wet insulation causes the ceiling to fall in.

- Insufficient coffee, tea, milk, hot and cold water, cups, sugar, paper towels, a filled cookie jar (it matters), and so on. These staples should always be kept on hand.

- Lack of engineering assistance. Never do section sessions without at least one assistant—more if there are lots of players. One of them should always be in the studio and listening on talkback to help you or anyone else in the studio.
- No place to throw out trash. Always have sufficiently large trash bins in the studio, and never leave empty or cold cups of anything on the floor.
- While it's bad to find an irreparable flaw on a recorded track sometime after the session, it is far worse if the track was played by session musicians. And while you hope it never happens, a track can become corrupted or lost accidently. Giving free time to replace the part (and a lot of sincere remorse) is often enough if it's something the band played, but if it was played by session musicians, you may have to pay for them as well. Critically listen to every session track in solo (usually when the musicians take their hourly break) and double- and triple-check every track before deleting and freeing up storage space. Back up everything and keep your backups off the premises.

Photo courtesy of Simon Leadley.

Figure 14.5 Scoring orchestra on break at Trackdown. Of special note, the diffusers on the walls, the height of the string microphones (circled RØDE NT5s), and the small screen in front of the rostrum that provides video playback so the conductor can meet visual cues in the score.

If a conductor is working in the session, be sure to leave enough room in front of the setup for him. You will save time and aggravation by making sure you can maintain eye contact with the conductor. He should also be able to see the record light go on so he knows what's happening. The conductor/arranger will need two music stands set side by side (or a podium) so he can read the complete chart without flipping pages in the middle of a take. If it is a scoring session, he will also need a large video monitor to be able to see the film (from a synchronized video playback). In the largest of sessions and studios, the film or video will be projected onto a large screen in direct line of sight to the conductor. The control room will also need video monitoring.

Studios that do a lot of scoring work have a conductor's talkback as well as a conventional talkback. The conductor's talkback provides a talkback to the conductor that does not go to the musicians. There is also a microphone on the conductor's rostrum or music stand that lets him talk back to the control room without disturbing the session. The conductor's talkback is also a part of a table in the control room where the conductor's copyist or music editor sits. This person follows the score and makes notes on the performance, takes, and cue numbers. He will often makes suggestions to the engineer as to what is coming up in the score.

If you don't have a conductor talkback, give the conductor a microphone to talk back to the control room and to cue the players through the headphones. If no one is wearing headphones, the talkback to the studio should be connected to a small speaker near the conductor.

When overdubbing with a conductor, wait until the very last moment to go into record, because many conductors (or arrangers) will give the players a "chart letter" and a count off into their entrance. If you go into record a little too early, you'll also record these count-offs and cues. It's also common for musicians to make "getting ready" noises before their entrances. Any extraneous sound can be later edited, but the client will prefer to not hear anything that shouldn't be there and will not want to take the time for you to edit out any annoying junk right then.

Mics and Mic Placement

Sections of horns, strings, and the rest of the orchestra generate pretty much the full range of sound. Which microphones are best for the array of instruments in an orchestra will depend on what those instruments are, but it's safe to say that almost every microphone the studio owns will be put to use in an orchestra session. And no matter what the microphone is, for a given instrument, it could be the right mic.

Ribbon or condenser microphones are usually the best choice for strings, horns, and most other "orchestral" instruments. Generally, small-diaphragm mics are best for the trumpets, high reeds, and strings, and large-diaphragms are best for trombones, lower saxes, cellos, and double bass. Windscreens should be avoided, with the exception of perhaps close-miking flutes and horns, where there is quite a lot of breath moisture coming from the flute's mouthpiece or the horn's bell.

Whether you use condenser or ribbon mics or a combination of the two will be a matter of taste and what you're trying to achieve. In general, ribbons will have a warmer, smoother sound, while condensers will create a brighter, edgier recording with more attack, particularly if you're close miking. At a distance from the instrument, the condenser will mellow. Ribbon mics have a sound that is particularly pleasing on horns and most reeds, such as saxophones. Some of the new modern ribbons made by Groove Tubes, AEA, and Royer have no low-output problems and sound very good on string instruments.

Strings

On a string section you should usually use low-mass, high-output microphones. Violins and viola are miked with small-diaphragm capsules, while the cello and double bass are miked with larger-diaphragm capsules (see Figure 14.6). The first and second violins will be miked with three to four instruments per mic so that the blend happens before the sound enters the microphone. The cello(s), the double bass, and possibly a single viola will all have separate microphones. If the section has many more cellos and double basses, mike them in groups of two. Close-miking violins, violas, cellos, double basses, and harps rarely works, and the players will keep hitting the mics with the bows or their hands.

Figure 14.6 Setup for a small string section.

With the exception of classical music, trying to record strings in the same room as anything else is difficult due to leakage. Obviously, leakage is less of an issue in classical or orchestrated scoring work, where the rooms are larger and the effect of leakage may be a desirable part of the sound. Figures 14.7 and 14.8 show two different scoring string sections at Trackdown.

Photo courtesy of Sue Taylor.

Figure 14.7 Medium-sized scoring string section. The section is in the middle of the studio, and all the connections are back to a breakout box behind the rostrum. In this case, a collection of larger-diaphragm RØDE NT1000 condensers was preferred.

Photo courtesy of Sue Taylor.

Figure 14.8 Medium-sized scoring string section. In this case, a collection of small-diaphragm RØDE NT5 condensers was preferred.

Violins and viola are miked from above. My choice would be a cardioid Neumann KM 84 or 184, an AKG 451, an Audio-Technica 4051, or a Schoeps CMC 64. Position them 3 to 4 feet above each three- to four-instrument grouping, and to the front of the grouping with the mic angled toward the center. Keep the mic, stand, and boom out of the way of the bowing and where no one can stand up and hit their head.

A short floor stand is best for double bass and cello. I prefer a Neumann U 87 or U 67, AKG 414 or 214, Oktava MK-220, RØDE Classic II or NT1000, or Groove Tubes MD1b, usually in a cardioid pattern. Keep the mic below where the bowing occurs and face it angled upward slightly toward the F hole. Eighteen to 24 inches is a good starting point on the distance between the mic and the instrument.

When strings must be recorded at the same time as a full rhythm section and horns, such as at a live pop concert or musical theatre orchestra, miniature microphones (that are often wireless) attached to the instruments may be the only solution for maintaining control and separation. While this solves a lot of problems in live performance (feedback, leakage, and so on), using them in recording eliminates the acoustic blend that is so much a part of an orchestra sound. String overhead mics are also used to capture some of the instruments' full sound, and this is mixed in with the close mics. Often with close miking of string sections comes the need for a generous amount of EQ and reverb.

If the acoustics are particularly good, a well-blended string quartet can be recorded with just a couple of microphones. Any of the stereo techniques could be employed. Figure 14.9 shows an AB approach. To record a solo violin for a modern-rock track, I might go for a closer, edgier sound with a close mic (see Figure 14.10). In the studio would also be a couple of distant mics that would be blended in with the close mic for a stereo image.

Horns

For an open ensemble sound on a pair of horns, position one bidirectional microphone between them with each player facing the other (see Figure 14.11). The two of them having good eye contact will also help them make entrances and cutoffs. For three horns of the same type and voicing, set a wide cardioid, such as a Neumann U 87, in front of them. (A wide cardioid pattern is one that has a very broad heart-shaped pattern and is not extremely directional—see Figure 2.15 in Chapter 2.) Many selectable patterned microphones have broad cardioid patterns because they have little porting. The longer the port, the narrower and more directional the cardioid pattern (referring back to Figure 2.16). Have the horns set up in a crescent about 3 to 4 feet from the mic. By miking the horns at some distance, the overall sound will open up and result in more of a jazz-band horn section sound as opposed to a rock-and-roll sound.

Rock-and-roll horns often use close miking (see Figure 14.12). I set up a five- to seven-piece rock horn section in a line with one mic for each horn, all mixed together to one or two tracks, with

Photo courtesy of Sennheiser.

Figure 14.9 String quartet miked with a pair of Sennheiser MKH 8040 cardioid condensers.

Photo courtesy of RØDE Microphones.

Figure 14.10 Solo violin close miked with a RØDE NT55 cardioid condenser.

Figure 14.11 Neumann U 87 in bidirectional pattern between two horns.

the first trumpet on one side, followed by the second trumpet, and the trombones and saxes/ flutes at the other end. If the saxophonists are also playing flute, a second set of mics should be available. When the saxs are played, the low mics are switched on, and when they switch to flute, the high set near their lips is turned on (and the sax mics are turned off).

Figure 14.12 Rock-and-roll horn section line.

I prefer AKG 451s or Audio-Technica 4051s for rock horn sessions. There are also many engineers who like the Shure SM57 or the Sennheiser 421 for close miking horns, as a dynamic mic takes off some of the horn's edge at that close range. Have the mics for each horn 6 to 8 inches from the mic to the bells and the height set depending on the musicians' height and where they play the horn (see Figure 14.13). Face the mic into the bell of the horns as a starting point. If this is too percussive, raise the mic slightly and tip downward toward the bell.

Figure 14.13 Mic placement for rock trumpet.

The sax mic is positioned on a short boom 4 to 8 inches from the bell to the mic (see Figure 14.14). If the sax player is also playing flute, the flute mics should be on booms and positioned above the player's lips, 2 to 3 inches away from the lips and angled downward toward the mouthpiece. Clarinets and many other small vibrating-reed instruments tend to sound best if miked from the front. The mic should be 8 to 12 inches from the instrument and positioned 2 to 3 inches above the bell of the instrument, angled downward. Some clarinet players also like the mic directly in front of the instrument's opening.

Figure 14.14 Mic placement for rock sax.

It is not uncommon for a scoring date to include almost entirely woodwinds, such as flutes, clarinets, oboe, English horn, bassoon, and saxophone. Miking them two to three instruments to a mic and in front and above gets very good results. Figure 14.15 shows a session of woodwinds.

Photo courtesy of Sue Taylor.

Figure 14.15 Mic placement for a woodwind session at Trackdown. In this case, a collection of small-diaphragm condensers, RØDE NT5.

Tubas are miked from above, as bassoons and English horns often are. One of the large-diaphragm condensers mentioned earlier or a ribbon, such as an AEA R84 or the Groove Tubes VELO 8, will work well. Position the mic 18 to 24 inches above the instrument, but slightly behind the musician so that when he gets up he doesn't bang into the microphone.

French horns are miked from behind the musician. The bell of the horn faces the rear. Use a short stand and position the mic about 2 feet off the ground and 3 to 4 feet from the bell. If there are a few French horns (usually they come in three or more), use a mic between each pair. Three to four feet further behind the microphones I might position a reflective gobo, since I like the sound bounce that blends with the sound coming directly from the horn.

For a mellower horn sound, I will pull the mics back a couple of feet and go with ribbons, such as those that were previously mentioned in this chapter.

Orchestral Percussion

Orchestral percussion almost always sits at the rear of the orchestra and in the biggest of orchestras can occupy the width of the orchestra (see Figure 14.16).

Photo courtesy of Sue Taylor.

Figure 14.16 Mic placement for large percussion at Trackdown. A larger-diaphragm RØDE NT1000 is used on the timpani.

Latin percussion and orchestra percussion have a great deal in common because they both have louder drums, such as congas, timbales, and timpani and mallet percussion, such as marimbas and xylophones. They also have hand percussion, such as tambourines, shakers, cow bells, wind chimes, cabasas, rain sticks, temple bells, and such. And of course, there is often a full drum kit. Miking a percussion section will use techniques common with drums and Latin percussion (see Chapter 10) and general stereo techniques (see Chapter 8) for other instruments.

Unless there is a problem of leakage from other instruments (or it's a live performance where there is a great deal of PA or stage monitor foldback sound coming into the percussion area), I tend to mike the larger and louder instruments, such as timpani (also referred to as *kettle drums*) or marching bass drum, at 2 to 3 feet from the vibrating surface and slightly in front of the instrument. If there are two or three timpani, a stereo pair may be adequate; if there are four or more drums, one mic between two drums is usually sufficient.

Tuned percussions are those instruments that are played with mallets, such as xylophones, marimbas, glockenspiels, tubular bells, and such. I tend to use a stereo pair if the instrument is featured and mix the two mics to mono if it's an incidental part (see Figure 14.17). The mics are placed a foot or two in front of the instrument and 2 to 3 feet above the vibrating surface. If mono, one mic will do for the glockenspiel or tubular bells. It's important to consider that many tuned percussion instruments have pipe resonators that extend downward toward the floor, and the sound from these pipes adds a great deal to the sound. For this reason, if there is no problem of leakage from other instruments, I might move the microphones farther in front of the instrument or add an additional pair of microphones 2 to 3 feet in front of the instrument and a foot off the ground. The right low mic is mixed with the top right mic and the left with the left to get a stereo pair. As always, how many microphones and where they are placed are determined by how the instruments sound in the spaces they are placed in and the style and texture you're going for.

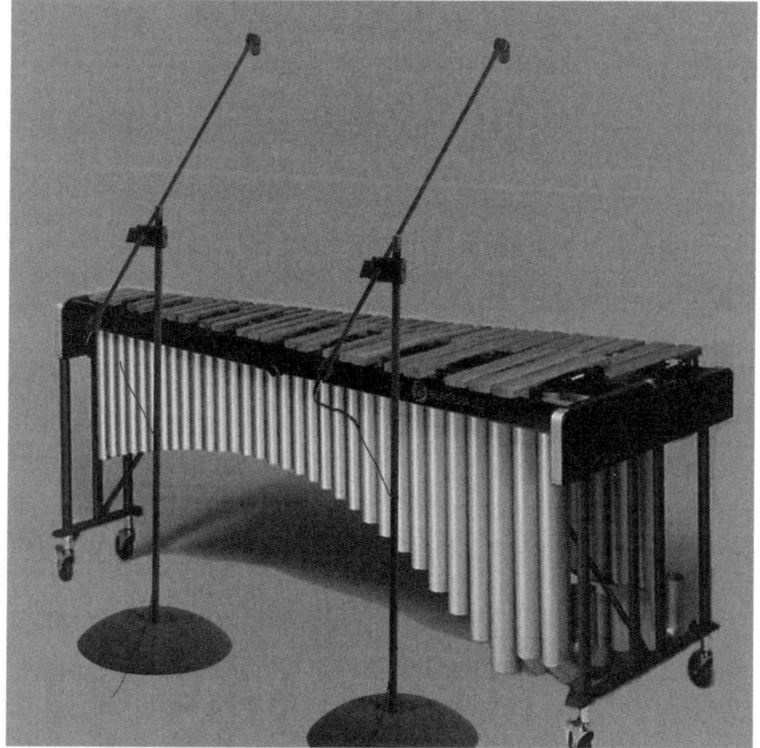

Figure 14.17 Mic placement for marimba using a pair of Sennheiser MKH 8040 cardioid condensers.

Invariably, the percussionist will have a trunk of noisemakers, and as he uses each, you may need to make some EQ and level adjustments. Most of the time, a couple of microphones set up where the percussionist has his trunk of stuff will give him a stereo field to work with where he will position his instruments. If he has a good stereo mix in his headphones of what he is doing, he will move the percussion in the stereo field for dramatic effect.

Some percussion (such as wind chimes) may be more appropriately recorded in mono with one microphone if it is a part of a classical piece, but a simple AB stereo technique with a pair of AKG 451s or similar will work well for pop or jazz, where the production has the high-to-low range of the chimes sweeping across the full field of the stereo mix. Or, in the case of a rain stick, the top-to-bottom flow (of the rice or beans) inside the stick would be translated into a journey of sound across the stereo panorama.

Choirs

Choirs are often an addition to a large studio recording, particularly in scoring. The various techniques in Chapter 8 can be used to record them. Given the space of a large studio, the singers should be spread out a bit more than if they were singing live (see Figure 14.18).

Photo courtesy of Sue Taylor.

Figure 14.18 Mic placement and singer positioning for a choir.

In conclusion, there are many different instruments in each family of instruments, and the best way to mike them will always be a learning experience the first few times you record them. As I mentioned in Chapter 13, if you've never been up close to a certain instrument, use your ears as a starting point for where to place the microphone. As for what mic to choose, if it looks something like a violin, start by miking it like one. Do the same for horns and for things that look like acoustic pianos or guitars.

How Many Microphones Does It Take to Record an Orchestra?

In 1938, Benny Goodman and his band were recorded with one microphone hanging from the ceiling of the Carnegie Hall stage, connected to a disk cutter. The recording was made by Albert Marx as a gift for his wife, and a second set was made for Benny. The discs were rediscovered in

Benny's apartment in 1950. Goodman took the newly discovered recording to his record company, Columbia. These recordings have not been out of print since then. (They were on vinyl and then CD.) Does it sound like a modern recording? Well, no, but it's an amazing recording of an amazing performance that marked a point when jazz was acknowledged as a part of the musical mainstream and as acceptable as the classics.

Many modern concert recordings have been made with just a stereo pair of microphones with excellent results, provided the performance was by a well-balanced, acoustically oriented instrumental, individual, ensemble, or orchestra. Impressive recordings have been made with any of the techniques described in Chapter 8 on stereo recording.

For most recording, however, a stereo pair will be used to pick up the entire performance, but all the instruments, either individually or in small groups, will be individually miked as well. This provides the opportunity to vary the balance and bring out instruments that are too weak in the overall mix or to adjust levels when certain instruments and sections need to be raised or lowered for dramatic effect. Individual tracks also allow EQ and other effects to be added to the various orchestral elements. The need to add drama in the mixdown is probably greatest when mixing film and TV scores, because the balance will often change to reflect the visual content in each cut of a scene and the emotional impact that the director/producer is looking to achieve. In the case of opera or musical theatre, even when the singers are part of the orchestra recording, it is inevitable that one or more vocals will need re-recording.

Whether the individual mics are mixed to a multitrack or a stereo/surround mix will depend on the production approach and the budget—it takes both time and money to record and mix multitrack. For most major studio productions, multitrack will be used if for no other reason than to have a means to fix imperfections.

As described in Chapter 4, when you're using several microphones in combination, always check to see whether there are any comb-filtering problems by hearing how multiple microphones sound when they're combined to mono. You may want to reverse the polarity of one or more microphones because one polarity combination might sound better than another.

Premixing Sections

- When premixing to a mono or stereo mix a section (horns or strings) that is part of a pop music production, I usually mix slightly more low-end instruments (baritone sax, bass trombone, cello, double bass, and so on) into the recording than it may seem to need when soloed. Often when the section tracks are placed into the final mix, the low voicing flattens out and tends to get lost.

- If I'm premixing a section, I may slightly compress the overall signal. This smooths out the blend of the various instruments that make up the section. Be aware, though, that if one instrument in the balance is raised or gets louder, it will affect the compression threshold and the relative balance of everything in the section. At other times, depending on the chart, I will use compression on individual microphones to smooth out the dynamics of a certain instrument (or three violins if I have one mic on a group of three).

- If there are enough tracks, the sections will be assigned to several tracks—for instance, strings (left and right tracks) would be first violins, second violins, violas, cellos, and basses (and some of these might be stereo pairs), brass would be trumpets, saxes, flutes, trombones, French horns, bassoons, clarinets, and so on (again, some might be stereo pairs). In post-production mixing, these combined tracks are often referred to as *stems*.

It's a Wrap

There is a palpable adrenalin rush when you record a large section or orchestra. No matter how many times I've done a big session, I've always felt a degree of trepidation, of risk. There is always the concern that something will go wrong, something won't be recorded right, or something will come up that wasn't planned for. But that's the key to pulling it off—the planning. And, of course, you always need a little bit of luck that everything will work or that if it doesn't, you can work around it. And in the back of your mind, you'll begin to worry that the air conditioning may fail. Or even worse, some dope down the street will crash into a substation and you'll lose power ... such will be the anxiety. But after everyone is gone and you do a playback, and the strings, brass, and the rest come through the speakers, you know you're ready for another day of big session recording.

Appendix A: Compressors and Limiters: A Brief Overview

Compressors and limiters are audio processing devices that restrict the dynamic range of the signal passing through them. There are two main ways in which compressors and limiters are used:

- On one signal during multitrack recording or mixing (channel insert)
- On a group or composite program output during recording or mixing (group insert)

The use of compression and limiting in pop/rock music recording and many areas of broadcasting is common.

Most amplifiers have what is called *unity gain*. This means that the output signal will be proportional to the input signal up to the point that the amplifier's maximum gain is reached. Then, of course, the amp will distort and clip. A compressor/limiter has an input level sensor that controls the gain of the amplifier: Hence, it is called a *variable gain amplifier* (VGA) (see Figure A.1). VGAs are compressors, limiters, gates, and expanders. When the input signal of a compressor/limiter exceeds a certain input level, the gain is reduced. Below the input threshold level, the input signal passes through to the output with no level change or gain reduction—that is, at unity gain. This is known as the *rotation point* or *threshold*.

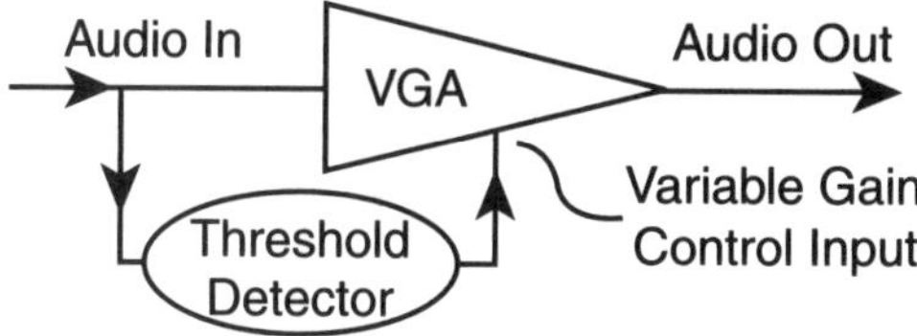

Figure A.1 Block diagram of a variable gain amplifier.

As an example, in Figure A.2 you can see that for input levels below 0 dB, the output level is comparable to the input level. Above 0 dB, a 10-dB increase in input level produces only a 5-dB increase in output level. This indicates a 10:5 relationship, or a gain reduction ratio of 2:1. Thus, for this setting, an input signal to the compressor varying in the range of –30 to +15 dB

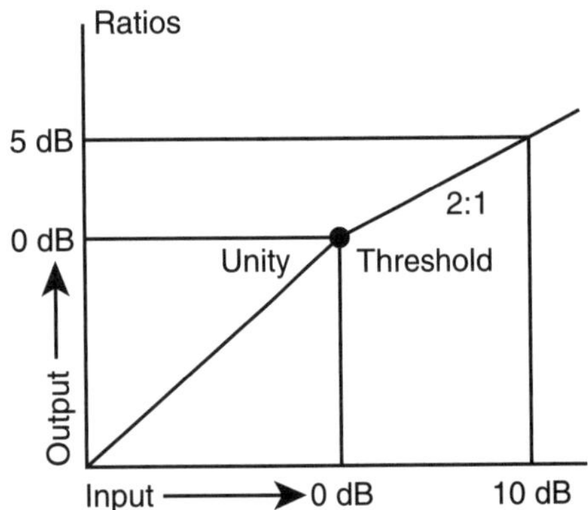

Figure A.2 Once the input signal exceeds the threshold of the compressor, the output will go up at a 2-to-1 (2:1) ratio. A 10-dB input above the threshold equals a 5-dB increase in output.

will produce an output signal varying from –30 to +7.5 dB. That is, its top 15 dB (above the 0-dB threshold) is compressed to 7.5 dB, thus reducing the overall dynamic range from 45 dB to 37.5 dB.

In other words, with a 2:1 ratio, for every 2-dB increase after the threshold is reached, the output will increase by 1 dB. For a ratio of 10:1, for every increase of 10 dB at the input, the output will increase by 1 dB. The difference between a compressor and a limiter is the severity of the gain reduction once the input signal exceeds the threshold. A device set for a ratio of 2:1, 4:1, or up to 8:1 would be considered a compressor, while a limiter would have a ratio of 10:1, 20:1, or 100:1 (see Figure A.3). The ratio control changes the rate of reduction of signal levels exceeding the threshold level.

For the purpose of explanation, a gate (or expander) is also a VGA. In this case, the VGA has unity gain until the input signal goes below the threshold when the gain of the amplifier is reduced. Chapter 10 described how to use gates on drums. In other words, with a 1:2 ratio, for every 1-dB decrease below the threshold, the output will decrease by 2 dB. For a ratio of 1:10, for every decrease of 1 dB, the output will decrease by 10 dB. The difference between an expander and a gate is the severity of the gain reduction once the input signal drops below the threshold. A device set for a ratio of 1:2 to 1:4 would be considered an expander, while a gate would have a ratio of 1:10, 1:20, or 1:100 (refer to Figure A.3). The ratio control changes the rate of reduction of signal levels dropping below the threshold level. In general, gates are traditionally used to eliminate leakage, as was the case when used on drums, and expanders have been used in various forms of analog noise reduction, such as Dolby and dbx.

The most basic function of compression in popular music is often to achieve a consistent signal level to a recording medium or in the mix and thus improve the signal-to-noise ratio (SNR), and/or to achieve a signal that has a more consistent dynamic range. In effect, the peaks (such as a bass

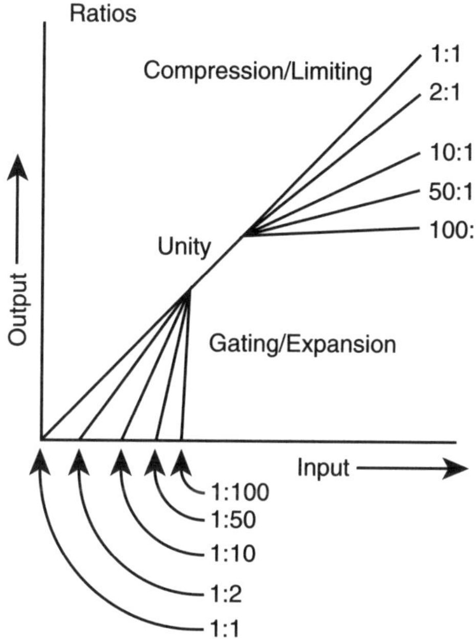

Figure A.3 VGA gain ratios.

pluck) are lower and closer dynamically to the sustain (see Figure 11.12). Compression on vocals can help with intelligibility, particularly when there is a full backing track and a dynamic singer.

The diagram in Figure A.3 shows several different ratios starting at the same higher and lower threshold. Note how the output dynamic range differs for the same input level. It is also possible to vary the ratio and threshold level simultaneously. When used on critical signals such as a voice, a lower ratio with a lower threshold seems to produce a softer, smoother, more pleasant, and less audibly obvious sound. Limiting ratios can make the sound very restricted and lack sparkle. Limiting would have a higher threshold and greater ratio. The threshold control changes the level at which the compressor/limiter starts reducing its gain.

Compressor/limiters usually have metering that indicates the amount of gain reduction applied to a signal (that is, signal level loss in dB).

The attack time control adjusts the time it takes the VGA to react to an input signal once it has exceeded the threshold. On many compressors it is adjustable and varies from fast (0.1 milliseconds), where it reacts almost instantaneously to ensure that no large transients slip through, to slow (up to 200 milliseconds), where it allows the transient to pass before compressing any sustained signal. Extremely fast attack times have the effect of causing the sound to lose percussiveness and clarity, so attack time adjustment in a sense controls how percussive a sound might be. A slower setting can in fact be used to add a percussive edge to a bass or kick drum signal, for example (see Figure A.4).

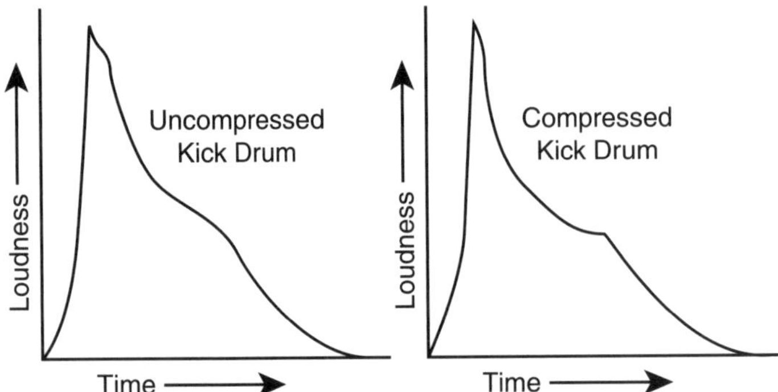

Figure A.4 Example of slow attack compression to increase transient.

In the case of a gate, the attack time controls how quickly the VGA will return to unity gain. If the attack time for a gate is slow, before the gate turns on, the transient of the sound will pass and not be heard. For most things, the gate attack should be fast so that it responds to the leading edge of the sound. The release time control adjusts the amount of time it takes for the VGA to return to its normal unity gain once the signal drops below the threshold (in the case of a compressor or a limiter). If the release time is too fast, the compressor is not likely to cause any residual gain reduction to the signal that occurs after the peak, but if it returns to normal gain too quickly, the sound will seem to "pump" or "breathe." This pumping sound can be very obvious and highly objectionable. On the other hand, if the release time is too long, the VGA will not return to normal gain quickly enough, and the sustain will not be heard.

In the case of a gate or an expander, the release time is how long it takes the gain to decline once the input signal drops below the threshold. If the sound has a decay that goes up and down across the threshold as the level falls away, a too-fast release time will cause the decay to turn on and off quickly and will sound like it's "tearing."

There is no one attack or release setting that is optimum for all situations; the variations depend upon what the sound envelope is like and what the user wishes to hear.

With a reduction in dynamics, there must be a way to readjust the overall output of the compressor/limiter, hence there is a makeup-gain output control that boosts the overall output. It does not change the now-compressed signal's dynamic range.

External Threshold

A common problem encountered when recording the human voice is sibilance (a *sss* sound). One type of VGA is generally called a *de-esser*, as it reduces the high-frequency *sss* content from the program. De-essing has little effect except at the moment of peak sibilance. There is no change in general frequency response. However, all frequencies are reduced at the moment of sibilance control. There are also a few very specialized de-essers that are able to reduce only the high-frequency portion of the sound. This function is handled by a DAW plug-in, but in the analog world, de-essers are commonly found in broadcast facilities. On more than one occasion, I have used a de-esser on cymbals for a unique effect. See Figure A.5.

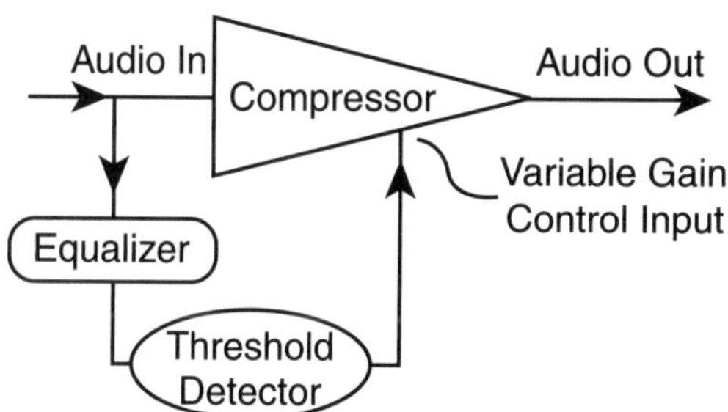

Figure A.5 Circuit diagram of frequency-dependant compression/limiting.

An external input to the VGA detector circuit can also be used as a *ducker* or *dipper*. A ducker is used in radio where the announcer on a talk-back radio show always wants his voice to be louder than the person calling in or the music. The announcer's voice is used to control the degree of gain reduction of the caller's voice or the music.

Overall program compression is used in many applications, such as mastering, PA, radio, TV, and so on. The result is that the average loudness of the track is increased, and peaks are smoothed out. By increasing the average level, a mix can be made to sound louder, even though the peak levels are identical. It does, however, reduce the dynamic range of the recording.

To preserve the positioning in the sonic field, the multiple compressors should have the same characteristics and be in a linked mode. Failure to do this will result in common sounds (such as the center of a stereo mix) shifting whenever one channel is momentarily louder than the others.

Most dual compressors (that is, two channels in one box) have the facility to link the two discrete audio processors to one set of controls, usually including threshold, ratio, attack, and release. As the term implies, this linking of two compressors is useful in stereo applications, such as for insertion over a full stereo mix or for stereo subgroups of horns, strings, or drums, for example. This linking means that both compressors respond to excess signal at either of the audio inputs and at the same attack time, thus both audio processors reduce their gain by the same amount. This ensures that no shift in the stereo image occurs.

Stereo-linked compression is usually set for subtlety. If any of the settings are too severe, pumping or breathing will be noticeable because the program material has such a variety of different sounds, transients, and envelopes. See Figure A.6.

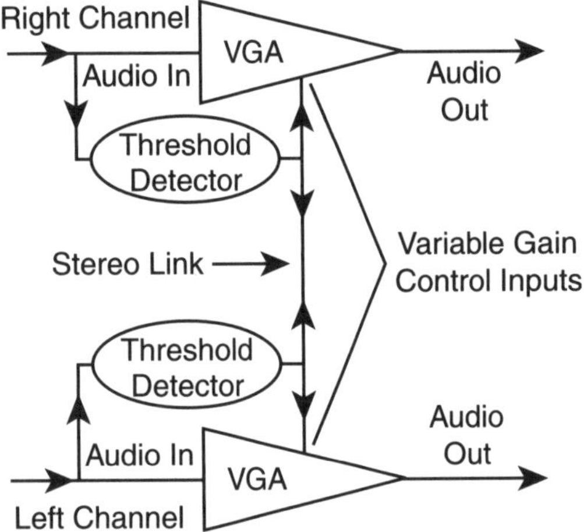

Figure A.6 Circuit diagram of a stereo compressor/limiter.

Over the years I've used gear in ways never intended. Here are a couple of interesting examples that were used on a couple of major releases. The bass setup (see Figure A.7) was interesting, but the hi-hat setup (see Figure A.8) created an amazing overdub sound on an Art Garfunkel recording. The drummer played a hi-hat while controlling the compression on it by blowing into a second microphone.

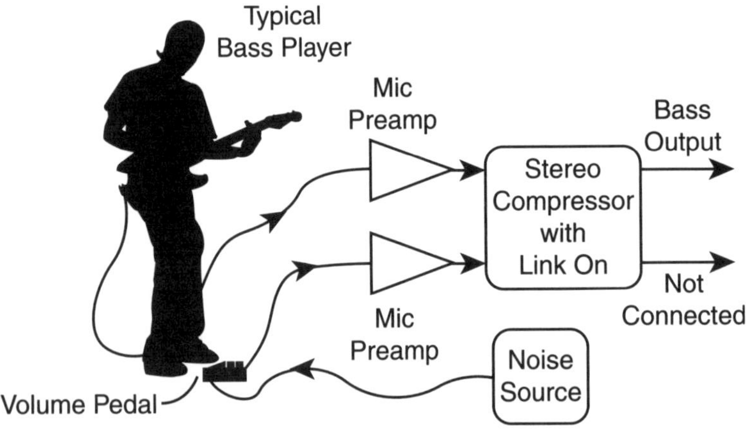

Figure A.7 Pedal-controlled compression on bass.

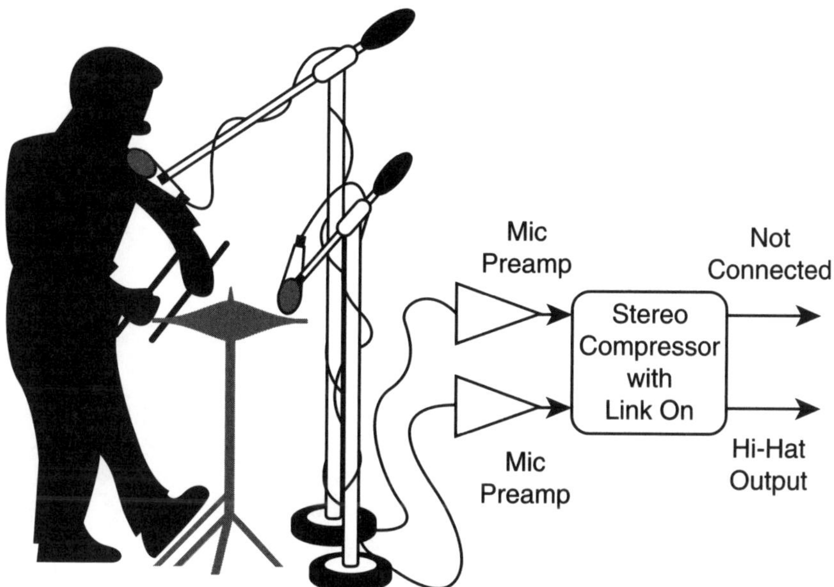

Figure A.8 Breath-controlled compression on a hi-hat.

Appendix

B An EQ Primer

Equalization modifies the loudness of specific frequencies in the sound. It is the most common type of signal processing, although it is usually not considered an outboard effect because almost all mixing desks have EQ.

Basic Rules

There are a few basic truths for adjusting EQ.

- EQ can't enhance or remove tones that don't exist. If, for example, you want a sparkly hi-hat or a vocal with a lot of clarity, you must use a bright microphone to start with. If the high frequencies don't come through the mic to some degree in the first place, there's nothing there to boost.
- EQ won't save a bad performance.
- For acoustic sounds, make sure the instrument you're recording sounds the way you want it to in the acoustic space before you mike it and begin to use EQ.
- EQ is dependent on the nature of the sound. EQ can't make a hollow-body guitar sound like a solid-body guitar.
- When adjusting the EQ, be sure you're making the sound better, not just different or louder. Take the EQ in and out and listen to the difference. Try to establish a reference for comparison so you know what the EQ is doing.
- Equalizer circuit designs use frequency-specific phase shift to achieve their results. EQ will not only boost or cut frequencies in a sound, but will also introduce phase shift that can affect the sound. The introduction of phase shift is more noticeable in boost EQ than in cut EQ.

The way to approach EQ is not solely as an additive process, but also as a subtractive one. A common mistake many make is to boost the high frequencies to get more clarity. But boosting the highs won't really solve the problem muddiness. You must remove the low-end rumble. When you take away the frequencies you don't want, all you're left with is what you *do* want. Because we hear one sound through another, you need to make room for the sounds you want by reducing or removing unnecessary tones, undertones, overtones, dissonant harmonics, and any noise, hum, rumble, or hiss.

When you're mixing, it can help to think about EQ in terms of filling a bucket of sound. If the bottom of the bucket is loaded with a lot of murky rumble on voice tracks, other superfluous sounds from a bunch of bottom-y synthesizers or a "big bottom" acoustic guitar, or drum rumble, you won't have a lot of room at the low end for anything else. Use EQ to open space for the essential elements of each overlapping sound. For instance, an acoustic guitar by itself has a lot of low frequency, and this richness sounds wonderful on a solo guitar. But as soon as you add a couple of rock guitars and a bass, when you raise the acoustic in the mix, it will tend to wash out the clarity and definition of the entire low end. This problem is aggravated when too much reverb is added to the acoustic, causing the reverb to rumble in the caverns with no purpose and cloud the whole track.

A better approach is to go for the impression or essence of the sound. By rolling off the very low end on the acoustic, it will sound somewhat thin by itself, but as a part of the mix nothing will seem to be missing. Your brain will fill in the nonessential missing parts, and those instruments that need low frequency will retain their clarity. (This phenomenon is known as *residue* or *periodicity* pitch.)

On the other hand, if the acoustic guitar is a featured instrument and possibly on its own someplace in the production, you might use less (or no) roll-off on the recording. You may, however, in the mix, roll off the low end of the guitar's signal that's only going to the reverb.

One of the biggest problems in many multitrack live recordings is low-frequency rumble on many tracks because of the air conditioning, external noise, and structural vibration. Get in the habit of rolling off the the rumble in the low end, generally 40 hertz and below. That being said, make the decision to use the roll-off on a case-by-case basis, as you may not want to use roll-off on instruments where the low end is an important element of their sound, such as kick, bass, floor toms, pipe organ, and so on. There will be a lot more clarity (provided the mic has clarity to start with), and it will reduce that deep woof and rumble which seems to plague many recordings.

Blending and mixing of overlapping sounds affect the overall impression of a given isolated sound in the total sound. In other words, what is needed in the way of EQ is determined by how a track (instrument, voice, section) sounds within the context of the entire production, not when it is in solo.

Let's use drums for an example. Suppose you have a microphone on the snare and a microphone on the hi-hat. If you equalize the microphone on the snare for the sound of the snare, you will also change the tone of the hi-hat (and vice versa), because the snare microphone will pick up some of the hi-hat. Even if you use a gate on the snare, when it opens with the snare drum beat, the hi-hat will be there as well. I've worked with people who insist on soloing the snare drum mic and then spend hours getting a "sound" for the snare. This can be an incredible waste of time (and completely debilitating for the drummer) because as soon as all the other drum mics are turned on—and in particular the overhead microphones—the overall sound of the snare will change.

Always approach equalization in total rather than in isolation. For instance, on a hi-hat I tend to roll off everything below 1,000 cycles and boost highs above 10,000 cycles. I do this because I'm using very little of the hi-hat microphone per se—since the overheads pick up plenty of hi-hat, and all I want from the hi-hat microphone is a taste of the "psst-psst" (that really close percussive sound that comes from the stick impact). The close mic provides specific direction, attack, clarity, and definition, while the overheads provide the overall sound of the hi-hat as it relates to the rest of the drums. The hi-hat microphone all by itself might sound extremely thin, but within the overall mix of the entire set, it will sound unclouded and vibrant with plenty of up-front impact.

EQ will also affect the leakage from other sources. For instance, if you have a bass amp cranked up right next to the drummer, you'll find that as you EQ the drums (in particular the overheads), the sound of the bass will be affected. If you try to EQ the bass out of the overheads, you'll most likely make things worse because the overall sound of both the bass and the drums will suffer from the effect of the equalized leakage. This is why I try to get the sound in the studio as close as possible to the sound we're going for. I then add EQ like seasoning. On analog tape I'll generally record it a bit brighter than I think it should be, because you tend to lose a slight amount of brilliance through the course of the non-digital recording process. Then, when I remix, I use whatever EQ is necessary to get the overlapping textures I'm looking for.

Finding What You're Looking For

Many times, the best way to find the frequency range you're looking for is to turn the boost/cut control up full-blast, and sweep it through its range of frequencies until you find the frequency that seems to be the most pleasing to you, or those frequencies that you want to diminish. Then turn the EQ boost/cut control down until it's at the right level for what you want to hear.

In many cases, when you find the frequency you want to boost and that is most appealing to you, it is often in what is called the *presence range*, which extends between 1,500 and 5,000 cycles. This is also the area where our ears are most sensitive. If you have a lot of boost EQ in that range, your mix will sound very mid-rangy and won't seem to have the broadband clarity and richness you're probably looking for. An approach I take is to find the fundamental tone range that I'm looking for and then move the equalizer's frequency up slightly, which brings out the basic tone as well as nearby upper harmonics and overtone colors of the sound. For example, if the frequency that seems to achieve the sound I'm looking for is around 4,000 cycles, I'll raise the frequency setting of the equalizer up to 5,000 or 5,500. The result will be a fuller texture with more clarity and openness. I think it makes the sound seem less electronic.

Bumping Your Head at 10,000 Cycles

When boost EQ is used, the headroom of the EQ's amplifier is reduced in the boosted frequency range. If, for example, an equalizer is set flat with 20 dB of headroom and we boost the signal by 15 dB at 10,000 cycles, the EQ amp has only 5 dB of headroom for the frequency range above that frequency and is likely to distort on a high-frequency peak (see Figure B.1). To prevent this, turn down the signal going into the equalizer, thus gaining more headroom for the amplifier. Most boards have some sort of input trim or some way of turning up or down the signal coming back from the recorder.

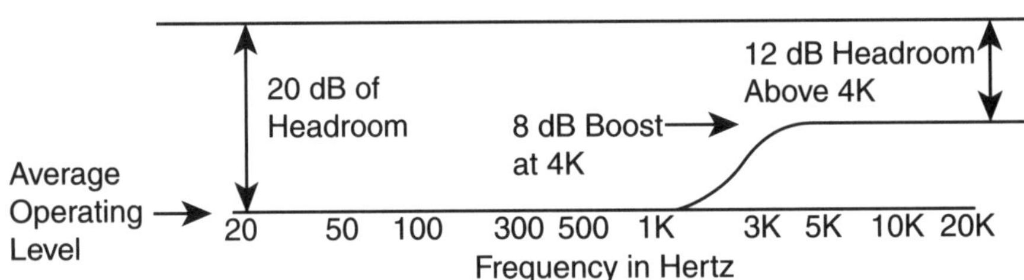

Figure B.1 Losing headroom with EQ boost.

Punch, Bottom, Mids, Presence, Tops, and Brilliance

There are certain types of expressions used in pop music that are difficult to interpret because sound is so difficult to describe. Years ago, the first record deal I ever made involved a record that was in 5/4 time, and when I asked the label head why he liked the record so much, he just raised his arm over his head in a strange, twisted gesture and said, "Because it kinda goes like this." Trying to understand what someone means when they are describing what they like can be challenging.

These are all rock-and-roll terms for different things. I'm sure there are so many more.

- *Punch* usually means the low-end attack. This is sometimes the very low-end sustain, between 50 and 250 cycles, and the attack in the area between 800 and 1,500 cycles. From there, the kick drum and the bass get their percussiveness. If someone says they want to "feel it move in my stomach," they want more punch. Same thing if they want to "see the speakers move" or have their "hair blown back," and so on.
- *Bottom* usually refers to low mid-frequency sustains in the area of 100 to 800 cycles or so. Usually this is "felt" in the chest area.
- *Presence* is the upper sibilance range that contributes clarity—around 800 to 6,000 cycles. It is the area where our ears are most sensitive. (Refer to Chapter 3 for more about ears.)
- *Tops* and *brilliance* would be above presence, higher than 10,000 cycles.

EQ Terms and Tools

An EQ curve describes the frequency versus loudness pattern of an equalizer. Equalization curves can fall into a few different groups. The following list describes them.

- A *roll-off curve* (or high-/low-pass filter) can be found on mixing desks labeled as a low-frequency or high-frequency *cut filter* (see Figure B.2). At a specific frequency point in the audio band, it begins to roll off so many dB per octave, and it continues rolling off until it is out of human hearing range. The point at which roll-off begins is most often fixed, but in the more expensive consoles the cut-off point is adjustable.

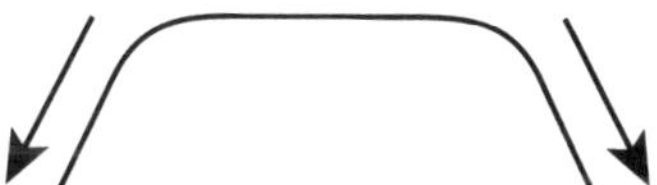

Figure B.2 Roll-off curve.

- *Shelving curve* equalizers (see Figure B.3) are found in most mixing desks. Unlike the curve of a roll-off equalizer, a shelving equalizer will stabilize or flatten out at a certain point. An equalizer can have a boost-shelf curve as well as a cut roll-off at the end of the shelf—for instance, a high-frequency shelf at 10 kHz and a roll-off at 16 kHz (see Figure B.4). In that case, you might boost the highs and cut off the very highs.

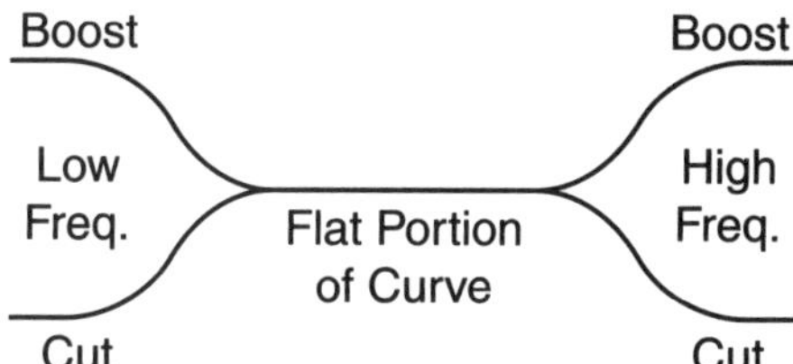

Figure B.3 Shelf curve—boost and cut.

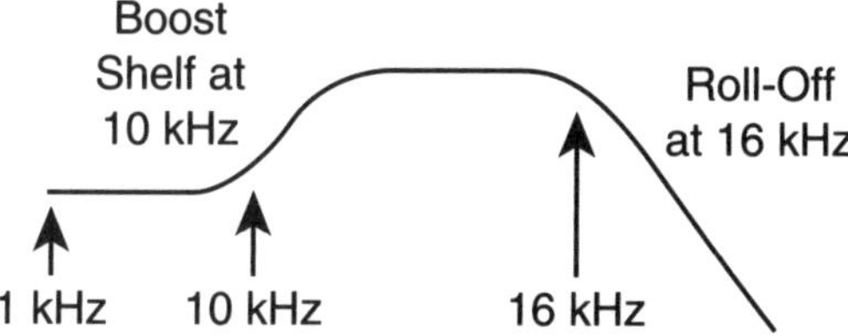

Figure B.4 Boost shelf EQ, then a roll-off.

- A *peaking or dipping equalizer* creates a bell-shaped curve in the sound's frequency response (see Figure B.5). The boost or cut is centered at a certain frequency but will affect a range of frequencies to both sides of the center frequency. A bell-shaped EQ pattern is commonly

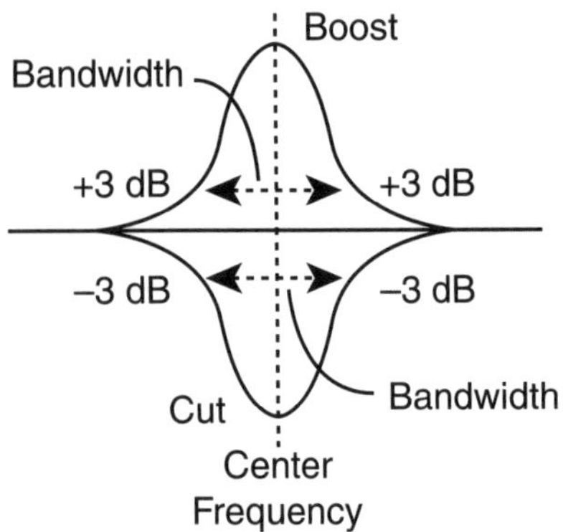

Figure B.5 Peak and dip curve.

called a *pass band.* It is generally found in the high-mid to low-mid ranges of an equalizer and as an alternative to shelving, and it may be switchable (pass band or shelf) in the high and low range. Bell-shaped curves (see Figure B.6) are centered at a specific frequency and then will affect frequencies to both sides of the center frequency. The bandwidth that is affected can vary from very narrow to very broad. Many equalizers have adjustable bandwidth.

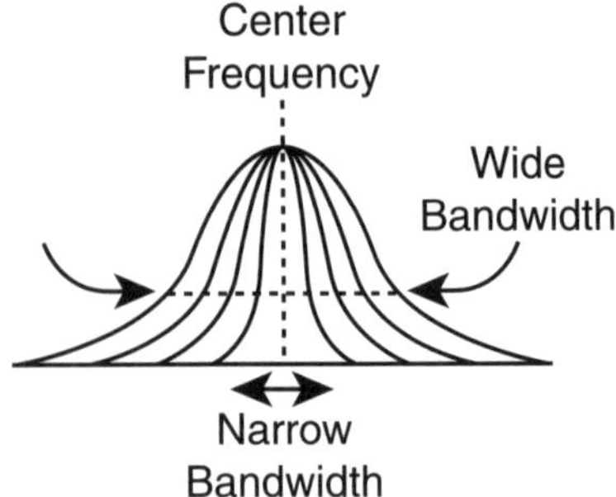

Figure B.6 Peak and dip curve at different bandwidths.

Types of Equalizers

Equalizers are grouped into three different types.

- **Simple tone control equalizers.** The simplest equalizer has a fixed single frequency with the amount of attenuation or boost variable within a certain range. For instance, the frequency choice is 8 kHz, 10 kHz, and 12.5 kHz, +/– 10 dB. (See Figure B.7.) Many small mixing desks and the simplest home studio mixer/recorders have basic two-band equalizers that may include a few selectable frequencies for each boost/cut control. A bit more elaborate, but within the same group, are program equalizers, such as those made by Pultec (see Figure B.8) and Lang, as well as modern copies of the same. These equalizers remain a popular outboard

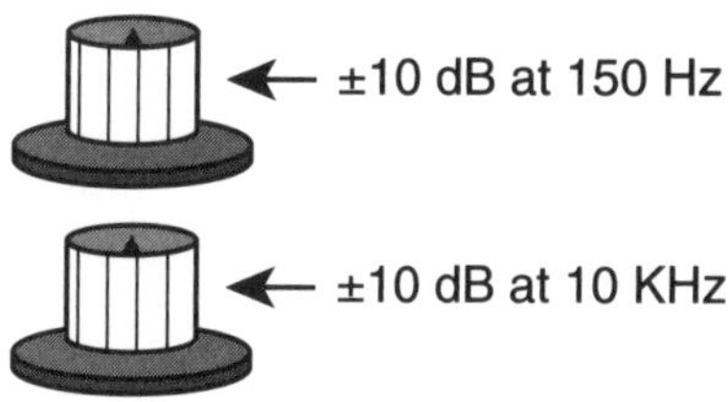

Figure B.7 Basic EQ controls.

Figure B.8 Pultec EQP-1A tube-amplified program EQ.

EQ because of their broad and gentle effect on the sound. The vacuum tube amplifier versions are particularly prized because of their warmth (due the nature of tube distortion).

- **Parametric (sweepable) equalizers.** Some console equalizers are of a parametric variety in that you can continuously boost or cut a sweepable frequency band within a range (see Figure B.9). There will be two, three, or up to six overlapping frequency ranges. For

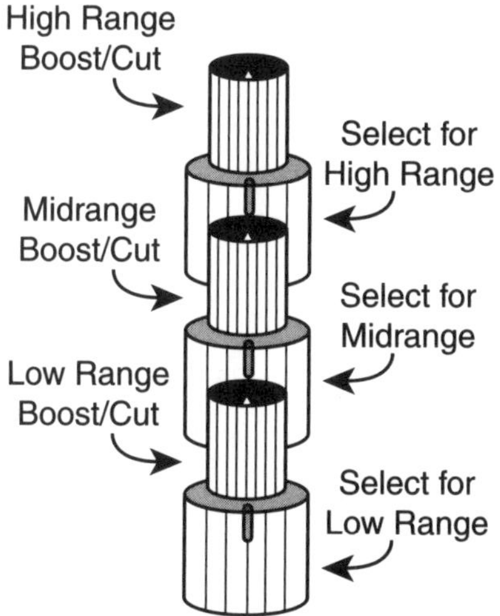

Figure B.9 Concentric parametric controls.

example, the low range will be tunable from 20 Hz to 1,000 Hz, the midrange from 500 Hz to 10 kHz, and the high range from 5 kHz to 15 kHz with +/– 10 dB (see Figure B.10). This type of equalizer will also have sweepable bandwidth for at least the middle ranges, and quite possibly all the ranges. Many consoles have sweepable equalizers (frequency and cut/ boost) but are not parametric, as they do not have sweepable bandwidth for each range.

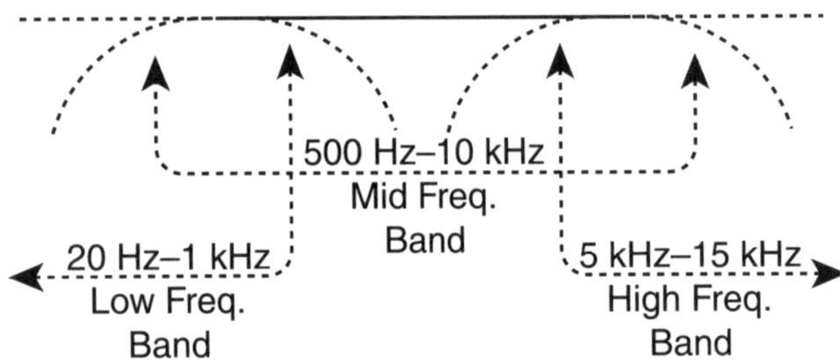

Figure B.10 Overlapping frequencies of a three-band sweepable equalizer.

- **Graphic equalizers.** Graphic equalizers have the ability to boost or cut at specific frequencies or bands (see Figure B.11). Most graphics cover the full sound range (certain specialized ones encompass a smaller range) and have a certain number of bands per octave. *Band per octave* means that the frequency intervals between controls are wider as the frequency goes up.

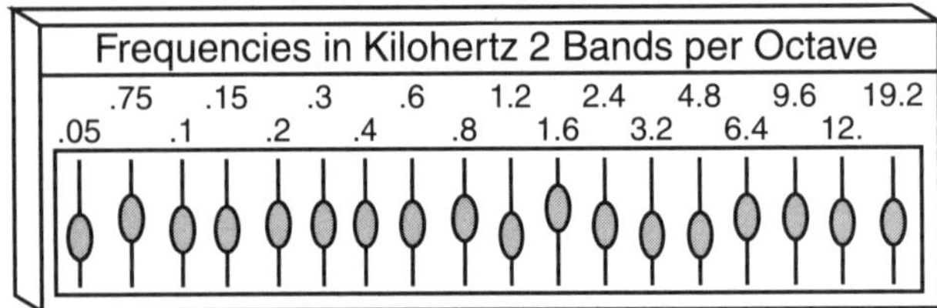

Figure B.11 Graphic equalizer.

Contrary to popular belief, the position of the graphic equalizer controls does not give a true visual indication of the frequency response curve of the EQ. Because each of the bands is very narrow in order to selectively control only its range, the frequency response curve will have sharp dips between each of the band control settings. Though the position of the controls might indicate a gentle curve, the electronics are introducing many hills and valleys (see Figure B.12). Graphics tend to be the least usable type of equalizer for recording, but they are very popular for room tuning and feedback control of PA and monitors.

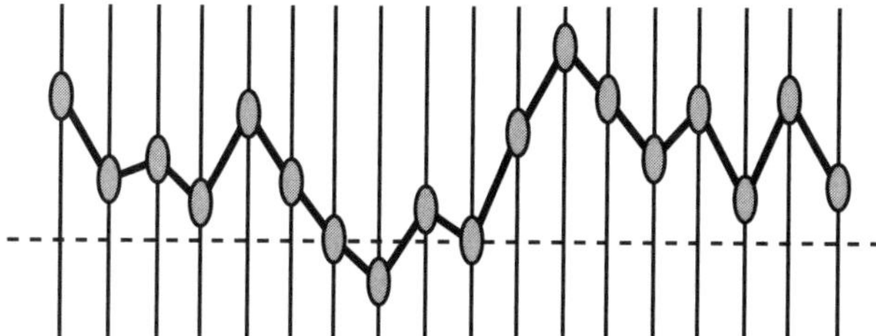

Imagined response based on the physical placement of the EQ controls.

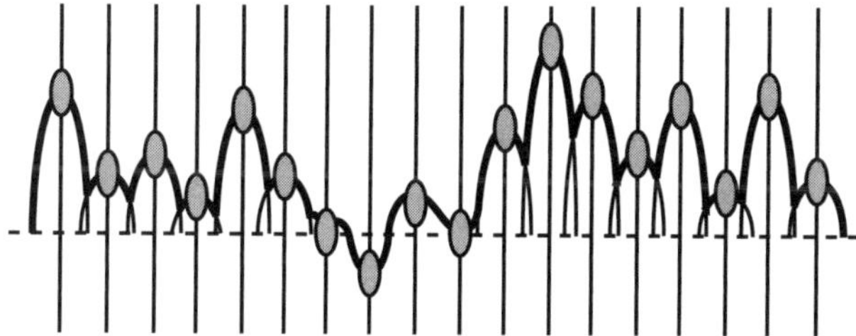

Dark line indicates actual response due to narrow band filters. Light lines indicate bandwidth of each control.

Figure B.12 Indicated and real EQ curve of graphic performance.

Index

D

E

F

H

M

R

T

U

V

W

X

Y

COURSE TECHNOLOGY
CENGAGE Learning
Professional • Technical • Reference

SERIOUS RESOURCES FOR SERIOUS MUSICIANS

From interactive CD-ROMs on the latest music software offerings to comprehensive books on music production, recording engineering, and the music industry, Course Technology PTR has a solution for every musician.

The Mastering Engineer's Handbook, Second Edition
The Audio Mastering Handbook
Bobby Owsinski ■ $34.99

This completely updated edition of the classic provides a thorough exploration of the mastering process for any kind of audio program, utilizing insights from the world's top mastering engineers.

Pro Tools for Video, Film, and Multimedia, Second Edition
Ashley Shepherd ■ $34.99

Offers comprehensive coverage of the extensive features of Pro Tools 7.4, giving you the skills you need to take any multimedia soundtrack project from concept to completion.

The Musician's Legal Companion, Second Edition
Michael A. Aczon ■ $26.99

Don't sign a recording contract before reading this book In clear language it explains the difficult legal concept you need to understand for a successful music career.

Your Cubase Studio
Steve Pacey ■ $24.99

This book goes way beyond the Cubase manual, showing you how to use Cubase in a practical recording, results-focused setting.

M-Audio Guide for the Recording Guitarist
Chris Buono ■ $34.99

This book helps guitarists work with M-Audio hardware and software so they can join the computer-recording revolution.

Music Theory for Computer Musicians
Michael Hewitt ■ $34.99

Teaches DJs, gigging musicians, and electronic musi producers the music theory concepts they need to becom better musicians.

New Comprehensive Guides from our *Power!* Series

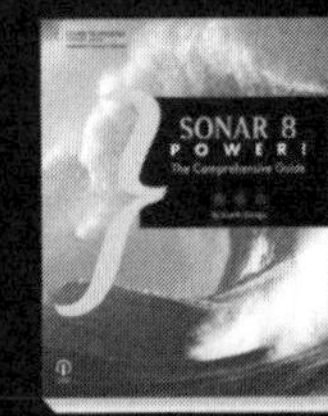

Order now at 1.800.648.7450 or visit courseptr.com.

Course Technology PTR products are also available at Borders, Barnes and Noble, Guitar Center, and Amazon.com